the|western|dreaming

the|western|dreaming

the western world is dying for want of a story

JOHN CARROLL

HarperCollins*Publishers*

HarperCollins*Publishers*

First published in Australia in 2001
Reprinted in 2001
by HarperCollins*Publishers* Pty Limited
ABN 36 009 913 517
A member of the HarperCollins*Publishers* (Australia) Pty Limited Group
www.harpercollins.com.au

HarperCollins*Publishers*
25 Ryde Road, Pymble, Sydney NSW 2073, Australia
31 View Road, Glenfield, Auckland 10, New Zealand
77–85 Fulham Palace Road, London W6 8JB, United Kingdom
Hazelton Lanes, 55 Avenue Road, Suite 2900, Toronto, Ontario M5R 3L2
and 1995 Markham Road, Scarborough, Ontario M1B 5M8, Canada
10 East 53rd Street, New York NY 10022, USA

National Library of Australia Cataloguing-in-Publication data:

Carroll, John, 1944– .
The western dreaming : the western world is dying for want of a story.
Bibliography.
Includes index.
ISBN 0 7322 6671 8.
1. Archetype (Psychology).
I. Title.
150.1954

Painting on cover: Poussin, *Self-Portrait*, 1650, Louvre, Paris
Photograph on cover: Maria Moro/Getty Images
Cover and internal design by Luke Causby, HarperCollins Design Studio
Typeset by HarperCollins in 11/14 Garamond 3
Printed and bound in Australia by Griffin Press on 79gsm Bulky Paperback White

7 6 5 4 3 2   01 02 03 04

contents

For Want of Story

This story is an enigma. Two men set forth on the most fateful journey of their lives. Clueless as to what is happening, their instinct is to flee Jerusalem, along the road to the village of Emmaus, twelve kilometres away.

They could be anyone, anywhere, at any time. Yet it is a Sunday afternoon in early spring, some year around 30AD in a remote province of the Roman Empire. The steel-blue light dulls the greys and browns of the arid hills, making of this a cheerless, unwelcoming journey. High cloud drifts grandly across the heavens, its eternal procession mocking the puny mortals inching along far below, sandalled foot before sandalled foot, gingerly plodding the stone-strewn rutted track. Gusts from across holy wasteland chill the men as they glance at each other out of dilated, haunted eyes — blank, apart from a dark flicker hinting at the void underneath, of dread. Their faces are gaunt and set, as they stammer out their shared versions of recent events. Over and over they retell it, that they might understand — and to hold off the silence, which threatens to consume them.

Can it be true it had been only today, early on this very same morning, that the terrified women found the dead body gone, the rock tomb empty? Winds of violation eddy through the stagnant Jerusalem streets. The sacred veil in the Temple hangs in shreds. The three crosses still stand on Calvary hill, outside the walls, their silhouette towering over the transgressive city, taunting. Little wonder two men seek asylum.

On the open road, a stranger is with them. How can this be? Where has he come from? Some nobody, they hastily suppose, some intrusive vagabond going nowhere. Failing to read their own fear, and forgetting the significant events pressing upon them, they make the normal human assumption. This moment, the here and now they inhabit and look out upon through their blurred minds, is nothing, just another arbitrary speck in time, another indistinct smudge on the scratchy meandering line of their bit-part scripts. Irritated by this one further jolt to the fracturing order of their lives, they note with disgust that the stranger's cloak is fouled with grime and age, his long hair unkempt. In his ordinariness, he looks a bit like Matthew, the tax collector, or a gardener such as the one Magdalene saw.

The third man queries their conversation. They stop in their tracks, gloomy, amazed that the stranger does not know what has just come to pass in Jerusalem. They tell him, ending with the empty tomb. Berating them as fools, he launches into a long lesson.

At last, they draw near the village. The stranger gives the impression he is going further, but as it is nearly evening, they persuade him to rest. So what is to be just happens, in the tiny public room of a local roadside inn, where he joins them at a rough-hewn slab table set for three. They watch with mounting apprehension, by the wildly flickering light of an oil-lamp, as he takes the bread. Suddenly his presence shimmers, filling the shadowy room. Bathing them in a pained and knowing look, he breaks the bread and gives it to them. As in a spell, they become their vision, hovering at a remove out in front of their physical selves, and dissolve into His eyes, His hands and the broken bread. Now they see clearly. It is Jesus himself, who in the instant disappears.[1]

The darkness of this night is in keeping with recent events, and they are left alone and bewildered, hunched over the table. Mark's *Life of Jesus* had ended without any risen Christ, with three women outside the empty tomb, trembling and amazed. 'Neither said they anything to any man, for they were afraid' run Mark's last words. Of the death that killeth death, not a sign. The frantic women do not even report back to the disciples.[2] If that is true of them, the ones with the surest knowledge, then what can the two men in Emmaus, who had a sign, have made of it? In their shoes, what would you or I make of it? In fact, the two around the flickering oil-lamp soon reconstruct: 'Did not our heart burn within us, while he talked with us by the way.' Within the hour, they set off back to Jerusalem.

How are we to read this story — the dramatic finale to Luke's *Life of Jesus*? Christ is also leaving Jerusalem. Perhaps he has had enough of human injustice and dim, fickle disciples. The drift is that he will keep going. But where to? Then the two he has lectured so vigorously invite him to join them. This has been the last time he will teach, and he is bad-tempered and perhaps even long-winded, as if sick of explaining the truth to the obtuse and the resistant — to everyone. And why these two? Why has history shone its immortalising spotlight, if only for a moment, on these insignificant beings, as they made their solitary and fitful way along the donkey route to Emmaus? Are they not us, one and all?

The story poses the ultimate question: On the journey of journeys, the road open, who is it that he or she may meet? This is the spot at which they yearn for the person who will point the way. Not that it is clear in the story that He has done this — the two unnerved men simply decide to return to Jerusalem, and it is far too early to tell how their lives have been transformed, if at all. And what does the right stranger *do*? If he saves them, then from what, into what? Furthermore, it may actually be the gardener, only the gardener, or an accountant, or the girl next door. It could even be a road of misfortune, such as the one on which fate decreed that Oedipus, believing that he had fled from his father, unwittingly met his real father, and killed him, thus sealing his own doom.

This thread leads directly to the question that is at the basis of all serious enquiry: What is truth? When the Greeks designated truth by their word *aletheia*, they built in a narrative. Truth is that which is *a-lethe*, not *lethe*, *Lethe* being the place of oblivion or forgetfulness, later the river running through the underworld. To drink the waters of this river was to extinguish memory. Oblivion is thus the natural human state, one in which individuals have forgotten what they know. They know everything, but are constitutionally blind and comprehensively so, containing within themselves a huge reservoir of Unknown. It would be identified in the twentieth century as the unconscious, following Freud, who also taught that they are inwardly driven to resist the unseen truth, as in the two men's instinct to flee Jerusalem and deny the stranger. Plato's version was that the all-knowing soul entering into a human form loses its memory.[3]

At the most, in times of gravity, when the 'heart burns within', they may *re-member*. Truth tears them out of the oblivion of being. The philosopher Heidegger translates *aletheia* into German as *Unverborgenheit*, meaning 'unconcealedness' or 'disclosedness', drawing on the sense of the *hidden* but not the *forgotten*.[4] Truth is a shaft of light breaking through to illuminate the mist-shrouded river. A mere broken piece of bread may do the trick, and the mists rise from off the eyes. In Magdalene's case, it was the voice that she recognised, when the gardener addressed her by her own name, intimately: 'Mary!' Moreover, as English has picked up, to be without Truth is *lethal*, death in life, its condition that of *lethargy*, a weariness of spirit in which all vitality has drained away.

A range of energies surface in the story — firstly the panic that drives the men away from Jerusalem, then the burning in the heart when the stranger speaks, the shock and awe around the table, and finally the resolve to return to the site of the horror.[5] But 'energy' is a feeble word for the demons that drive. What the third man *does*, if he does anything that will endure, is to arouse 'sacred rage'.[6] Sacred rage is the energy of truth. It is the fire that burns within, waiting to be piped forth by the music of *aletheia*. It is the stranger's medium.

So, the question becomes: who or what bears the Truth? Will the stranger be in disguise? We have assumed that the two men are rattled in their perplexity, and thereby too anxious and self-absorbed to notice who is with them. They may, alternatively, be shrewd, and resist the call, sensing with dread what it will ask of them. For as we are told, they stop abruptly, their mood suddenly gloomy — surprising, as there is no reason for this, apart from a stirring in the inner Unknown, where of course, the stranger is recognised. The normal human reflex out on the open road is to avoid risk, stick with what is known, pretend one is at home and dream on through life, and on, wedded to the security of oblivion. But the two men cannot help themselves, poor fools, inviting him in to join them for supper.

And is it that once they have seen him, he may disappear, for he is no longer needed? Is he now alive in the two who have been torn out of forgetfulness? This is less obscure in the case of Magdalene, told by the gardener, after she has recognised him: 'Touch me not!' He is now untouchable, and what is more, although she wants to hang on to this moment of all moments in her life, keep it forever, in fact she no longer needs to cling to the past for the charisma of being has entered into her.[7]

On that fateful journey, it need not be a man — perhaps, rather, an image. When an image truly becomes an *icon*, it lights up with remembering. In the story, the nature of the stranger's presence is not specified. Is it a ghost, is it a flesh-and-blood

Jesus, is it some form intermediate between body and spirit, or do the men hallucinate? A mountain of Christian theology would futilely debate just this point. John follows his *Touch me not!* story with Thomas, who is sceptical of all this mumbo-jumbo, boasting that he will believe only when he has stuck his fingers inside the real-live physical wounds. In other words, there is confusion and fear in all quarters about who or what the third man is.

We receive him, if at all, in the form of a story. If that story is told in the right way, painted or sculpted in the right form, composed in the right key, and the people on their own road to Emmaus are receptive — the story cryptically intersecting with their own — then the very foundations of being may be illuminated by the light of Truth. That is what culture does. It may be the thing that saves, that taps the sacred rage. It is the subject matter of this book.

The Western world is in the process of being thrown back onto its deepest resources. The stories are close by, ready to lift us out of our lethargy. Some have unwittingly found them, their lives driven, as it were, by a hidden god, or demon. Even they, however, the fortunate ones, would gain a poise and a fortitude if they knew. For the rest, it is a question of life itself.

The spirit cannot breathe without story. It sinks to a whimper, deflating its housing characters, and condemning them to psychopathology — literally, disease of the soul. So it is for the young in the contemporary West — teenagers, those in their twenties, the hope and pride of their societies — and with them, swathes of their seemingly more assured elders. A malaise holds them in thrall, struggling to live in a present without vision of any future, or connection to even the organic tissue of being, their own personal past.

He is eighteen, a year out of school and still with no regular work. There have been casual jobs — bartending, clearing gardens, that sort of thing. Girls are too strange and threatening; he never learnt to talk to them. Sometimes, when he is drunk with his mates, his eyes will glaze over and another self will slur abuse across a bar. He doesn't seem to care. He keeps his head lowered to avoid looking forwards, and the closest he comes to reflection is to scorn his parents for the monotony of their half-hearted pursuits, just getting through the day with the help of television and, he suspects, sedatives other than alcohol — scorns them for being like him. Catch him unawares and stunned eyes, an embarrassed grin and a spirit flailing around inside an alien body implore: 'Tell me what to do. Tell me how to live. Have pity on me; I am lost.'

She is twenty-five and successful, her schedule crammed with bright moments — nights out, ecstatic affairs, a new car, skiing in picturesque mountains, a swirl of acquaintances — and she has travelled some of the world. While she cannot be sure she will keep the one stable thing in her life, her job, that doesn't matter much, for she doubts she wants to, the solid professional path of her father unattainable but also unappealing. So she surfs the days, the months and the years, with each episode soon forgotten, as if it were but a passing wave returning, spent, into the timeless ocean out of which it rose. She induces oblivion, as if to wipe out the shadow she fears looming up inescapably over her.

They are dying for want of Story. So they taunt each other: 'Get a life!' So they mock each other: 'You are a waste of space.' The more hopeful among them question at the end of the day, if they are honest, and at the end of the most intense of days — a day of love, of adventure, of calamity — they question: 'Is that all there is?'[8] Indeed, *is* that all there is? The less hopeful have closed themselves off to expectations, lest they be disappointed.

They are dying for want of Story. Some delve into the East, drawn by its depth of spirit, or become fascinated by indigenous peoples like the Australian Aborigines who appear to live by their ancient stories and sacred sites, sustaining a blood bond with Nature. If there is political passion, a sense that I, too, am responsible for the world I inherit, then it will almost certainly centre on that same Nature, where it is believed that the gods still move. But the Western myths that animate sky, sea, mountains and bush have dimmed. On another front, many found in the life of Diana, Princess of Wales, a tragic story that they could scrutinise for clues as to how to live with dignity and value in their own time.

They are dying for want of Story. Contemporary slang provides a clue, in the mock serious ideal of the 'living legend'. A legend is a story with such gravity as to defy time, its subject entering the Halls of Fame, joining the immortals there. Clark Kent, popular cultural hero through the twentieth century, humiliated by a real life of bungled journalism and failure to attract the woman he loves, dreams himself a completely different story, that of *Superman*. Thus it is that paranoia drives its victims into either delusions that they are men who had unequivocally powerful direction, such as Napoleon and Superman, or delusions of persecution — 'I am followed, therefore I am!' — another fabrication of story to impute meaning to the chaos. The modern age's most sophisticated hero, Hamlet — the one it has most read, discussed, and watched on stage and cinema screen — has as his dying request to his friend Horatio: 'Tell my story.' This is the man whose own incapacity to do what he should has left the stage littered with corpses, a dithering paralysis in relation to life that makes him, once again, the hero of the time. Hamlet's final absurd hope as he sprawls across the wreckage of his life is that there might have been a form, justifying his existence. He dies for want of a vindicating story.

For both parent and child, the old bedtime ritual is often the one most warmly remembered. It was then that the world was given magical shape, the child identifying with fairy-tale characters and mythic heroes, enraptured by the story in which it is Me who rides through the enchanted forest and kills the fiery dragon, Me whom the glass slipper fits. The spirit soars; there is a place, a mission, a way of living, the monstrously huge world outside not so daunting. Once upon a time!

Without the deep structure of archetypal story, a life has no meaning. Take Odysseus. His many trials on his ten-year voyage home at the end of the Trojan War — a boys'-own adventure series, cowboys and Indians stuff — make sense to him, and become interesting to us, only because he has an overarching story, which tells him where he is going and why. In his particular case, it is the narrative of homecoming, told in such a way that it became the canonical story of the long voyage home in the Western tradition.

Then there was Antigone, gaining the courage to defy the State and risk her own life in order to bury the decomposing body of her outlaw brother, left out as carrion for birds and dogs. She is the only one big enough to take on the dread of being the daughter/sister of Oedipus, who killed his father and married his own mother, with whom he sired four children, Antigone being one of those four. She is driven by a sense of definitive story, that of her own family and her obligations to it, which it is left to her to bring to fitting completion. She is the last one able to restore sacred order to the horror of her family saga. We humans can bear almost any pain if we can find purpose in it.

Western culture runs on stories, starting with Homer's mythic recounting of a few episodes from the tenth year of the Trojan War. The Greek formula put it: *mythos* is *pathos*. 'Pathos' comes from the verb *paschein*, meaning both to experience and to suffer — hence its other modern English derivatives: passion, sympathy, pathology, apathy and empathy. Experience requires wholehearted engagement — that is, passion — with suffering its ever-present companion — hence the tragic vision. If you want to live, you must accept the totality. Furthermore, this is possible only under the authority of myth. Take away the charged archetypal story, fail to keep it animated, and you take away life.[9]

Roberto Calasso captures some of this ancient Greek understanding:

> *When something undefined and powerful shakes mind and fibre and trembles the cage of our bones, when the person who only a moment before was dull and agnostic is suddenly rocked by laughter and homicidal frenzy, or by the pangs of love, or by the hallucination of form, or finds his face streaming with tears, then the Greek realises he is not alone. Somebody else stands beside him, and that somebody is a god. He no longer has the calm clarity of perception he had in his mediocre state of existence. Instead, that clarity has migrated into his divine companion. A sharp profile against the sky, the god is resplendent, while the person who evoked him is left confused and overwhelmed ...*
>
> *What conclusions can we draw? To invite the gods ruins our relationship with them but sets history in motion. A life in which the gods are not invited isn't worth living. It will be quieter, but there won't be any stories. And you could suppose that these dangerous invitations were in fact contrived by the gods themselves, because the gods get bored with men who have no stories.[10]*

It is not just the sacred stories that have faded. In the closing decades of the twentieth century, the orthodox life-narratives also crumbled. A changing economy made it increasingly unlikely that many could count on a lifelong career awaiting them on entry into adulthood, a vocation that was secure and would provide the financial basis for a comfortable life. At the same time, belief withered in a lifelong marriage companionship, building a family, leading into a contented old age, the rocking chair in front of the fire. *Necessity*, in one of her recurring guises, was closing in once again.

What was left was making the most of the little things: a job here done with heart and soul thrown into it, an intimacy there in which love rose above the petty concerns of the egos involved. But even for such modest achievements, there had to be a story behind the scenes lending authority to each step taken — the story that fits, linking to the higher truth which could release the sacred rage.

Without Story, the temptation has been withdrawal into self, chit-chat about the everyday, as if describing how I drank coffee at nine-twenty-seven this morning anchors existence. Complaint comes, too — how bad my mother was when I was a baby, my father in teenage years, my society thereafter. The temptation is exacerbated by a surrounding culture of therapy and counselling. Behind its caring façade, the reality is that each puny ego is left alone to whimper *me-me-me* at the void.

There arose a linked fear of big story — archetypal, classical, what some called 'grand narrative' — that it would show *me* up as being of no consequence. If I am a nobody, then I would rather fail in peace, in oblivion, and deny that heroes exist. The wiser response has come from popular culture, with film, television and tabloid press taking the boy or girl next door and recasting their lives as something special. These 'real-life' stories address the vital unconscious knowledge in each person that the local and particular, ordinary old *me*, is shadowed by a grand story, a truth shaping and vindicating its existence.[11]

John Ford set out deliberately in his Westerns to give mythic weight to ordinary lives. He spelt his vision out in a narration over the concluding images to the cavalry film *She Wore a Yellow Ribbon* (1949):

So here they are, the dog-faced soldiers, the regulars, the fifty-cents-a-day professionals, riding the outposts of a nation. From Fort Reno to Fort Apache, from Sheridan to Stark, they were all the same: men in dirty-shirt blue and only a cold page in the history books to mark their passing. But wherever they rode, and whatever they fought for, that place became the United States.

*O*nce upon a time — so start the favourite stories that children ask to hear over and over again. With adults, it is not different. Mark opens his *Life of Jesus* with the Greek word *arche*, John with '*en arche*'. The translation is 'in the beginning', 'at the foundation' — or perhaps, rather, quite simply 'the fundament'. We are being told that we will be led to the 'sacred site'[12] where the presiding stories were created — the *archetypes*, types formed in the beginning, once upon a time.

One is tempted, when standing back to survey the vast span of Western culture, to imagine chiselled over its portal, as motto: 'In the beginning was the story.' Indeed, this is a permissible translation of the original Greek of the first line of John: 'In the beginning was the word (*logos*).'[13]

A culture is its sacred stories. In each case, it has one or two, perhaps three, major channels, which in turn are diffused through myriad tributaries forming the beliefs of a society, right down to the petty habit that may have given us wayfarers our excuse to visit Emmaus. Without it, there is no map, just the mist of oblivion. Humans, like the gods, get bored when they have no stories, and sink into lethargy. Culture is the power to lift them up from their prone animal state, the power to reveal the truth. That truth may engage universal moral laws, as in the case of Antigone. Then again, it may be pure in the spirit, which 'bloweth where he wills, and thou hearest his sound; but canst not tell whence he cometh and whither he goeth.'

The Australian Aborigines call their sacred stories 'the Dreaming'. It comes from the time before now, before ordinary time, yet a time 'everywhen'. The central task of each individual is to tap into those eternal stories, find a right relationship to the powers they represent. *Mythos* is *pathos*, or as the Australian Aborigines put it, not to live the Dreaming is to die. One interpreter has called the process the 'obliteration of the ephemeral':

> *Dreaming can be conceptualised as a great wave which follows along behind us, obliterating the debris of our existence and illuminating, as a synchronous set of images, those things which endure.* [14]

Here is a people that knows the truth about Story, the truth about culture.

Midrash, the Hebrew tradition called it, the process of each age taking up the ancient, sacred stories and retelling them in a way that spoke to the new times. Every living culture is inwardly driven to *midrash*. One of the major protagonists in what is to follow in this book, Nicolas Poussin, was referred to in these terms. His most successful contemporary, Gian Lorenzo Bernini, called him 'the great story-teller'.

So what was in the beginning? *Necessity* was there, as the ancient Greeks conceived of her, the supernatural force more powerful than any of the gods, she whom the Greeks held in such awe that they never personified her in their art — such would have been the sacrilege. In her control over human destiny, she determined the grand as well as the particular patterns. Her three beautiful daughters, the Fates, wove the thread of each individual's destiny, a thread that could be neither cut nor loosened, however powerfully heroic (Achilles) or wilfully crafty (Odysseus) the poor human yoked to the merciless tale that was his life. Fate binds. We can imagine them, those three ravishing nymphs, dancing gaily around in a circle together, and glancing down on their handiwork far below, at the moment two poor creatures tramping the track to Emmaus realise they are not alone.

Necessity — that chilling, pitiless name the Greeks gave her, in order to stress their own impotence over anything of significance in life, and in recognition of its force, far more coercive than anything biological or sociological — inherited genes or confining social institutions. Modern English usage reveals an enduring faith in *Necessity*, and the inviolable thread it spins for each individual destiny, in such expressions as 'it is *bound* to happen' and 'poor boy, you're *bound* to die.'[15]

In the beginning, *Necessity* also dictated the stories through which we humans would be able, if we were so inclined, to interpret our own singular lives, make sense of them, and even find some consolation for the torment inflicted upon us by the yoke of that same *Necessity*, herself. A small stock of stories they were, finding their completion in the Jesus cycle, told like most of the others, in the beginning, in Greek. Together, they staked out the sacred site that would found the West and make it great.

Or was it Athena? The cool one with the flashing grey eyes, she was patron of the arts, crafts and sports; of just wars; of the olive tree — she, above all, goddess of Truth. Statues of her would appear, as if on cue, as if rising out of the Western Unknown, during every great phase of *midrash*, starting with the temples dedicated to her on her own Acropolis, the one that oversaw fifth-century classical Athens.[16]

Homer opens *The Iliad* with the three words: 'Wrath, sing, goddess ...', letting us know that only the voice of a divinity may carry what is to follow, and in song. The Dreaming is too big for mere mortals to tell, the *mythos* of those superhuman beings who strode the earth in the days before ordinary time, who established the types for everywhen. Homer does not name the goddess, but it could only be Athena.

In *The Odyssey*, he is more explicit:

> *From some point*
> *here, goddess, daughter of Zeus, speak, and begin our story.*

Or, as another modern translator opens his version:

> *Sing in me, Muse, and through me tell the story.*[17]

So, we may also presume, it is the goddess Truth who from the beginning has presided over the Western Dreaming.

This book assumes a background argument. It draws heavily upon a period roughly pivoted around the sixteenth century, during the last great turning point of Western culture. This was the Rebirth, the last fundamental *midrash*. There were three new world-views that came into existence. Together, they have governed what has followed. It has been orthodox to recognise only two. Firstly, there was Humanism, at the core of the Renaissance, with its credo of reason, free will and the pre-eminence of the human individual, a culture founding modern science and technology, and producing later liberal and democratic derivatives. Secondly, there was the Protestant Reformation of Luther and Calvin, with its reorientation of Christianity around doctrines of faith and grace alone, individual conscience, and this-worldly vocation, with its own later secular derivatives.

Concurrently, the Old Masters were rethinking the formative stories, and producing in their art an earthily tragic picture of the human condition. The visual image becomes the messenger of truth. This might be called the Third Reformation. The place is principally Italy. The time starts around 1440, with Donatello, and has ended by 1670, soon after the death of Poussin.

This was not just a reworking of stories that were all presented whole in the beginning. A feature of archetypal story, as Frank Kermode has pointed out, is that it compels those who come under its thrall to bring it to its logical completion.[18] It demands to be filled out. That the *Lives of Jesus* provide no more than fragments of the Magdalene story forced those artists who retold it fifteen hundred years later to fill in the gaps, including how she spent the rest of her life.

Keeping the argument in mind, the book sets out to present the fundamental themes of the Western Dreaming — they come in the form of stories. There are nine. They will be pieced together from the major works that gave them narrative flesh, around half of their number receiving their most telling *midrash* to date from the Third Reformation.

Why the term 'Reformation'? Because it is almost always the *forms*, as Plato introduced them, that matter.[19] 'Reformation' is thus a more exact and fitting term than 'Renaissance', the focus on forms underlining the ever-present need to rework and thereby reinvigorate them.

The assumption used in selection holds that with any story, it is the major telling that counts.[20] All of importance, for instance, that may be known about Achilles is to be found in *The Iliad* — Homer establishes the archetype of hero and does so definitively. Similarly, the principal dimension of the story of fate is determined once and for all time by Sophocles' *Oedipus the King*. The form is never improved upon, every later *midrash*, lesser. Everything is to be gained by concentrating on the best and forgetting the rest. There is a canon, and a ranking.

The task requires method. From the outset, the method is that of *midrash*, to retell the stories, in the company of some interpretation. When the authoritative source is a work of art, this involves translation from the visual images into words, in effect continuing the spiralling motion of the culture forwards, just as the painters and sculptors had themselves taken up written narratives, together with philosophy and commentary, and metamorphosed them into pictures.

These stories are not at a distance, of largely academic interest, some detached account of the mess and the glory fictitious others have made of their lives. A principle governing what is to follow is that we ourselves are all on stage, plunged into the thick of the action, inhaling the stench, receiving the blows, sighing the sighs — the protagonists. Archetypal story has that special immediacy, demanding participation, obliterating the debris of our existence, illuminating the things that endure. Or it is dead. Nevertheless, when from time to time we are forced to interpret, to make better sense of where we are, we shall gain a little distance. The scholarly baggage, essential to keep the caravan in provisions, will be displaced into endnotes, which are not peripheral.

The reason for choosing to open this book with the 'Road to Emmaus' is simple: as parable, it is the key to the nature of our enterprise.[21] As parable, it insists on the inescapability of mystery. Every detail remains obscure — open to question and doubt. All we are left with is the inner confidence that this story is important, that somehow and somewhere it bears a deep and central truth. The story hounds us, it haunts us, yet it will not reveal any clear formula. It says: Do not press too hard for a definite shape, for a definitive reading. I am not like that. Do not ask to know who or what power moves behind the scenes — you will not find God or whatever through me. Indeed, any urgency in the drive to interpret will be a symptom of lack of knowing, and the insecurity that leads to doctrine. The story in itself is all. Relax and let it be! Then it may work its fill.

The Australian Aborigines from time to time say to Westerners: 'You have lost your Dreaming!'[22] They are, of course, right in part. The Christian churches are custodians of a treasure lost to themselves, and the universities are tending the same way. As these institutions founder in metaphysical emptiness, their words as dead leaves, all the texts and icons are there in their midst, waiting to have life breathed back into them.

Third Reformation art is the major modern contributor to the Western Dreaming as it might speak today. It is far from the whole. Not all the retelling has been through painting and sculpture. The other great tradition in Reformation story is 'classical' music, exemplified in such works as Bach's *St Matthew Passion* (c.1727–44). And ever present are the great ancient texts, waiting to be taken up once more.

Those who find art obscure may experience archetypal story through other media — music, for instance. The *St Matthew Passion* reveals what forces may be unleashed by tapping into the Dreaming. While Bach is literal with Jesus' last day — Matthew's written account unchanged — his *midrash* is into sound. A volcano of controlled passion rages for three hours as the choruses — solo and collective — act out and reflect upon the unfolding story. Through the fury, there are pockets of stillness, and grace notes.

The Dreaming is like the stranger on the track to Emmaus, but silent — not haranguing or even tutoring. The wayfarers of the modern West do not really know where they are going, or why — perhaps just *away*. They sense he has come from afar, and now accompanies them for a long stretch of their road. He is just there, a presence. Indeed, does he speak at all? From time to time, they seem to listen, and occasionally their hearts burn within. Somehow they know, and that he is there to guide their journey, but for much of the time, they behave as if they have forgotten what they know, and do not even notice him.

He will keep going, as in the story, whatever they do, and even for another five hundred years if necessary. For them, however, entering a new millennium — they who have come to realise that neither the Humanist nor the Protestant Reformation is more than a secondary guide, incapable of tapping the sacred rage, for they had no stories, his time has come. How else might they recover their Dreaming? 'The gods get bored with men who have no stories.' As it is towards evening, they should invite him in, to abide with them for supper.

THE STORIES

I.

God is Dead — *Pneuma*

It is the Deluge. An expanse of grey water, flooding an entire valley, merges into a mountain in the distance shadowed by sheets of rain, rising into a grim sky tending black. A pale moon reflects feeble light, hinting at the withdrawal of any warmth or vitality from the world. Church spires and the roofs of submerged houses can be made out above the still-rising waters, the waters of catastrophe.

Standing in the bow of a punt, a mother passes a golden-haired infant cloaked in red up to the father, who is bending down from a craggy outcrop and, she assumes, safe on dry land from the voracious waters. She had been quietly at home when the rain started, going about her daily chores, soothed by the drumming on the roof. But it did not stop. For the first few days, her son would crawl outside and squeal with delight as he rolled around in the mud. Then the waters began to rise. Her husband stopped going to work. They watched with mounting consternation as their ordinary lives were steadily, remorselessly washed away.

Now the father, extending his right arm rigidly down, fingers on the child's chest in a parody of benediction, stops him, his own mouth opening with dread, screaming: 'No!' The rocky land he has explored is snake-infested — indeed, out of the corner of his eye he sees a viper draped around a tree close by, looking straight at him, its head poised to strike. The trees are stunted and dead, and the piece of cliff rock from which this man leans down has split off from the land mass and is about to crash into the water, taking him to his doom.

Dark rocks nearby provide the backdrop to a giant python that slithers upwards, its head directed into a parallel scene. The flood pours over a cataract, down which a long rowing boat has plummeted, stern first, bow diagonally up. It is on the point of plunging under.

In the bow, projecting upwards like the tail fin of a diving whale, two men perch precariously. One manages to keep erect, his form like a high-board diver about to spring, reaching upwards in a gesture of prayer, imploring the heavens for mercy. His companion strains with all his might, left hand clamped on the gunnel, to hold him up, right arm tightly around his hip, back bent, barefooted, toes gripping the rib timbers. As the boat hurtles backwards and down, it is as if these men walk up it, using the ribs as rungs of a ladder. They may go no farther, hovering there in the instant, like trapeze artists at the apex of their flight, but with no partner to catch them in their down somersault. The praying man is already starting to arch over backwards. In a moment, he will plummet into his watery grave.

Here is quixotic individual humanity, its final hope to influence the gods through prayer. Dream on, proud mortal! If anything governs this scene, it does not respond to such entreaties. It questions: Who are you to aspire to justice? By what presumption do you think you could sway powers strong enough to flood the whole world? Your prayer is absurd, and you know it.

You imagine you have free will, that you can influence your destiny, set it right, counter the misfortune in store for you. You are learning about free will. You are learning about the vacuity of your cathedrals, the flimsiness of your homes, even the futility of your compassion — that fellow there, his arm around you, do you think he moves the gods to pity? If there are gods.

But do not waters of forgetful dream, waters of peaceful death, all seem like the signs of oblivion? Enveloped in dense mist, thick low cloud, blinding sleet, closed in grey, are these not the veiling waters of *Lethe*, letting you know that the goddess of Truth may be near?

Back inside practical reality, a shaft of incandescent lightning spears through the black sky, counter to the flood, the one manifestation of fire in this twilight world, lightning the weapon of Zeus, king of the gods. It is the voice of power, but with no redemption in it. It snakes towards the white-shawled head of the mother.

Here is the final lesson, that life means one long, unremitting initiation into Fall, into endless night. Everyone is damned. The ultimate necessity, which is death, keeps his court, and no-one escapes from him, neither man nor beast, neither woman nor saint.

The figure of the man aloft in prayer intimates crucifixion, hovering in the vertical, attempting to rise from the earth, which is now in flood. But any possible foundations for surety of human stance are washed away. Death is death; it rules life, whoever you are, whatever good fortune you think you enjoy. Just look on the young family, their experience hitherto as good as human life gets! As Zeus once reflected while pausing to scrutinise the heroes fighting on the plains of Troy far below — and they the greatest of humans:

Since among all creatures that breathe on earth and crawl on it there is not anywhere a thing more dismal than man is.[1]

This simple story is a paradox. The overall mood is at odds with the individual narratives. A calm shimmers out of the catastrophic night. Every particular is horror, but transmuted in the totality. Out of the annihilation, out of the obliteration of every human hope, the poisoning of every human desire, to the point of scoffing at both parental love and self-sacrificing friendship; out of the nothing that remains of human existence, there rises a tune. It is like the mournful cry of the dusk bugle, carrying the voices of the warrior shades to the living.

Even the praying man, pitching himself absurdly into thin air to transcend the earth and its profane physicality, achieves a moment of grace suspended under the heavens. Were he to look down, he would, like Peter walking on the water, sink — 'Oh thou of little faith!' His rational self is in despair, but for the moment he has jettisoned it, opening himself to a spirit that holds him there, aloft, and the god answers, his voice a shaft of brilliant silver illuminating eternal night.

This is prayer. Out of the depths of tainted flesh, of raw exposed wounds, out of the annihilation of self — all he is and was and might have been — he is liberated. Freed from the petty bounds of being, he flows out into union with the infinite oneness, out into the distant, timeless unity. This *is* his Cross, on which he prays. Thus, it is not, as Reason would argue, analysing the scene, that death is the one escape from the horror and absurdity which is life, but rather, the tragic religious view that out of the ashes of annihilation, out of the suffering, we may be reborn. Here is the key to the exhilaration, of a death that killeth death. Grace comes somehow violent.[2]

The scene universalises. Is the entire endeavour, of everybody who grinds through the everyday, merely one of survival, in good times to the tune of *Is That All There Is*? Is not all striving, at its heart, a reaching for the heavens, standing on nothing, a quixotic attempt to rise above brute matter and profane time? The waitress who does her job justice throws her entire being into placing the fork down just right. Her belief is no illusion. Out of the still centre of the annihilating paradox, the silver javelin may flash.

The figures, one by one, around the scene are touched. In each particular, they glow, the python having lost its menace, changed into some queer vertical momentum. Gone is the despair. In tandem, the praying man and the family trio defy the mortal gravity, poised weightless in mid-air, held by the *pneuma* that distils through them. The lightning shines through the whole scene, a luminous clarity recasting the black night as a curtain about to lift, revealing some paradise to come. It is a still, serene incandescence, an all-suffusing grey-silver aura flaring from where all humans belong.[3]

God is dead in the modern West. He is just as comprehensively extinct as the dinosaur, but with none of its enduring charm. No child's imagination is captivated by His memory. No mourners bearing flowers pilgrimage in search of His tomb, which in any case does not exist. He has gone, without trace. So how did He die? When did it happen? Indeed, what was the *He* or *It* that died? Does His identity even matter, except as a comparative aid in recognising what has replaced Him?

Some still refuse to accept reality. But the facts are all around, for anyone to see. If a painter today were to portray God, as Michelangelo did on the Sistine Chapel ceiling — the old man with the long grey beard, touching the hand of Adam — who would not be convulsed by laughter? And when some antiquated theologian begins to argue that there is an all-powerful, all-seeing Lord up above, watching over events, guiding them, and thus there must be reason and justice — even mercy — lying behind the death, for instance, of a little girl who accidentally runs out in front of a car, the modern response is to judge him not just inhuman but insane. Or when the remnants of Church Christianity in the West, and they are few, among even its meagre number, get down on their knees and pray that God intervene in their lives, are not the rest of us tempted to roll our eyes in disbelief?

Kierkegaard had already in 1846 mocked the arrogance of believing that God might be the slightest bit interested in human suffering.[4] This Danish philosopher was the last reflective Christian in the deep traditional sense of faith circumscribed by belief in Christ and the Lord God of the Bible. He was, equally, the first serious post-Christian philosopher, three years earlier having charted, in his book *Fear and Trembling*, the virtual impossibility of believing in that same God any more. The era of the cosy, comprehensive metaphysics of Catholicism was irretrievably over, and with it what he dubbed nostalgically as religion for children. Then, in 1882, the modern chronicle of evaporating belief in a single all-powerful person reached its culmination in Nietzsche's *Parable of the Death of God*:

> *We have killed God — you and I. We are all his murderers. But how have we done this? How were we able to drink up the sea? Who gave us the sponge to wipe away the entire horizon? What did we do when we unchained this earth from its sun? Whither is it moving now? Whither are we moving now? Away from all suns? Are we not perpetually falling? Backward, sideward, forward, in all directions? Is there any up or down left? Are we not straying as through an infinite nothing? Do we not feel the breath of empty space? Has it not become colder? Is more and more night not coming on all the time?*[5]

In other words, this was not just a limited issue, of faith in God and weekly attendance at church. The entire edifice of Western belief was at stake. Collapsing like a house of cards would be any confidence that life has purpose, and by extension, that there is meaning to why we are here, where we come from, and what happens to us at death. Kill God, Nietzsche put it, and human life becomes either horrible or absurd. His further prediction that even the order of visual perception would disintegrate was fulfilled in abstract art and the theory of relativity.

In the broad sense, of a complete collapse of meaning into nihilism, Nietzsche's prophecy has turned out to be wrong. God was indeed gone, but the force of the sacred continued to drive through the human condition. A religious imperative seems to be innate, a sort of third instinct, apart from *eros* and aggression,[6] reaching for the beyond. It insists that everything profane, starting with the human body, undergo metamorphosis 'into something rich and strange'. Pealing on out of eternity is the *pneuma* refrain:

> *The wind (pneuma) bloweth where he wills, and thou hearest his sound, but canst not tell whence he cometh, and whither he goeth.*[7]

The Greek word *pneuma* means all of spirit, breath and wind. The 'sacred breath' is potentially all around, caught in the image of the wind that bloweth.

As much as ever, there is the experience of the rising out of self to conjoin with the greater oneness. It may happen in ecstatic intimacy, in empathy with a companion, in quiet wonder in some garden, or in a room that has suddenly shone like lit crystal. Form continues to be found in work, sport, pastime, talk — that state of grace in which mind, body, task and the surrounding environment achieve union, a higher harmony together; and the person moves, for a moment outside time, with a superhuman, god-like poise. Thus, the modern West has its own meditative exercises through which the ego and its daily worries are transcended, techniques for becoming *un-self-conscious*.

Faith that there is a soul in the creatures and things that inhabit the world, if only the human individual can find the right relationship to them, lives on.[8] However, these are all forms and faiths compelled from behind the scenes by the Dreaming truth.

The sacred presence no longer manifests itself as the Lord God above. How, then, did this revolution come about, the greatest theological upheaval in Western history? How was it that God gave way to *pneuma* — the spirit, the wind, the breath that bloweth where it wills? With the Deluge, we have already entered the modern West. Poussin told this story in 1664, two centuries before Nietzsche announced the death of God. So when and how did it actually happen?

The first time was back in the creation vortex out of which the culture of the West was born — at the end of the beginning. As always, our approach is through a story — Mark's *Life of Jesus*.[9] Bearing the awesome gravity of Greek tragedy, drawing on Hebrew tradition, told with the stalking night tones of the Deluge, it is cast on the brink of an unbearable terror. The generative core and anchoring authority of the Christian Bible, it is not a gospel in the literal Greek sense of *euaggelion* — good news. It is far too tortured and dark for that. It documents, moreover, the site and the circumstances of the primal death of the Judeo-Christian God.

Mark opens with Jesus' baptism, he alone seeing the breath of *pneuma* descending, hearing a voice from the heavens: 'Thou art my dear son in whom I delight.'[10] God speaks at the outset, but thereafter, with the exception of a couple of passages, barely a reference is made to him.[11] The story is exclusively Christ, seen through his own eyes, felt through his own being, the most desperate existential psychospiritual drama in the Western Dreaming. Its central thread is *pneuma*. His intercourse is here on earth, with the impure *pneumata* that possess the sick and the deranged, the wayward and the feeble of mind — in other words, everybody.

His teaching comes to focus on his own life, articulated through three main themes: *pneuma*; *I am*, which he asserts is the key to truth; and *the story* itself. Know who *I am*, is his message, and you shall know everything. Then the *pneuma* will be with you, in you. The cue is from the Old Testament, in the words its God uses when naming himself to Moses, the most important line in the whole epic Hebrew Bible: 'I am that I am.'[12] Here is the axiom of being. When God exists, then He defines everything — as primal and categorical being, who serves as first cause of all happenings and as the centre of all meaning. His existence answers all questions. Thus, Jesus' contrasting insistence that nothing matters apart from his own *I am* is fundamental and revolutionary. He is replacing God with himself. The new divinity is thus lodged in material, earth-born being, *pneuma* shaped by the *I am*, the potential within each human individual, initiated by his example.[13]

Jesus' own spirits steadily flag through the first half of Mark's narrative, due mainly to the failure of his chosen disciples to learn anything.[14] Then he undergoes metamorphosis by fire, his *I am* incandescent. This is preparation for the inexorable End logic, which begins in Chapter 14. After the Last Supper, Jesus descends to the Garden of Gethsemane. It is night, and he is distressed — 'My soul is exceeding sorrowful unto death.' Alone, he addresses his God: 'Take away this cup from me.' It is the cup of destiny, of the portion of good and ill the Fates mix for everyone, the cup of suffering.[15] His tone is resigned, past caring, but with his last request, he wants, like Oedipus, to change his fate, although without any of the Greek hero's dynamism. Either he is praying here for divine intervention — knowing this to be futile and wrong — or his words are whispered to himself, in weakness and temptation, a sign of his dispiritedness. He has lost faith in his destiny. He has lost faith in his vocation. At this critical moment, nearby, his three leading disciples have fallen asleep, and the chapter ends with Peter's public denial of having known Jesus.

The core End narrative follows — from arrest and trial, through crucifixion, to deposition and entombment — told in the long Chapter 15. Various groups mock Jesus — indeed, they take up one-third of the chapter — setting the mood of relentless hatred against one lonely man. Just before death, Jesus addresses his God for the last time, with words that form the climax to his life story, his summation of what he has learnt, the significance of it all: 'My God, my God, why hast thou forsaken me?' Then he screams, and lets go.

The End lacks any intimation of the presence of God. There is Christ, there is *pneuma* and there is the darkness. The climactic words have as their charged undercurrent: I abandon God, who is no more to me. And God is truly not with him. Modern scholarship argues that the title 'son of God' was not applied to Jesus during his own lifetime — he was the 'Messiah'.[16]

Mark completes his story with nine terse and terrible verses — Chapter 16. There is no Resurrection, no good news, just an empty tomb and three women so afraid that they run away, and will tell no-one of what they have seen.[17] One of those women is Magdalene. If she is mute with fear, we can imagine the effect on the less assured others.

This is a story of fire, fear and failure, anathema to fanatics and Fundamentalists. The fear is absence of God, and the impact that has on an unhinged and stunned Jesus. The new theological equations, generated from death by godless crucifixion, are extraordinary in their implications.

In Mark, there is virtually no moral law — no teaching stories in praise of worthy human actions, no warnings about wicked ones. The couple of inclusions are timid, as if the author is merely going through the motions, feeling under obligation to say something about goodness.[18] In fact, it is Luke, probably learning from Mark, who makes this vital distinction clear, in his third chapter. He identifies ethical religion with John the Baptist, whose mission is that of the standard Hebrew prophet, coming in from the wilderness to storm at the people: 'Sinners repent, or be damned!' John's entire focus is on moral impurity, offering baptism by water to cleanse it.[19]

Ethical religion is being singled out for relegation. It is always premised on an ultimate authority, transcendent and just, imposing a moral balance sheet, endorsing forgiveness. As Dostoevsky, himself an Orthodox Christian, put it: If God is dead, then everything is permitted.[20] No God, then no moral law. That is the orthodox logic, and all the Christian Churches have been true to it, baptising with water — even the Protestant ones, and in spite of their founding theology. This, however, makes them, one and all, Churches of John the Baptist, not of Christ. In essence, they have stood on a twin foundation — unquestioned faith in a just and merciful, all-seeing God as one leg; moral rearmament as the other. Here is the key to their modern Western downfall.[21]

At the core of Church Christianity's violation of its own formative story is its doctrine of 'sin'. Christ often uses the word, but the Greek original, *hamartia*, had the literal meaning of *missing the mark*, as in, say, a spear throw. Thus it is, rather, a *pneuma* term, alluding to something like *loss of way*. Aristotle uses the same word, in his theory of tragedy, for the *flaw* (or error, frailty, weakness) in the hero.[22] Mistranslation recast the biblical *hamartia* in ethical guise — a characteristic moralising of the *Life of Jesus*.

Even explicit ethical comparison in the Bible needs to be approached with caution. Take Jesus' line: 'I came not to call the righteous but sinners to repentance.'[23] 'Repentance' here is *metanoia*, meaning literally 'change of mind' — or, more loosely, change of perception, even transformation of consciousness. 'Righteous' is *dikaios*, which can mean *right* in the sense of well balanced, innocent and fitting, or equally, can mean having a right relationship to Law. So the *pneuma* translation might read: 'I came to call not the sound but those who have lost their way, to spirit change.'

John the Baptist is different from his moralist predecessors in knowing that he is not the one. He announces that a man with far mightier powers is about to arrive, one who 'will baptise you with sacred *pneuma* and with fire'.[24] The subtext is that ethical religion — water religion — is being superseded by *pneuma* religion — fire religion — and the two have nothing to do with each other.[25] This, moreover, is made possible by sacred force being brought down to earth, and planted within the human entity, in an *I am* that suffers unto tragic death. Jesus teaches by example, putting himself on stage, saying: I am all that is; do not look elsewhere, not even up above. Join with me on this, my life journey, totally exposed, and feel what it is like to be human. Learn what you will need to save you — fire and *pneuma*. Know the sacred rage!

Mark's Jesus, a few days before his death, comes upon a fig tree that is flourishing in full leaf but fruitless — it is out of season. He is hungry. In a fury, he curses the fig, which the next day is wasted down to its roots.

This is Jesus' version of bringing on the Deluge — he uses fire, not water. He singles out an innocent tree — being true to its nature its only crime — and scorches away all its living attributes. There is precedent, that of the Hebrew God appearing in a burning bush to address Moses. God was indicating that encounter with divinity burns away all past identity — the chosen mortal forced to start again in terms of his *I am*, start from nothing.

Jesus is at the same time cursing himself. In a couple of days' time he will be nailed alive to a vertical stump. Once the raging fire has crossed the earth, reducing it to a smouldering wasteland, the only thing left standing will be the Cross. Jesus' disciples look on, astounded, rigid with fear, knowing that they, too, are that incinerated tree, dry of sap, denuded of leaf — all sense of self annulled.

After these events, which happened around 30AD, a millennium and a half will pass — dubbed by some the Dark

Ages — of God ruling in His heavens, served by His earthly rock, the Church. Then the story recommences. At the formative moment of the three Reformations, Mark's death of God returns, and with it the accompanying pall of the withered fig, for those sensitive enough to sniff the new chill wind whistling over the steadily rising waters.

Poussin makes it explicit, in the first of his *Four Seasons* cycle of paintings — *Spring*. Up in the sky, he paints in the old man with the long grey beard looking down at Eve, in the process of standing up, pointing at the apple above her head. God's reaction to what He sees is to fly off into the distance, waving farewell as He departs the human universe. The image is comic, Poussin inverting traditional theology, having Eve and Adam inheriting the world while God banishes himself. The artist is deliberately mocking Michelangelo's God — as medieval and thereby obsolete. The date is 1660, the place Rome.[26] The cycle will be completed four years later with *Winter/Deluge*, the painting that marks the end of the Third Reformation.

Poussin was not the first. He picked up the inference from his great predecessors. God is absent from Raphael's *Deposition* of 1507. And in the 1440s Donatello had already sculpted in Padua a bronze *Christ on the Cross*, this Jesus straight out of Mark's narrative, alone and forsaken, without God. The face is modern in its earthly realism, harrowed with pain and despair, bearing in its gaunt contours the shadow of the withered tree. Donatello would draw out the explicit form in a life-size Magdalene statue carved in 1454, she drained of all sap, hideous, a body shrivelled in the searing crucible of life, worldly identity obliterated in the hope of gaining the saving *pneuma*.

Luther, too, was sensitive enough to feel the chill wind. His rage against Rome and the Papacy was that they had failed him, leaving him on the brink of nothing to believe in. It was the same Protestant rage that stripped the churches of all their holy bric-a-brac, smashed the statues of the Virgin and saints, scrapped the sacraments and demoted the priesthood — the fury driven by the abyss, against trifling aids to spiritual wellbeing. Luther might as well have engineered his own flood, submerging the Roman Church and all it stood for. He wrestled in 1531 with the 'death that killeth death', as he put it, in his *Commentary on St Paul's Epistle to the Galatians*.

The Second, Protestant, Reformation was thus under siege by the shadow of Mark's Jesus. Assaulted by doubt, Luther and Calvin launched their simple and austere axiom — faith alone, grace alone — and with it a fog of fatalism as despotic as that enshrouding Oedipus. They postulated a God so harsh in his distance, inscrutability, lack of compassion, and cruelty that the modern interpreter is inclined to read him as a product of *negation*.[27] Fearing his non-existence, the Reformers are driven to the opposite extreme, just as those who are insecure in their faith tend to fanaticism. Moreover, the Protestant God was so random in his 'grace' as to behave more like *pneuma*.

Luther propounded the 'darkness of faith' — elusive, inaccessible, utterly incompatible with the light of reason. Its single commanding story was that of crucifixion. Here was the death that might killeth death — the one remaining answer, he thought, to the horror. It was as if he was anticipating the Deluge, attempting to read its portent.

Then there was the First, Humanist, Reformation. It imagined that the death of God was its cue to lead the West down an entirely new road, one of its own creation. It staked its entire endeavour on God's extinction. Nor was He to be magically metamorphosed into some other form of sacred force. In the strict Humanist canon, *pneuma* is itself mere superstition — off with the fairies. But this became problematic, and virtually from the outset.

The Humanist problem was simple, put most eloquently by Holbein and Shakespeare, in their respective masterpieces *The Ambassadors* (1533) and *Hamlet* (c.1602). The latter became the story that would endure at the core of the modern West's understanding of itself.[28] Proud heroes were cast centre-stage under the spotlights, believing only in themselves, their intelligence and their freedom of will. They were those who would lead the West for the next five hundred years, directing its civilisation, masterminding its technology, its politics, its virtuosity in most spheres of human endeavour. They would be fine as long as they kept moving, magnificent in their dignity and their glory, adorning the world with their brilliance. But once they paused to look around, and down, they found they were all Hamlets, skull in hand, with no answer to the Deluge.

They had yoked their existence to the wrong knowledge. They discovered that their truths — those of secular philosophy, science, literature and music — when subjected to the darkness, turned into an instruction to the praying man to be realistic, pause, look around, look down. This is the knowledge that can merely disenchant, coolly pointing out that you are about to plunge to your watery grave. Thus it was that the most eligible young men and women in the world, however wealthy, influential, creative and wise, were sunk once they found the grey water upon them. For they who were unmusical in relation to the grace notes, God was gone centuries before Nietzsche wrote his requiem. As their life inexplicably drained out of them, they found themselves alone, no silver shaft spearing through the darkness.

Once *midrash* has recommenced, the re-formed Dreaming moves under the authority of Mark. The killing of the Western God liberated metaphysics, untethered it like Homer's stallion, after a long stalled winter, to range over spring pastures.[29] So it thunders across the human landscape, whinnying and tossing its proud mane, fuelled by fire and *pneuma*. After a sleep that had lasted a dreary one and a half millennia, it finally happened.

Once the story gets going, it sets off in new directions. Mark's Jesus is not alone in filling the empty space left by the death of God. In particular, vivid ancient Greek presences return, opening with death by grey water. Two other stories come into focus.

A man sits on a lump of marble surrounded by the ruins of a Greek temple. He has dark, coarse features, thick muddy-brown hair and a beard streaked with grey. A river winds away behind him through cultivated plains towards hills in the distance. Clouds scud across a pastel-blue sky. Order presides, a sublime ethereality, as if Athena rules. The ruins of her temple instruct that power does not lie in ritual worship, nor in stone cathedrals built in her honour, but in art and breath. The goddess of Truth insists on a balanced creation — between the human part, which is transitory, and Nature.

The man is Matthew. Years have passed since that day when the stranger entered the room in which he was collecting taxes, and he received his call. It seems little has happened in the intervening decades. He spent the first couple of years travelling around Galilee with his teacher, but he hardly remembers those times. His story is not as might have been anticipated, after the fateful encounter — his Emmaus — propelled along a purple road of inspired mission and achievement. Like the others, he fled in fear that Thursday Jerusalem night, and only later heard third-hand what had happened — most of it rumour. Then, still young and confused, he started drifting, settled here, moved there, did this and maybe should have done that, not much eventuating. Carried along by the rhythm of profane time, he has not been someone given to looking back. In any case, it was all so, so long ago.

Inexplicably and from nowhere, one day it presses upon Matthew that he has to write his account of those once-upon-a-time events. We meet him now, after decades of restless journeying in search of whatever. He has sat down by this river to start. He holds pen and paper, strains his thoughts, but nothing comes. His being is clogged up with beast, goat thick with soil and slumber — with ordinariness.

Suddenly an angel alights close beside him, with fiery-red bushy hair, robed in white, and Matthew gazes up into a pale face smiling down at him. Gentle and encouraging, it looks almost human. Matthew notices that a chubby hand is on the paper, pointing to where he must write the first word. His mind, now bathing in golden light, relaxes, clarifies, and it all comes back to him, the story unfolding before his inner eye.

This is grace. Smooth, mild — unaccompanied by suffering — grace in this, its other mode, comes easily.[30] Matthew senses not only his pen speeding across the paper, as if automatically, guided by some hidden hand, but his entire being streaming out beyond the perimeter of his edgy normal self. For the first time, he feels himself a centre of gravity — yet, paradoxically, a centre without boundary, his own territory infinite — not that he owns it, but possession in terms of him being its point of view. He also notices that the cloud formation and its reflection in the river both mimic the angel's wings, and the curve of the river the arrival path.

So the sacred presence is all and at once — beside him, behind him in the water, and beyond him in the heavens, without distinction — and he, too, is all and one. In this, his *metanoia*, he has become river and tree, hill and mountain. When *pneuma* rules, its breath dissolves the limits, synthesising world. Matthew has found his form. His vocation can finally take flight.[31]

But this is not all. Suddenly, another presence is there, having risen out of the concealing mists. No-one, not even Matthew, is quarantined from the Deluge. As the angel comes into focus, Matthew senses a linen mantle, also white, appearing just in front of him, draping itself over a stone slab, just like the one on which he sits. It is his own mantle. It suggests the form of a man kneeling low, bent forwards flat over the block, arms stretched back and up as if tied behind him at the wrists. His head is down, neck bared, prepared for execution — in fact, the head has already gone. Legend has it that Matthew will suffer a martyr's death, by beheading.[32]

At the moment of awakening to his vocation, as writer of the story, he awakens to his own death. Yet that death, in spite of the gruesome facts, is not horrible. Here it has undergone *metanoia*, transformed in the shape and character of the white drapery into something light and innocent, even delicate and serene. Moreover, a triangle of immense power, formed by the angel, the linen shroud and Matthew, governs the scene. Little wonder that the classical temple has been blown apart, as if by the dynamite of this triple presence. At the centre of force is the page. Matthew is learning that he is his work. It is the key to his existence. Under its authority, his own death turns into a joyful celebration.

Danae is just like Matthew. It may not seem so. For her, the visitor — or stranger — is not an angel as such, but Zeus, the king of the gods, disguised as a shower of gold. Who would not give everything to be her? Who has not glimpsed what it is to be her? Danae is a beautiful young woman, locked up in a high bronze tower by her father, because he fears that she will be seduced and the illegitimate progeny will grow up to kill him. So it has been foretold — the grandson-to-be, Perseus.

One day as she lounges dreamily on her bed high up in the locked bronze tower, her pet dog sleeping beside her, sheltered by burgundy-red velvet curtains at its head, it happens. A brilliant explosion of golden stars floods in through the open window, her exposed flesh tingling as it moves down her body, her palms and the soles of her feet throbbing. Caressed by some invisible warm breath, breasts flushing, her core rises helplessly, joyously towards it. As she sinks back in ecstasy, her swooning gaze discerns the outline of the god's face in wisps of grey cloud wafting through the cascading sparks.

Her father's trusted gaoler sits close by, at the foot of the bed, a hideous old crone, steel keys jangling on her belt. But she, too, is enraptured by the shower of gold, forgetting herself and her job, impulsively blushing, and opening her own lap as if to say: This is a far more welcoming place. As if! Quickly, her own more rational, sober self, past interest in divine *eros*, intervenes. It sees the stars as gold pieces, which she then tries to catch in her apron. Such is negative *metanoia*. Age turns not only beauty into ugliness but receptiveness to the light into petty calculation. Danae, too, will be old one day.

Grace is divine drunkenness.[33] God has returned in pagan form. Danae is the new Dionysiac Eve, torn out of the oblivion of being by another truth, fused in the crucible of fire and *pneuma*. Indeed, according to one version of the story, her father's punishment was due to his doubting the divinity of the god of Bacchic abandon — Dionysus. That foolish father then locked Dionysus out of his city, Argos, further provoking the slighted god and thus ensuring his own doom.[34] It is a story in which the repressed instinct returns, and in a torrent, Dionysus shooting his own spirit arrows of intoxication unerringly into the daughter's heart, his own father exploiting the result. The irony is that Danae's father, doubting that Zeus is Dionysus' father, ends up with that same king of the gods siring the grandson who will murder him.

What moral law has the authority to stop seduction by the king of the gods? His presence overrules any 'Thou shalt not fornicate outside marriage', or whatever. Danae's dog sleeps through the visitation, its instinctive wisdom that his mistress is not under threat. Where Greek Aphrodite and Eros — or Roman Venus and Cupid — are present, so is *pneuma*, and the ethical turns into a mean old hag. This order is metaphysical, not moral — to the extreme of scorning the ethical as life-denying.

Everything going on in this story is fated, minutely scripted by *Necessity*. But so what? Danae does not care. For her, this moment is enough, outside time, worth fifty years of pleasant coffee interludes, fifty years of storm and exile. Who does her father think he is, trying to prohibit life, and how pitiful, locking the door when her lover is not just some uncouth local, but the magnificent supreme divinity, who may enter at whim by the window? Her dog knows better than her father.

Furthermore, as always, the Dreaming story generalises. Whenever a lover enters the room, if he is not imagined as king of the gods and she as goddess of beauty, things have gone wrong. The humans will drown in their own profanity, no light to their Deluge.

Danae is more graced than Jacob, not needing to wrestle all night with an angel for her blessing.[35] When Zeus arrives, he does so as an unexpected gift, irresistible archetype of sacred desire. He will not depart like Hamlet's father's ghost, needing to say: 'Remember me!'

The three stories — death by grey water, Matthew and Danae — guide the West through the archway into a modernity that makes metaphysical sense. Once through, no Lord God sits up above any more, watching benevolently over His flock. His place has been taken by a sort of sacred ether, in which *pneuma* moves with its grace notes. All creatures that walk the earth, and other things that dwell there, are potentially of Matthew and Danae — to be touched by the wind that bloweth.[36]

It may be there when the fisherman casts his line, or the memorandum perfectly expresses the argument, or the waitress places that fork just right. Then again, it may stir when the recovering patient addresses her surgeon with tears of gratitude; or the football fan explodes with delirious, howling triumph; or a surprise encounter turns out to be chosen. Above all, it is there when one of the archetypal stories begins to speak through a life, charging the air.

And when the lethal waters come, as they surely will for one and all, washing away human hope, extinguishing ego, may we not follow our great ancestors and suspect that it is the grey-eyed Athena introducing her own truth, her own *not-lethe*? The mist-drenched atmosphere, under the stillness of the steady, pouring rain, is sober and collected. It is just how the West has imagined its goddess of Truth, with her fusion of beauty and right. She is to visualise, engaging, the owl eyes challenging: You, you prove yourself! Show who you are, what you are made of, whether you are up to it — my test.

But wait a minute — what is *she* doing back on the scene, and her father, too? Why hasn't she gone the way of the Christian God, into the museum of holy fossils? How can the sceptical modern West possibly conceive of these two, for instance, take such throwbacks seriously? To be sure, it may well not be them. Perhaps when the world turns into a strange and wonderful curtain of finely orchestrated greys — as it does here before our very eyes — snakes slithering the earth at will, water everywhere, and a serene grey-eyed calm descends over the hopeless catastrophe that is the human narrative — perhaps these are not signs of the presence of the divinity. Could it all be just coincidence — random?

Athena of the flashing grey eyes, born out of her father's head, owl-wise, is the ideal creation of king divinity, exactly how he must have wanted it — Zeus, the lightning-bolt god. She is a difficult beauty, not just a pretty face like the goddess of love, Aphrodite. Mistress of the arts and sciences and sports, of skill and stratagem, of just wars and, thus, of barbarity civilised, of the city itself — Athena is goddess of Truth. Yet snakes adorn her shield, lest anyone take her to be too intellectual, she a warrior goddess, and her cool eye is renowned for turning its victims to stone.

Needless to say, Truth is a subtle intelligence. The challenge for us mere mortals is to piece together the obscure clues, if there are any. Poussin set an example in *Winter/Deluge*, his last finished work, his own final judgement on human life, and on a death that might killeth death. He showed his reverence by radiating the scene in grey. And while Athena was traditionally linked with water, just as Zeus was with lightning, the key to who rules Poussin's twilight world is planted off in the top-right shadows, hardly to be noticed — an olive tree.[37] The olive was Athena's gift to humanity. Here, it is the sole living vegetation, indicating her presence, in its *metanoiac* mode — on first recognition, quiet and unassuming, then surreptitiously taking over the entire scene, as it looks down on the human predicament.[38] Lightning and olive tree rule, father and daughter, a balanced divinity. And just as he illuminates with heavenly fire, she steadies the frenzy, calms the dread, imposing a higher order — letting those wretched humans sense that they may be, in spite of all, looked after.

The wisest of the Greeks, the tragedians, would from time to time forget their normal inhibitions and cry out: 'Zeus, whatever he may be; Athena, if she exists.'[39] But they knew that forces personified in something like the way their great and ancient stories told them, in the form of Zeus and Athena, guided the events that were their lives. How else might *being* gain coherence? How else could *stories* get started?

They knew what it was, moreover, when an ordinary mortal, not different from themselves, miraculously gained superhuman form, on the field of battle, for instance, or of sport, growing huge of stature and deer-swift of foot — or rose high in the air, superb and quixotic, like the praying man in the bow of the plummeting boat. When the warrior went storming up and down the plain, invincible, scything down the petrified enemy like a field of ripe wheat, it had to be that some god was breathing through his ordinary, mundane self. Diomedes, for instance, had his head and shoulders lit up by Athena, shining like a harvest star.[40] Signs were always close by that mortals were not alone.

Cheshire-cat divinities or spirits, or demons they might be, never to be trusted, or recognised with confidence, but divinities all the same. One might slight them, scoff at their backward followers, but failing to take them and what they represented seriously was to not take oneself and one's own life seriously. We have been returned to the heart of the fateful enigma. When the valley is inundated, swamping its inhabitants in despair, the truth may be bugling you out of the oblivion of being. Or gold stars flood in through the window, but you think they are coins.[41] Or from behind your clammy, ordinary self, some angelic presence dictates the story. Either disenchantment or *metanoia*! So it is that the death of God has liberated the West to return to where it started: *in the beginning*.

2.

Magdalene

No Western story has left more varied and enigmatic traces in the last two thousand years than that of Mary Magdalene. Wherever a purity of breath rises through the grime of fallen worldliness, freed from its everyday scales, then we are in her presence. Moreover, there is no clearer example of a *mythos* that inspires pathos, of the dynamism of one of the formative sacred stories, breathing spirit into particular lives.

There was Diana, Princess of Wales, hers the cardinal story of the second half of the twentieth century. While the modern Diana myth is deep, hard to read, the primal force driving through it is Magdalene. *Fallen earthiness* followed by *metamorphosis* are the defining movements in the archetype. In Diana's case, there was a life lived on the suffering edge of a failed marriage, an unstable character prone to chronic eating disorders, fruitless affairs; and some petty interests, including the enjoyment of expensive clothes — she liked to look stunning. And there was a simple desire for a share of ordinary human happiness. Diana, too, showed her open wounds in public.

The metamorphosis came after years as a 'basket case', with Diana rising from the tear-drenched ashes to gain a public dignity and, slowly, find a role for herself in her mission as the 'people's princess' to her 'constituency of the rejected'. Her own saving medium was that of touch — the film footage played again and again in the week in 1997 between Diana's death and her funeral always showed her touching.[1]

The preceding tragic story to engage the public imagination had been that of Marilyn Monroe, and once again, the mythic source was Magdalene. In her films and her life, Marilyn developed an almost explicit whore persona, playing the 'sex goddess' who spends her time flirting with men, proposing her wanton availability through wiggling hips, pouting mouth, fluttering eyelashes; and tempting them with various modes of undress — often, she is after their money. She is 'good', but not in an ethical sense. Her characters are naive, at least on the surface, embodying a bubbly girlish innocence and enthusiasm, the lovely blonde Marilyn with the simpering baby-doll tinkle of a voice.

This time, however, the narrative diverges. There is no fulfilment and little happiness in the Marilyn story. She dies, also aged thirty-six, from an overdose of sleeping pills, her career in ruins — directors loathing her, studios fed up with her unreliability, and her last film, *The Misfits*, a commercial flop, although arguably her own best performance. Her many tormented marriages and affairs have come to naught.

Her story beguiles not because of its particularity, the successes and sufferings of one particular woman, but because it taps into archetype. Who, in themselves, in their mundane self, is interesting? Moreover, the force of this legend is greater for it being incomplete. Marilyn is failed Magdalene. What this means is that we, the onlookers, project onto her the full story — which we know backwards in our cultural bones, for she is vital to our Dreaming. We fit Marilyn to the archetype. We cannot help ourselves in this process. The archetype is so powerful that not only is its logic inflexible, but it demands the full story — it forces us to complete it. The pathos we sense in the modern sex goddess is due to the second, implicit half to the legend, the one she fails to fulfil in her life. She then becomes our means for hearing the eternal story, the particular vehicle accessible to our times. And as always, like children, we demand to hear the favourite story over and over again.[2]

In the twentieth century, Magdalene was also there, as the good-hearted prostitute, for instance, in John Ford's first major Western, *Stagecoach* (1939). The same figure recurred in *Pretty Woman* (1990), a film in which a life is transformed, not by a man with the authority to forgive but by the experience of love. Character is freed, to the degree that almost everyone who comes within this woman's orbit is infected by her simple and spontaneous goodness — it helps that she is attractive, but that is just another Magdalene trait.

Magdalene is archetype of human metamorphosis, of every truly changed life. Her hidden authority can be felt, negationally, even behind German metaphysics — the predominant force in modern philosophy — and its core concept, introduced by Hegel, of *aufheben*.[3] The best of secular thought intuited that its own central truth had to do with taking the essential thing and overcoming it while at the same time transforming it into something higher. But it had lost touch with *pneuma*, so it groped away in high 'dialectical' abstraction for two centuries, with its muddled threads spilling into theories of social revolution, individual therapy, and reforms to the nature of existence.[4] Modern thought was unwittingly being driven mad by the simple and concrete story of Magdalene, vainly seeking its own alternative. Hoping to reject *mythos* altogether, it walled itself into a charnel house of dead words.

At the other extreme, mocking 'high culture', it is Magdalene who anchored the century's most popular reworking of the gospel narrative, the musical *Jesus Christ Superstar* (1970). She is the one who gives Jesus the strength to keep going, their union celebrated in the song *I Don't Know How to Love Him*, which is thick with pathos because of the hidden, unsayable truth that it is also his song.[5]

She is everywhere, as blueprint source of formed sacred passion. It is she wherever an authenticity of chaste voice rises in song above the ruins of a ragged character and a disappointed life. So who was she?

The scene is Magdala, a fashionable resort town by the Sea of Galilee where rich Romans and Jews own luxurious villas, a town known for its urbane morals and religious tolerance. Jesus has accepted the invitation of Simon, a pious local Pharisee who is intrigued by him. He lounges Roman-style at one end of the triclinium couches that border the banquet table on three sides. Simon reclines opposite, his feet being washed by a servant.[6]

There is a commotion among the servants at the villa entrance. Suddenly, the dozen or so other guests around the table are startled to observe a woman bursting through, and gliding her way quickly and silently to stand behind Jesus. The colours of her velvet dress dazzle the stately marble-columned room, a flowing ruby patterned with deep-green leaves, and green sleeves extravagantly fluted, embroidered with gold. One of its loose shoulders has slipped down, exposing silky olive skin. She wears gold bracelets, and red toenails draw attention to bare feet. In spite of the casual restraint of a yellow ribbon, auburn hair spills abundantly down her back. Fiery dark gypsy eyes flash around the room, then settle.

Jesus senses her close behind him — he has been watching the wide-eyed stare of Simon tracking her, the host pale and stuttering with rage. Now he looks around and sees this unknown woman sink to her knees, tears from lowered eyes streaming down her cheeks. He recalls noticing her across the street on his way here, how she had suddenly looked at him and stopped, as if she had seen a ghost. She must have followed him.

She is bent low, loosening her hair, which cascades down, obscuring her face. He feels the tears splashing onto his dusty feet, which gentle hands caress, hair wiping them, then being kissed, then wiped again. She never looks up, and he sees her mouth hanging open in voiceless anguish, so pained and empty that she wants to sink out of existence, at the shame of what she has done with her life.

Was it miracle or curse, that infinitesimal speck of time in the street when her eyes were opened? The instant that changes a life, catching her unawares, has been like concentrated acid dropped on tender skin, the more caustic for him having been no more than the mirror. He senses her fighting against a huge weight of humiliation crushing down on her drained and tainted body.

One hand fumbles to find some hidden pocket, from where she produces a small alabaster flask. She uncorks it, and pours rare and costly perfumed oil onto his feet, tenderly massaging, regularly on impulse breaking her motion to kiss them. Tears continue to flow from bloodshot eyes. The large, airy room is filled with the powerful fragrance of myrrh, enough to induce a dreamy intoxication in the guests if their host's darkening mood had not infected them.

Jesus recovers from his surprise. He concentrates, bathing her in his own meditative gaze. Now he knows her, and his own mind. Meanwhile, the resentment of Simon spears at him across the table, the host mumbling under his breath that if Jesus were whom he claims to be, he would know the immorality of this woman. And to let her touch him!

So Jesus turns to face Simon and poses a riddle. A man is owed money by two others — one owes five hundred *denaria*, the other fifty. Neither had anything, so he forgave them both their debts. Which one will be more grateful?

Simon tentatively replies with the obvious answer. Jesus tells him that he has judged rightly, but turning to the woman, he launches into a stern rebuke:

Simon, seest thou this woman? I entered into thine house, thou gavest me no water for my feet: but she hath washed my feet with tears, and wiped them with the hairs of her head. Thou gavest me no kiss: but she, since the time I came in, hath not ceased to kiss my feet. Mine head with oil thou didst not anoint: but this woman hath anointed my feet.

Wherefore I say unto thee: Her sins which are many are forgiven, for she loved much. But to whom little is forgiven, the same loveth little.

Simon flushes bright red with humiliation and rage and confusion. From the moment this gutter slut violated the sanctity of his home, he has been subject to insult upon insult. The great teacher whom he invited in as his guest of honour has offended him, in front of his closest friends and most prestigious associates, all intrigued to meet the rumoured miracle worker. This so-called holy man now indulges that notorious whore's excesses as if he were one of her after-dark visitors. Not only that, but he makes fun of Simon by posing him a riddle so simple that any schoolboy could work it out, yet punishes him for solving it. Then he questions Simon's hospitality, which has been proper, it is true, but then this is a God-fearing household that wastes not. And how can the servants be expected to proceed normally with their washing duties when chaos descended from the moment of Jesus' entry?

Worst of all is the confusion. Simon is an intelligent man, well-read, and practised in discussion. He prides himself on his scrupulous understanding. Jesus has just reversed the logic of the riddle, which had love following from forgiveness, with the more that is forgiven, the greater the debt of gratitude. Moreover, the teacher had repeated that logic in his last utterance. But he has deliberately baffled them with this scandal of a woman, forgiving her *because* she loved. How can that be: has he got it the wrong way round? In any case, we know the nature of her love.[7]

While Simon is lost in these torrid thoughts, one of the two disciples who had accompanied Jesus to the feast, Judas, reclining next to the host, explodes in rancorous support, snarling across the table that this precious oil should not be wasted. It is worth a small fortune, the wages of her sin — where else could it have come from? — as much as a craftsman earns in a year.[8] The myrrh could be sold and the proceeds given to the poor. Simon notices that Judas wears a prayer scarf like his own tied around his head, with the inscription over his forehead in broken Hebrew: 'Mine eyes are ever toward the letter of the law of the Lord.'[9]

Yes, thinks Simon with rising indignation, that is right. To accept this woman, whom no decent person would give the time of day, is to turf all law out the window, starting with the Ten Commandments, extending to every *Thou shalt not*, including adultery — she is a walking epidemic of temptation to married men. You may as well tear up the ritual rulebook and demolish the churches, for their foundation is trust in moral discipline. I myself am a good man. I love my wife and children, regularly attend the synagogue, keep the Commandments, act as a pillar of the community and, yes, I seek more, and am drawn to some of your teachings, but this is too much. It is anarchy to go along with you here. We are weak, and need the limits of the law.

Jesus, letting Simon be, looks at Judas and is pained to see how this flimsy but furiously ambitious ego, foolishly driven to compete with him, now seems so belittled — a hurt boy doomed never to grow up, his fists clenched. Judas has seen his counterpart, that other fallen one, welcomed with love. Cursed with insight, he foresees how much she will gain. He could wonder at it, or recoil in envy. She, by her very existence, challenges with Jesus' own formula: 'Courage. *I am*. Don't fear!' Crying out, he twists up inside: 'Help the poor!' — the concealed plea of he who is so hopelessly without. 'Help me!' This Magdalene would never lavish her precious oil on his feet. To cap it off, he is now tortured by a yearning for the embrace of this woman. His last despairing view is that Jesus, who is rich in everything, gains more — her adoration. Hereafter, Judas will have only one purpose in life: to annihilate the presence that has humiliated him.

Diminished, he gathers himself in search of another identity, which he finds in the moral law. Securely steeled in his new armour, wearing his creed on his forehead, he proclaims himself defender of the faith — that is, the Church. He points accusingly across the table and, boiling with self-righteous hatred, rants forth the scriptures. He has to stamp out of existence what he cannot have, what he cannot be.

To this, Jesus calmly replies that they will always have the poor, but he is here only once. This woman, who hath not ceased weeping, has done a fine thing — out of spontaneous, whole-hearted love. Turning back to her, he slowly raises his right hand over the bowed head.

Simon waits for more to be said, but an aura of peace has descended on Christ and Magdalene, an oasis within the electric silence. Surely, he is going to parade her past life before her, rub her nose in it. Surely, he is going to demand that she give up her wicked ways. Surely, he is going to test the sincerity of her remorse, and check this excessive weeping and kissing. Surely, he is going to lay down a strict programme of prayer and good works for the community. Yet all is quiet.

He starts to sink, Simon, for he is a balanced and reasonable man, open to the wind that bloweth. He realises that Jesus, speaking to him, is doing more than undermining stock moralism — that is Judas' level. Simon is not a petty man. A higher legal ethic is under assault here, which would hold that one who has the rare authority to forgive does so in order to attract the love of those stricken with remorse, so as to redirect it. Other guests, obscurely glimpsing the drift, are starting to murmur: Who does he think he is, this teacher? By what authority does he assume the power to forgive? But Simon no longer doubts.

One at the table begins to understand. The second disciple who had accompanied Jesus reclines next to his Master. John, the youngest of the twelve, the beloved one, is tunicked appropriately in green. Since Magdalene sank to her knees, he has been agog with astonishment and fear. The episode, he senses, is of climactic gravity. Then, as Jesus raises his hand in forgiveness, John finds his own right hand elevating itself in tandem with the back of his Master's hand, as if in echo or salute, or perhaps himself hoping to receive the charged rays or some understanding into his own exposed palm.

The sin word *hamartia* harasses him, like grit in the mind's eye. Somehow, it holds the key. Transgression is not what Jesus is talking about. Otherwise, Simon would be right. Her past, what she has done, no longer matters. The tears of her love have washed it away. It is as if being in the vicinity of Jesus has enabled her to purify herself. What is meant by *hamartia* is something like 'loss of way'. Magdalene had strayed. Jesus is helping her gain balance so as to find her right direction. John, who is himself still unsure, feels tingling in his own palm the power of that right hand opened over the dishevelled mass of auburn hair, the *I am* ringing in his ears. He can feel it drawing her upwards, her own *pneuma* low and ill, soothing her, calming her, as if cleansing by water, then slowly sparking it, kindling it, into a love and a capacity for touch that will flame outwards.

It will be John, decades later — an old man — who alone will recount the sequel Magdalene story, of the encounter in the garden. And the canonical first line of his narrative, 'In the beginning was the *logos*', will refer back to this scene so many years before — this story and this word — where for him it all began.

But loss of way is Fall. Stumble and Fall! Magdalene, in sinking to her knees, was stumbling. I, John, in raising my right hand clumsily aloft, am stumbling. To live is to lurch into fallen worldliness, engage with it, become it. So Judas' *letter of the law* banner is denial — identity printed across the brow, like a convict number, to mask the insecurity. His energy is diverted away from life, so as not to risk humiliation, in fear of an *I am* careering around so rattled and self-conscious that when it sprawls out, it will not get back up. To love much enables this woman to stumble, and when down, bare herself to *pneuma* and to fire, then stand up.[10]

Pneuma is all. It is the charged air descending beneath the open palm of his elevated right hand. It is the fragrance suffusing the villa. It is the drift of drunken breathlessness through the assembled guests — now snuffed out. It is the lift in her spirits weaving through the cascading hair, lightening the tears.

And so it works its fill, drawing out, first of all, Simon. He is alert, but unsure, *pneuma* not enough to hold him. Its charm flits past Judas, taunting him as it sails on towards its chosen ones, among whom he, in his flat and foreign being, is not, he who has gone faint with dread. Coldness to the wind that bloweth then releases the reviving gale, and it is a black fury from within, driving to obliterate anyone or anything graced by that breath, his lack.

Here, then, in this beginning, the insidious pathology was born, the one to blight humanity forever — *pneumaphobia*.

What did she gain? What might one do with a life so radically changed? The doors to Paradise did not open. Hers is not the sort of tale that ends with: 'And she lived happily ever after.' So she waits for the test, month after month for more than a year. Her drama, like her temperament, swings from one extreme to another. Now, as if becalmed on an endless tropical night, the air heavy and clinging with melancholy torpor, nothing moves. Her ship lists motionless, comatose. Yet she is permanently on edge, frazzled, incapable of focussing on anything.

For what was she forgiven — in order to be whom, do what, go where? 'Forgiven' was not even how she had experienced it. She was wayward, yes, but that was out of not being able to bear the ordinary, the everyday, and the people she saw accepting the falsehood, willing to live by the laws of oblivion. So she turned herself into the prostitute partly in rebellion, partly to goad them, try them out. In a way, she just didn't care — was careless. Like Simon, the others she encountered all failed. They dismissed her, mistook her for the fallen nobody that was their own true selves. He alone took her seriously. He alone saw through the surface self and its woe, embracing her, celebrating her.

There comes a day when she finds herself in Jerusalem — something has impelled her this way, far from home. She does not know it is Passion Week. Fretful at the rumours, she rushes up and down the town but cannot find him, day after increasingly delirious, fruitless day! Then it is early Friday morning. She joins the jostling, chanting crowd streaming from the Temple towards Calvary.

Only when the Cross is raised does she, from the back of the mob, see him. It is her turn for time to cease. She sinks down with a visceral groan — such as to bring tears to the eyes of the black pitiless Furies. Then for six hours — each a lifetime in its crawling agony — she is up there, her own nerves hammered, suffering herself every dread memory. As he cries out and expires, she comes to — with clarity — as if released for an instant from the drama, and she stares into featureless and cold empty space. How can I be in a world without him? All is gone: no sense, no love, no me!

Both hands up, stifling mouth and nose as if to contain the horror, cover the wound, she finds herself still managing to edge forwards through the crowd. It is John who now touches her lightly on the shoulder in acknowledgement, her presence having been deeply on his mind since Magdala. Mary the mother is the only other principal who has not fled in fear. But the three can do no more than look on, helpless bystanders, until the crowd disperses, and Joseph of Arimathea gets permission from the Roman governor to take the body down and lay it in his own tomb.

Down it comes, the strong young men at the head and knees staggering under the weight, gripping the white linen winding-sheet in which it is cradled. The mother lurches backwards, fainting with grief, three young companion women catching her in her fall. Lost in herself, she will be of no further help.

The head spills backwards onto the chest of the rear pallbearer. John moves close, hands clasped together under his chin, attempting prayer, and looks down at his Master's face. Can it be, she knows he is inwardly wailing, asking, imploring, can it be that you are no more?

Now, at last, is her moment. She steps quickly between the pallbearers to his side and takes the dead left hand, the blood still wet. Clammy, it flops down into her palm, cold as tomb flagstone, and heavy, so heavy, as if bearing gravity itself within. She seizes it. All the withheld fire, many months pent up and all the while gathering to a crescendo, is concentrated here. Now it flares forward. Might she, her entire being focussed through that imminent *Touch me not*, by means of interdicted feel, bring this hand back to life?

She leans in to him, her right hand moving up lightly to finger a sweep of the white linen — shroud to be — that somehow rises up behind his left shoulder, blowing past the head of the pallbearer and away. Palm open, she runs it through her fingers, stroking it with the outer edge of her hand, as if it were him — and perhaps it is, for *pneuma* seems to breathe through this cloth. Suddenly she is calmed, and can muse almost effortlessly, free of the heavy weight of tragic reverence. He has changed — and in that change is her own metamorphosis by fire. It is all right.

But his face, as now she looks, is agony — no death mild as a twilight breeze here.[11] Tilted slightly back, lids down, mouth open, it is as if he is struggling to rise above the violence, to gather his fractured being into one last ray of concentration, groping for her. And he finds her. She can feel him suddenly ease into her, a serenity breathing between them. The hand is effortless in hers, and warm now, hovering there. His body, too, feather-light, floats. So they swoon together, stumbling up out of the pain. *For she loved much.*

Such is the power of Magdalene's touch. He said that with faith — he meant something like 'right being' — one could move mountains. Her mountain is his corpse.

Little surprise, then, that in the Sunday pre-dawn two days later, it is she alone who is at the tomb. Seeing in the obscure half-light that the rock covering the entrance has been rolled aside, she rushes to tell Peter and John. They accompany her, running, and crawl one after the other into the burial chamber carved out of the rock face, where in the dark interior, they make out that the body has gone. The linen wrappings and head-cloth are all that remains. The two disciples then go off home, John recording that he now believes.[12]

Magdalene stands immobile, ungainly, weeping again. She thought he was here. She was sure. Yet she also knew she had to come. But they have taken him away, and with him, her precarious bearings. In panic at the vortex that has gripped her, pulling her down, she turns around and sees a gardener. It does not strike her as strange that, without her sensing his approach, he is suddenly close behind her, asking: 'Woman, why weepest thou? Whom seekest thou?'

She pleads desolately: 'Sir, if thou have borne him hence, tell me where thou hast laid him, and I will take him away.' He addresses her: '*Mariam*!', in an intimate voice she recognises. She bows her head and whispers: 'Master.'

From the palms, those that stroked the linen shroud and held the hand; through the limbs of blood, bone and flesh; to the eyes that saw the face, her whole body-being is transmuted into some vibrant thereness. She sways radiantly towards him.

But towards what does she sway? This figure did not look like him, its obscure form that of a stranger, at home in this garden. Nor did it strike her as some frightful spectre, such as the twelve reported whirling by them across the Sea of Galilee. So she assumed in her confusion, seeing the shape of a man, that he belonged here. He stands so close to her, this stranger who knows her — how could she mistake his identity? Or was it that she imagined him, conjured up her beloved in her own mind? No, that cannot be it, for then he would have appeared in his familiar form, to be recognised. It must, surely, not be him, at least as she knew him, but perhaps some presence from the beyond, whatever that means, and it or he is still here, or so she fancies. Her only certainty is the voice, speaking her name, '*Mariam*!' It is real.

He embraces her, but not with arms. *Pneuma* cocoons her in his tender voiced prohibition: 'Touch me not!' These three words, vague state that she is in, she seems to hear spoken as she sways towards him. The meaning takes time to surface, her understanding to clear: that his hour came and has gone. His time is past. He is no longer in tangible form: first the dead hand, now the enigma — as she instinctively knew when by his side, clasping one hand, her other moved to touch the fluttering linen. She is now on her own, but on her own not needing him, for he is in her, and at last she has gained the fullness of being.[13] She is herself. She is what it means to be self.

In disguise, he returned to meet her. Why is that, she wonders? Was he indicating that he would return, will return, unexpectedly, unheralded, and as anyone, even the ordinary local gardener? In actuality, maybe it is the gardener, for an instant possessed by the Jesus essence, whom she has met here. Is her Master instructing her to turn now towards them — that is, towards everyone — as if they are, one and all, him? Is he continuing the lesson about what, through knowing him, she has become, telling her what to do with her change?

Sinking down, not this time to her knees but to sit gracefully on the ground, her ruby dress spreads royally, gold gleaming in the oblique rays of the rising sun, auburn hair ablaze. She looks up at him, but her eyes steadily glaze over as her concentration shifts to the diaphanous veil, which she holds to her left ear. A breath of wind catches it and streams it away behind her head, murmuring out into the distance that will be hers. Now, she who was touch is hearing. And she listens. That opulent, sensual body — with its silky-skinned allure, its warm heart and its waywardness all strung together into the sordid story that had slumped at his feet in Magdala — is now metamorphosed into the wind snaking along the veil and out yonder.

He looks on — whoever he is — still standing close enough to touch, and is saddened that he must let her go, force her to go. His *Touch me not!* had been as much a caution to himself, against the temptation — no inner demon could interest him in thoughts of earthly power, wealth and glory, but this is different. He, too, was a man, and could so easily have chosen her, and with her, love in all its forms, he who, above all other mortals, in his unapproachable solitariness, had great need of it.[14]

'I don't know how to love her.' In this garden, he disguised as the one who furrows the soil and sows the seed, she ornamented in ruby velvet, gazing up at him from the dew-covered, early morning grass, welcoming peach-ripe his every touch — what is going on? What was the truth the story dared not spell out, strewing clues chaotically around like full-bloom rose petals in a gust of wind? In the primordial garden, Eve was tempted and seduced, the first fallen woman, and then was driven out to labour and suffer in shamed exile. Back in the garden, this time in a most unlikely place, in front of his tomb, Magdalene supersedes Eve.

Meanwhile, the right hand of her reluctantly metamorphosed self warms the alabaster flask which, having appeared from the hidden pocket, rests on the ground. She flicks away the cork and frees the vapour, her hand the agent of the transforming fire. The breath of her myrrh rises, curling around in the air that bloweth, suffusing the world.

The three-part story of Magdalene fixes once and for all time the portrait of Fallen being.[15] Without the consequent movement into balance, the archetype of Fall would make little sense. Fall without rise, if only as a potential, is as meaningless as black without white or *vice versa*.[16]

Magdalene contains two destinies, or two selves, in one soul. They fuse. There is a tragic self, which must spend the rest of its life struggling free from ever-present worldliness. 'Miserable wretch that I am, trapped in myself' is her cry.

Donatello sculpted this Magdalene, life-size, in wood, fulfilling the archetypal requirement to complete the story. The scene is set some years after the Crucifixion. Magdalene is haggard, with harrowed, desiccated face, teeth missing, mournful, sunken eyes, mouth pinched with pain and dread, throat shrivelled, scrawny body clothed mainly in calf-length hair, matted and filthy. Everything feminine has been corroded. Donatello rams home that flesh and blood is our conditioning reality. This Magdalene appears as *body* — of the earth — identical to her earlier self, but in negation. Its first, erotic mode is a beautiful femininity; its second, physical ruin and stigma.

Yet she has youthful arms and hands, as if uncorrupted by her relentless self-denial. Since his death, her life has been dedicated to freeing herself from bodily existence, with its all-too-human desires and ambitions. Hands move into a gesture of appeal, almost able to pray. Above all, her figure taken as a whole, in the round, once all its hideous details have been absorbed, has a haunting lightness to it, an extraordinary aura of grace — free from self, from the suffering.[17]

Her suffering pours out from love for he who is gone. She has been changed by vigilant devotion to what he was, what she knew, by sorrow for him, for herself, for everyone. Such is the completeness of her love, she has lost her old form, gradually shed it like a chrysalis. She has even come to look like him — as he was at the end, in despair up on the cross. It is his gaunt and harrowed face, living on, shadowed in the lineaments of hers — both together reduced to elemental being.

The other Magdalene is polar opposite — forgiven, a full-blooded woman in the round, embracing and cherishing herself, free to touch. Her past, her worldly being, does not need to be renounced, for it is constitutive of what she is. In its reintegrated form, it is essential to her strength. She is released on that Sunday morning to assume her mission. While Mary the mother is swamped by the tragedy, this Magdalene stands up and turns towards the world. Her story is of the gaining of inviolable presence through traumatic initiation.[18] She flings her right hand outwards. There may be anguish shading into horror in her face, but she is rising through it. Her work will be in the world and for the world, where she will both command and nurture.[19]

Magdalene's truth is a paradox: the two selves are contradictory, yet they belong together. Both her paths intertwine. Her lesson is that the human condition is simultaneously at war with the world and in love with it, potentially in harmony with it. Destiny is on earth, in mortal bodies, from within which individual humans are driven, onto which the ravages of their experience are etched, but also out of which they rise.

The story that has sown this tough paradox is therefore still not complete. If we wish to imagine the mature Magdalene on her own pioneering journey of saving touch, we can do no better than jump two millennia into the modern era and reflect on Princess Diana. The mission of Diana, caring for her constituency of the rejected, also included two selves, neither whole in itself.

In the modern story, it may seem that Donatello's Magdalene was better represented by the saint of monastic Catholicism, Mother Teresa, who had dedicated her life to working selflessly for the dispossessed in Calcutta. She died in the same week in 1997 as Diana — a timing, one might conjecture, determined by cultural fate. Mother Teresa's death was met by public indifference in the West, as if to say: You are not our ideal. We do not want to be you. The world-denying self on its own is not right. It's Diana we love.

In fact, Mother Teresa had no past and, consequently, was nothing like Magdalene. Diana was herself, in part, 'wretch that

I am', shaken by deep feelings of unworthiness, identifying with the forsaken and the downtrodden. Equally, she was a beautiful young woman who loved earthly pleasures and indulged them as best she could, given her own flawed character and destiny. And while, on the one hand, the Catholic saint was rejected, on the other a glamorous fairy-tale princess, as such, would not have captured the public imagination. What moved people were royal wounds on open show — Diana's meek vulnerability and pitiful unhappiness — followed by metamorphosis, which in her case happened in a normal manner. Lacking the encounter with a Christ figure, there was no cataclysmic moment of awakening. Her finding of her way proceeded mysteriously over time, by hidden gift of *pneuma*. Herself awakened, she became able to pick out the sick and the stigmatised in a crowd, go up to them and give them all her attention, her own medium that of empathy's succouring touch.

Diana astounded a sceptical modern world, her tragic story shaking it out of its mental lethargy. For some odd reason, this world could not get her off its mind. It was in the being and the life of the 'English rose', not those of anyone else — however virtuous, excellent or celebrated — that it sought a sign of how to make sense of the human condition, find a dignity in the midst of fallen worldliness. Here, it sought its *mythos*. It was precisely the dynamic union within one soul of the two Magdalene selves striving for meaning and grace that spoke to the times.[20]

The crux to the Magdalene story, as Raphael saw, is the *Deposition*, or *Lamentation over the Dead Christ*. This is the covert middle Act, not told in the written *Lives of Jesus*, a single movement of complex plays on the nexus of body and spirit.[21] It is the moment when Magdalene indicates what she will do in the future with all her gathered presence. The episode at the villa of Simon the Pharisee serves as prologue, the *Touch me not!* meeting as epilogue.

Her accompanying symbols are the skull and the crucifix, summing up her task as the 'death of death'.[22] This means in practical terms that she has to take on the body, which would soon be decomposing, every passer-by turning away in disgust — and fear.

She has to get the corpse to shed its weight. She has to neutralise the force of gravity. Her story stresses that the metaphysical either/or is between rule by the laws of Nature — including the higher moral law — or rule by *pneuma*.[23] Here is the vital spot, either the nothingness of a dead fish washed up on some beach or *I am*. On one hand, there is the profane way of life that asserts that on Monday morning at seven-fourteen I drank coffee — its truths are all of this form, and insolently, *pneumaphobically* proud of the fact. On the other, there is, extinguishing ordinary time, her invisible veil streaming in the wind — indeed, what could be more apparent?

This story is about the power of *pneuma* and *aletheia* — focussed through love.[24] It is pith to the saying that faith can move mountains — in itself so abstract that common sense can happily ridicule it. If the concreteness of this *mythos*, its directness in choosing the most extreme and simple terms in which to set the problem, does not speak, then nothing will. Magdalene invites every curious wayfarer to accompany her on her own private Emmaus road to the corpse.

First comes the bluntly rational proposition that a dead body is dead — organic matter subject to the laws of Nature, scientifically knowable, every stage predictable, with nothing more to be said. It is no different from a dead fish. Hand it over to the coroner! The *mythos* then conjures up its spell in defiance of this logic of ordinary experience, shining through the profane fog shrouding the river of Truth, to light its other order.

Let us enter again through the Dreaming door Raphael opens on the story. He positions his cast, sets their features, orchestrates colours, and invests the scene with feverish dramatic intensity — every figure on edge, caught in the singular motion that discloses its essence.[25] Above all, he so engineers the vectors linking the hands and faces of Magdalene and Christ, weights their angled bodies, that once viewers have worked themselves into the scene, felt themselves inside the tragedy, all attention fixes on the clasped hand.

The dank air of the underworld streams out at her from the empty tomb, sneering that death is death and that Nothing rules. She leans in to him, blood-crimson dress fired gold, wildly fluttering long auburn tresses and diaphanous ribbon, eyes almost shut down with the load of choked-back horror, and mouth agape. By now, we know her well, our own companion, her whole biography condensed here, the wayward young woman who fell at his feet and did not cease weeping-kissing-wiping-oiling transformed by the tender prohibition into a passion of touch, her life medium. All the force is accumulated here into an extraordinary presence of being, to give it back to he who once gave her all. Nail-bitten her hands, blistered with shame, shame at her past and shame in general, at the lowness of the human state, the right one strokes the pure-white linen while the left, aching with sacred pity, gently embraces the morbid-green, lifeless hand of Christ. She who is love draws breath into her touch. No tears flow, for she is with him.

That hand hovers in the dusk, under another law than gravity. If viewers, or listeners, are able to maintain their concentration, narrow themselves down to almost naught, a thread of illuminated sight focussed on these two — cast into the net of the bitter, fickle Furies of human destiny — then they will see not just it, in its lightness, but the whole body. The spiritless pallbearers struggle to hold it, finding it unendurable, heavier by the minute, sinking them in *pneumaphobia*. Yet the chosen onlooker will see it somehow shed its weight, the whole physical body-form floating, easing into her, and the two beings — although from either side of the great divide — becoming one, one *pneuma* sighing into eternity.[26]

And so it is that Magdalene lives on, as ever, at the heart of the Western Dreaming.

3.

The Hero

I s there anyone more admired in the West?[1] Modern times also seem to need him, gravitating towards national heroes, sporting heroes, community heroes. With reckless desperation, we seize upon minor achievements and blow them up into larger-than-life deeds. The search for political lions covertly drives lead news and documentary stories run by the organs of public opinion. Accordingly, the media speaks for its audience when it douses in vitriol real figures who disappoint. It is being inwardly compelled to project the standards of hierarchy and obligation set in the beginning by Achilles.

'My hero!' floats around dreamily, attaching itself to pop stars, screen legends and television celebrities. The terminology is used negligently to include those who have merely survived under extreme circumstances — mountaineers, lone around-the-world sailors, disaster victims. In the local golf, boating or tennis club, average players who win trophies, and see their names in gold letters up on an honour board — they, too, feel a bit of a hero. All believe they have been touched by the gloss of immortality. And indeed they have, as the saying goes, got a taste, but it is only a taste, as mindfulness of the full archetype will make clear.

The need for the hero has to be understood in relation to the fateful Deluge question for each individual in a secular age. What can I hold true? What sense can I make of my life? Is there a cause that will provide me with firm direction, enough to keep moving in the face of mortality? Or shall I, too, look down and see the absurdity of my life? Am I a 'waste of space'? The hero is a lone star, appealing to modern individuals who experience themselves as fundamentally alone and, in relation to the issue of Truth, with little confidence in communities or institutions. The hero, moreover, is an anchoring ideal in an age of uncertain male identity.

Some, indeed, are 'ordinary' — the boy next door, for instance, who as a fireman enters the burning building to rescue a child, later receiving a bravery award. Yet his moment of heroism lifts him out of the pack, making him larger, so that others hardly recognise him through the sparkle of their admiration. One of his number puts it, reflecting on his work:

> *The firemen, you actually see them produce. You see them put out a fire. You see them come out with babies in their hands. You see them give mouth-to-mouth when a guy's dying. You can't get around that shit. That's real. To me, that's what I want to be.*
>
> *I worked in a bank. You know, it's just paper. It's not real. Nine to five and it's shit. You're lookin' at numbers. But I can look back and say, 'I helped put out a fire. I helped save somebody.' It shows something I did on this earth.* [2]

Then there was the most influential film character of the twentieth century, the Western hero. The cinema between the 1920s and 1960s served as the principal new Church, the one to which most took the weekly pilgrimage that mattered — to sit in front of the silver screen on which their hopes and dreams might take flight. John Wayne came to personify the Western, leading by a vast margin all other performers, of every type, in the number of times he was accorded the title of America's most popular actor. He was again voted first in 1995, sixteen years after his death.[3] It has been said that he best represented twentieth-century America, the lens through which the people saw themselves and their country.[4] And America, with its imagined frontier beyond the settled traditional communal orders of the past, its Wild West, stood for the entire West.

What Wayne — identified by his screen persona — was may be gleaned as much from what he was not. Contemporaneous with 'existentialism' and such works as *Waiting for Godot*, Camus' *The Outsider*, and the film *Rebel without a Cause*, he shared the solitariness, the estrangement from everyday life and its ties and customs. However, he did not find life absurd, or nauseating, nor did he spend his days in gloomy introspection, wondering whether he could be bothered getting up. Lack of belief was not his problem.

The screen image relied for its psychic indelibility on his colossal *is-ness*. It was as if one of the giant phallic rock formations in Monument Valley, where John Ford shot his major Westerns, had come to life, nonchalantly swaggering into focus! The force of the films, their compelling energy, centred on Wayne, with other characters, the story and the direction all serving as little more than backdrop. He stood for what it can mean to be a man, with such concentration of being, animated by a near-demonic life force, that out of his very wildness, some sort of sacred aura was conjured up.

This is a life with character and direction, while stripped of the normal human supports — family, friends, social position, pastimes — able to remain unyielding in the face of some of the worst misfortune that may strike. Its message is that it is possible to *be*, even when born into the lawless fluidity of attachment to person, place and belief typical of the modern world.

The Western hero came with variations. Sometimes, there was a simple moral contrast, with the good fighting the evil, as in *High Noon* (1952). Sometimes, there was the descent-into-hell motif, the hero journeying through the underworld, suffering a symbolic death, finally to be reborn purified — as obliquely in *The Searchers* (1956). Then again, he might be the stranger who rides in from the outside, restores order, then rides away — as in *Shane* (1952). There is a touch of Emmaus here, and also a customary polarisation between ordinary humanity, which needs the cosiness and confines of community, and the superhuman individual, who does not belong. Only he who may never settle, he who is constitutionally solitary, will prove big enough to counter radical disorder.[5] And the story form is elastic, the *Star Wars* film series, for instance, continuing the typology.

The hero archetype also drives through the most popular television genre — the police or detective show. The 'honest cop' found its literary model in the novels of Raymond Chandler. The everyday life of his private detective Philip Marlowe, consisted of binge drinking, shabby clothes, the lure of scheming women, and crooks beating him senseless. It was all conducted in a sleazy Los Angeles where nobody believes or trusts in anything but their own profane and corrupt interests, the only hope wealth, yet the wealthy drown in their own despair, that of boredom.

Marlowe is hero with a trace of Magdalene. He is saved from his own fallen earthiness by purity of intent, that he has a master, whom he faithfully obeys, and who gets him up in the bruised, hung-over mornings. His master is Truth, that of the case he is working on, however badly he is paid or unsavoury the client. It enables his daily metamorphosis. Like John Wayne, he is the lone, just man, selfless and courageous, although himself gravely flawed.

The leading candidate for love story of the twentieth century was *Casablanca* (1942) — the film regularly nominated by critics and audience as the greatest of all time. The main character, Rick, played by Humphrey Bogart, has lived in torment since a brief affair eighteen months earlier in Paris, terminated by her disappearance. She arrives by chance with her husband at his bar in Casablanca — a place that is *nowhere*, of no significance, yet a place that has Rick's singular, fitful, solitary presence stamped all over it, making it *somewhere*.

The arrival pitches Rick into rapid swings between fury and drunken despair. By the end, she wants to go with him but he nobly sends her away. The finale, however, as her plane takes off, is not the dark grief of never seeing her again, but Rick turning to the Captain of Police and, with some lightness, uttering the famous line: 'Louis, I think this is the beginning of a beautiful friendship.'

Rick is a modern hero. He combines a surface world-weary cynicism — 'I am only out for myself' — with a deeper gravity. It is signalled in a gravelly haggard voice, a slow-moving unflappability, looking any intimidation straight in the eye, and a loyalty to his one pure thing — the memory of Paris, however badly it has scarred him. What makes him a hero is his courage to do what has to be done. Although it will cast a black cloud low over the rest of his life, he sacrifices his love for a higher cause, with a consolation prize for himself — male friendship. Under that brooding cloud, which is there from the start of the film, he endures as a dogged presence, sunk deep into its own being through suffering. Rick is indifferent yet warm, broken yet vital, his very human charm that of total self *in-dwelling* — almost, but not quite, as W. H. Auden puts it, 'snug in the den of yourself'.[6] This self with nowhere to go, nowhere to hide and nowhere left to yearn harbours charisma potent enough to recapture her heart. It makes him impossible to rattle.

In the contemporary West, however, the reverberations of the hero archetype are to be heard most distinctively in sport. Sport has surreptitiously pervaded the modern cultural consciousness to the point that only it has the power to generate a grand collective world carnival — the Olympic Games. The men and women who strive for gold medals — whether on track or field, in pool or at any of a dozen other venues — are all Dreaming, their lives in thrall of the *pneuma* formed in the beginning by Achilles. So, too, are the billion-strong global television audiences who adulate the star athletes.

The hero archetype finds its fullest modern sporting expression in the team game that is followed most widely and with the fiercest intensity — football. Groups of fast-moving men at the peak of their physical form, wearing their colours, wheel in formation around the opposition, sizing up the place for attack, menacing, then surge forward, cutting the defence to pieces, crushing resistance, and forcing retreat in disarray. Here is the civilised surrogate for war. The players display all the attributes of valour — courage under bodily assault, excellence and selflessness — and its off-the-field resonance. Retired footballers gather together to reminisce with warm, self-deprecating humour about tough games and purple passages of play, and pass on to juniors the legends of yesteryear.

The football crowd, too, discards its modern atomised identity, releasing itself into some primordial Dreaming rite, as witness. A tribe of tens of thousands of cohesive beings, it abandons itself to its own visceral roar, rising like the thundercrash of the deep ocean swell, then fading away with a rolling sigh, straight out of the creation labour of existence. Is it merely coincidence that the circular dimensions of the ancient walled city of Troy are close to those of the great modern football stadia?[7]

The Western Dreaming opens on the plains of Troy, amongst heroes in battle, confronted by death. Homer tells his story with sheer literalness, unglossed in its vivid terribleness, an almost inconceivable frankness not softened with sentimentality or even piety. Death is its still point, the hero its life force. We are ushered into a higher ether, the air thin, stark and crystal, almost inhuman — another reason for attributing the story to Athena. In its sung phrases, there is no blurring, no evasive gushing, no compensating for what is not. Consider the death of Erymas — the tone:

> *Idomeneus stabbed Erymas in the mouth with the pitiless bronze, so that the brazen spearhead smashed its way clean through below the brain in an upward stroke, and the white bones splintered, and the teeth were shaken out with the stroke and both eyes filled up with blood, and gaping he blew a spray of blood through the nostrils and through his mouth, and death in a dark mist closed in about him.*[8]

The Iliad forms the hero — its *en arche* parallel to the Hebrew God forming Adam. Thereafter, for the best part of three millennia, variants will appear, disappear and reappear, adaptations, hybrids, yet nothing will touch the epic force of the Homeric original.[9] Here is a case in which *midrash* is superfluous, for everything that comes after is lesser.[10] For once and for all time, the hero is cast, his a complete order, with its own ethos and *pneuma*. It breathes across the human landscape with tragic gravity, transmitting it.

George Steiner has alerted us to the peculiar centrality of Homer to the English language cultures. Their presiding *mythos* should have been national. Possibilities include King Arthur and the Knights of the Round Table, Robin Hood, and Shakespeare's Henry V. But it did not happen that way. Achilles and Odysseus became the twin figures to reverberate through the entire literature, from the Middle Ages to Joyce's *Ulysses* and on. From Agincourt to Armada, from Trafalgar and Waterloo to the Battle of Britain, it is the Homeric wave out of the Dreaming that picks up the particular events and immortalises them. It is cadences of *The Iliad*, part mediated by Shakespeare, that resonate through Winston Churchill's rallying speeches delivered to the British nation during the darkest hours of the Second World War.

The Iliad and *The Odyssey* are the texts most translated into English — in frequency swamping the Bible. Moreover, the tradition refuses to abate, a dozen new translations having appeared since 1945, some of extraordinary quality and most to wide critical interest, acclaim and robust sales.[11] It is as if England and its language diaspora have been staking a claim to the ancient Greek sacred site, shifting it, in the manner of Lord Elgin when he shipped home to the British Museum what remained of the marble statues that had adorned the Parthenon.[12] It was instinctively following fifth-century Athens — the creative centre of classical Greece — which had taken *The Iliad* as its bible. So England somehow won the torch, then sent it out by messenger to wherever in the globe its language had taken root.[13]

Perhaps the language culture raised on Tyndale and Shakespeare developed an ear so finely tuned and sensitive that, discovering the peerless height, it became irritated by everything else, hearing in the foothills only rawness and discord, so it insisted on translation after translation, that someone get it right. Or might it be Athena once again, that the story sung by the goddess of Truth, once truly heard, makes all else ring flat?

The period of Greek heroes, as Roberto Calasso has observed, lasted for only two generations, from Theseus killing the Minotaur to the murder of Agamemnon on his return home from Troy. 'History' was a brief and extraordinarily cruel period. It had been initiated by Zeus relaxing the rules, allowing gods to couple with humans, giving birth to heroes — whose exploits were then scrutinised and manipulated from above, a sport accompanied by laughter and derision. This history shifts abruptly from men who kill to men who understand, from Achilles to Odysseus. Odysseus is the last of the heroes, the cunning rogue, master teller of stories, who has the detached curiosity of the traveller and, as such, can take fate as a test, and withstand it. He already prefigures the next age, that of ordinary humanity.[14]

Homer's principal story is narrowed to a short episode from the tenth and final year of the Trojan War. It closes before the impending death of Achilles and the fall of the besieged city. This war had been caused by the Trojan prince Paris absconding with Helen, whose infamous beauty left men breathless and weak-kneed. Helen was wife of King Menelaos of Sparta, whose elder brother, Agamemnon, then assembled together and led an avenging Greek army to retrieve the wayward queen, whose very name meant 'Greece'.

Homer works indirectly with his characterisation. The basic role of the hero is mapped out through Diomedes, who is so formidable in battle that the Trojans assume some god must be fighting for him:

> ...he went storming up the plain like a winter-swollen river in spate that scatters the dykes in its running current, one that the strong-compacted dykes can contain no longer, neither the mounded banks of the blossoming vineyards hold it rising suddenly as Zeus' rain makes heavy the water and many lovely works of the young men crumble beneath it. Like these the massed battalions of the Trojans were scattered by Tydeus' son.[15]

Diomedes is courageous, single-minded, and excellent in his deeds, thinking nothing of his own safety, fighting for a cause higher than himself — an epitome of manliness. In type, he is already, in the beginning, obvious — a normal mortal who is outstanding at what he does, especially when Athena moves by his side. He serves as an anticipatory model for Achilles, who was once like him, the exemplary warrior. Homer leaves it to standard war sagas and sporting chronicles to celebrate simple valour. He is engaged by a deeper story, as his first, prophetic lines make clear:

> Sing, goddess, the anger of Peleus' son Achilles and its
> devastation . . .

For the main stretch of the twenty-four books of *The Iliad*, the giant refuses to fight, slumbering idly by his ships, enjoying the pleasures of companionship, talking, feasting. Meanwhile, the battle goes on, and things are not too bad. There is honour and glory in the fighting. There is relish and daring. Certainly, too, there is fear and shame, and dreadful realism in the descriptions of death in war. The mood, however, is sanguine. Disasters are averted. The to-and-fro swings of fortune are borne. There is some underlying balance to the heroic order.

Achilles, however, is not in his proper place, remaining idle while his lesser comrades fight and die. He is breaking the law of hierarchy. His sense of obligation should still his anger — 'all this heartrending insolence' — at having been insulted by his king, Agamemnon, who has confiscated Achilles' slave mistress, whom he loves. It is due to Achilles' own warrior prowess that the Greeks have won so many victories and have so much booty. His resentment subsides only late in the piece, with Trojan victories, and the realisation of the Greeks that they cannot win without him.

It is when Achilles stirs that the mood begins to darken. The manner in which the great hero takes up his proper place in the order of things perpetrates far worse sacrilege than his idleness had ever done. Achilles' form is superb, so much greater than that of all other men that it is better he does not exercise it. As the Japanese director Kurosawa puts it in one of his films, the good sword stays in its scabbard.[16] But Achilles does not stay sheathed.

We are given a premonition of what is to come in Book 16, devoted to Achilles' bosom companion, Patroklos, in battle. The colouring of Zeus' intervention blackens, sweeping 'ghastly night far over the strong encounter'. Patroklos, the one warrior who has been shown as gentle and kind, becomes besotted with killing, berserk for glory. He even pours scorn over the corpse of one of his victims. In a unique intervention, Homer himself adds a rhetorical judgement: 'you spoke bitter mockery over him, rider Patroklos.' Gone is the blithe, lyrical quality of the earlier scenes. Now, battle is a terrible business, sickening and horrible, a cold nightmare of pitiless carnage.

Yet Book 16 is mere prologue to what occurs when Achilles himself enters the fray. He is so much the superior warrior and in such a torrential rage for blood that what follows is butchery. No-one can stand up to him; there are no fair and brave fights between equals, just slaughter, rampaging mass slaughter. Achilles is superhuman — made explicit, in that his mother, Thetis, is a goddess. 'Superhuman' will become one of the defining attributes of the hero — larger, stronger, brighter than normal humans.

Many whom he kills are stripling youths, this 'man with no sweetness in his heart'. Lykaon is unarmed, cutting branches from a fig tree, when fate puts him in the path of Achilles. He falls in supplication, one hand grasping the knees, the other the huge ash spear, and the plea for mercy is useless. Achilles slings the mutilated body, as if it was a piece of kelp, into the river and speaks 'words of vaunting derision over him.'

The one thing strong enough to check Achilles is Nature itself. The god of the river Skamandros becomes outraged at this man's excess:

For the loveliness of my waters is crammed with corpses, I cannot
find a channel to cast my waters into the bright sea since I am
congested with the dead men you kill so brutally.

In fact, the river manages to catch and trap Achilles, and almost
succeeds in drowning him.

Thus Achilles violates the natural as well as the human order.
This is not the only instance in which humans overstep their
limits with respect to Nature. The gods are angry at the
impudence of the Greeks in building a large ditch and mound of
earth to protect their ships. After the war, the gods will create a
nine-day flood with waves to destroy wall and ditch and restore
what was, as if to say: Who do they think they are, these
humans, ignorant of their place, to presume powers over Nature?
Like a child destroys a sandcastle, Apollo wipes away a Greek
wall that has cost much labour.

The hero does not choose his path. It is fated. Achilles knows
that he carries two sorts of destiny: either to remain at Troy, in
the end fight, and win everlasting glory but be killed, or to
return home and live a long life in happy obscurity with his
family. Given this 'choice', he advises all others to go home. But
does he follow his own advice?

Earlier, he decided to stay by his ships rather than sail home,
even though he does not fight. Already in Book 11, he calls to
Patroklos to ask him to go and find out who has been wounded,
and Homer observes that 'this was the beginning of his evil.' And
what decides Achilles to remain by his ships? Is it his anger at
Agamemnon, or his need to win glory and avenge his
humiliation, or his sense of unfinished business — he has to fulfil
his vocation as hero — or his reluctance to leave companions who
are fighting? It is all of these things, to some degree or other. The
reasons, one and all, do not matter. Achilles stays.

Moreover, his 'choice' to enter the fighting, that great tribute
to human free will, how is it made? Does the reasonable man sit

down one evening and make a mental list of all the arguments for fighting, and weigh them up against all the arguments against? It is not at all like that. It never is. It is not even that he seeks human immortality, imagining the stories that will be told of his timeless deeds. Achilles grants the request of Patroklos to enter the fray. His companion is killed. Then passion takes over. In a fury of grief and anger, Achilles rushes into battle. Once the demonic is awoken, there is no choice. Choice, anyway, as the cynics have long maintained, is the privilege of weak desire: when you do not care, you can choose, but what you choose is of little significance to you.

'Check yourself!' is the imperative that peals through *The Iliad*, the bell of both warning and judgement. The warning to the hero is directed at times of grace, to beware of the heady exhilaration. You are carried away; don't be carried away. Check yourself, even though you cannot. You will be judged and condemned by the command, even though it is humanly impossible for you to obey it. If you complain that this is unfair, then just look at what men are capable of unchecked — Homer shows you.

Personality matters little in the heroic order — whether a person is complex and interesting. Psychological nuance is a decadent curiosity. Here, there are few references, Agamemnon described by his office, 'king of men', Odysseus by his quality, 'resourceful'. Achilles is acknowledged by his nature, 'god-like'. Homer concentrates on what counts in a man, his character, and how it stands up under the pressure of war, in the face of death. Its essential constitution is simple and unchanging.

Needless to say, Achilles enjoys his huge power, as all run in terror before him. From this perspective, his great form is splendid, 'shining like the flare of blazing fire or the sun in its rising.' He is glorious, and he brings glory to his own, the Greeks. Even Hektor, the brilliant Trojan hero who has inflicted grievous suffering and loss on the entire Greek army, shivers when he sees him. He flees, suffering the humiliation of running three times around the walls of his city — the terrified citizens watching from the ramparts — glorious Achilles hard on his heels in pursuit.

Then follows Achilles' worst violation: defiling Hektor's corpse. He ties it by the ankles to the back of his chariot and drags it around in the dust. At night, he leaves the body out unwashed for the dogs to feed on. He cuts the throats of twelve Trojans as if they were sheep to sacrifice at the funeral pyre of Patroklos. The first sacrilege, cutting holes at the back of Hektor's feet, by the tendons, in order to thread ox-hide through them, mocks himself, although he does not know it. Very soon, fate will wound him in just that physical place — the Achilles heel — and mortally. The glory, now, is tainted. It is not like that of Diomedes, clear and exhilarating.

Once Hektor is dead and the Trojans have retreated into their city, the fighting is over. The completion of the story follows, in Books 23 and 24 — both guided by funerals, the first that of Patroklos, the second that of Hektor. It is late; things must be redeemed, completed with rites of great sorrow. What was best is gone or soon will be, and for those left alive, there is little to live for. Any who get back home will spend the nether-lives that follow in a wheezing inertia closeted in memories of Troy. The abstracted minds of old soldiers will be locked up in that fighting, occasionally surfacing with a slight smile and a glazed eye to recount stories of the heroes there, and of the horror and of the stalking dark angel. But now is the last act, the carrying out of appropriate funeral ceremony. The goddess sings it in a sober twilight voice.

Achilles' first reparation is acted out in the form of funeral games in honour of Patroklos. He sets the games up, organises them, provides the prizes, and adjudicates. He does so with tact, fairness and generosity. He himself does not compete. The contending warriors squabble over who won, accuse each other of cheating, or complain that their prize is inadequate — the fierce competition for honour and trophies produces the normal human pettiness.

Achilles settles all conflicts with a magnanimity and grace that shames the others. The young Antilochus suddenly becomes generous in a bitter dispute with angry Menelaos, and the dispute is settled. He has come under the influence of the tone set by Achilles. When the best charioteer comes last because of an accident, Achilles awards him a special prize. He chides Aias and Idomeneus for arguing: 'It is not becoming.' He stops the armed combat between Aias and Diomedes before one seriously wounds the other, and gives equal prizes to both. He thinks of the wise old man Nestor, and gives him a present, in memory of Patroklos: 'I give you this prize for the giving.' The old man is grateful, happy to be recognised, which is fitting, both for his age, and for the good advice he has given throughout the war.

We witness Achilles the gentleman, the just and benevolent head. He channels the violence of the warriors into sport, and binds them together in tribute to his companion, and as right conclusion to the great battles.

We are reminded of many things in this book of *The Iliad*. We are reminded that the gross flouting of decency in the preceding episodes was not the work of some human monster — a criminal, delinquent or psychopath. No, it was the best of men, the most civilised, the man with the finest sense of tact and propriety in the entire story. We are also reminded that Achilles did not transgress out of ignorance. Achilles knows everything. He knows what is right. He knows all about limits. He advised Patroklos carefully about his own limit: not to go too far, not to get carried away.

What Achilles knows does not check the great man himself. What he does is done for his lost friend: Patroklos is worth it and nothing else matters. Were the ghost of Patroklos to visit Achilles and implore him to take care, not to go too far, not to ruin himself, that advice would be useless, and the ghost itself would be left to admire 'man-slaughtering' Achilles embracing his destiny. Achilles accepts that he must die soon. Now, for the moment, he must do what has to be done: run the funeral games.

Achilles knows that the truth about himself is dreadful. He is the one to reflect on experience, to question the meaning of it all in the face of *The Iliad's* prevailing concern — death.[17] Hektor may indulge in hopeful illusions. Achilles does not. That he fights with unquenchable fury does not prevent him answering Lykaon's plea for mercy with a poignant and telling argument:

So, friend, you die also. Why all this clamour about it?
Patroklos also is dead, who was better by far than you are. Do
you not see what a man I am, how huge, how splendid and born
of a great father, and the mother who bore me immortal? Yet even
I have also my death and my strong destiny, and there shall be a
dawn or an afternoon or a noontime when some man in the
fighting will take the life from me also ...[18]

By the end, Achilles is sick of the battle. Priam, reflecting his mood, speaks of fighting on: 'if so we must'. Achilles had just mentioned the two urns out of which Zeus draws evils and blessings for mortals, mingles them and adds more of one or the other. His own father had been blessed, but then evil came:

There was not any generation of strong sons born to him in his
great house but a single all-untimely child he had, and I give
him no care as he grows old, since far from the land of my fathers
I sit here in Troy, and bring nothing but sorrow to you and your
children.[19]

Achilles is past boasting and gloating. He is even past lamentation. And seen from the distancing perspective of his wisdom, glory, too, has lost its savour.

The last book of *The Iliad* centres on the visit of Hektor's father, Priam King of Troy, to Achilles. He comes to ransom the corpse of his son so that it can be taken home and given an appropriate funeral. Achilles' second payment for his impiety is to agree to Priam's request. Some preliminary divine pressure is necessary to quell his anger and his high sense of the tribute in retribution due to Patroklos.

Even more necessary is the correct approach by the heartbroken king. Priam steals unseen into the tent of Achilles on the twelfth night, he prostrates himself embracing the knees of the hero, then he kisses his hands. Achilles is seized with awe as he gazes on the godlike old man at his feet. That old man was the one who had most reason of all the Trojans to curse Helen — the face that launched a thousand ships. Yet it was he who forgave her, addressing her as 'dear child' one time when she came to him, recounted in Book 3, abusing herself, 'slut that I am.' Priam's first words are:

Achilles like the gods, remember your father, one who is of years like mine, and on the door-sill of sorrowful old age.

He asks for compassion, describing himself as the most pitiable of all fathers, for what other mortal has had to do what he now does: 'I put my lips to the hands of the man who has killed my children.'

Achilles the gentleman's sense of proper hierarchy is touched, and he starts to weep for his own father. The scene is suddenly one of wondrous intimacy, with both men in tears together, the sound of their mourning moving the house. When their sorrowful passion is done, Achilles stands up, and takes the old man by the hand, setting him on his feet, moved by pity for his grey head, admiring his iron heart, 'aged magnificent sir'. He sits him down. He has servants wash Hektor's body and prepare it for departure, not letting Priam see it lest he, Achilles, again lose his temper and kill the supplicant, thus extending his evil. Achilles cannot trust his own power of restraint.

He invites Priam to supper, after which the old king asks for a place to sleep before he returns to his city. For the first time in the twelve days since the slaying of Hektor, the father finds himself able to eat and sleep. Now his sorrow begins to mellow, to take its proper channel. Again, restoration is due to Achilles the gentleman, who makes Priam the parting gift of guaranteeing him as many days free from fighting as he needs to carry out a funeral, with full rights of honour. Achilles will hold the Greeks back for what turns out to be another twelve days.

Out of the gravity of war, out of the killing, with blood over the hands, true courtesy is born. The courtesy of Achilles in the last two books of *The Iliad* is something for innocent boys and girls to marvel at, and in their awe wish to sit at his protective feet, secure and well, until the day when they are big enough to take on a little of the mantle of Achilles themselves. It is in Homer's last two books, not in the preceding battles, that Achilles becomes great of soul.[20]

The Iliad ends with the image of brilliant, man-slaughtering Achilles sitting holding the hand of the 'aged magnificent sir' whose life he has ruined, reflecting on what he has learnt. The two look on each other and are in awe at the other's godlike form, these best two of men, and they weep together at the harshness of human fate, and the *Necessity* that has determined their respective roles in it. They treat each other with courtesy, and that makes the difference.

Thus the Western Dreaming is, from the beginning, non-tribal. It views any possibility of redemption — *metanoia* — as situated in the individual, for the individual. That the hero may sacrifice himself for tribe, community or nation is incidental

— or that ordinary humanity may respond to his feats collectively, as does a football crowd. His oath is to Truth. Significantly, Achilles, who gives no sign of group attachment, serves at the altar of *friendship* — what for him articulates Truth. He stipulates heroic individual being as the first locus of Western meaning — a psychic presence, a life trajectory, a story set within an encompassing frame.[21]

The ethos of the hero is unmoralistic. Its world is not one of sinners and the cursing of sinners. Evil characters do not appear on stage — there is no Judas. There is no real blaming. Even Helen is forgiven — the gods were responsible, not her. Neither is Agamemnon condemned, whose weakness causes much misery. He was deluded, a madness clouded his mind with rage, and again, the gods did it. So what! We all go through periods of delusion.

Good is not separated from evil. It is not that some individuals are saved and others damned. All are subject to fate. All die, and descend into the underworld. Form is available to everybody — although, perhaps, some are so deformed in body and spirit that they are worthy only of the contempt of others. Nor is the story-teller ever righteous or superior. It is not the business of humans to make ultimate judgements — events, fated events, will make those judgements for them. Accordingly, Homer never distances himself from the trials of his men — the furthest he goes is 'Rider Patroklos!', that sad, pained, rhetorical admonition to the doomed hero who will not listen, for whom it is already too late. Do humans never listen?

According to the heroic calculus, men are either larger or smaller, and belong as such on a continuum or, rather, in a hierarchy. All are subject to the same laws, ethical and spiritual, and all are flawed. For some, the demands are greater, in temptation, in actual excess, in reparation, in obligation. Larger means stronger; smaller means weaker. The hierarchy is in part to protect the weak, of whom less is asked. At the top, there is

Achilles. Odysseus is much the lesser man, although cleverer, luckier and happier. Lesser does not necessarily mean worse. Sophocles learnt this most important lesson from Homer — his Oedipus, who is neither notably good nor notably bad, is big, and so is his Antigone.

We do not hate the desert for being dry. We do not hate the lion for being fierce. The heroic view does not judge the desert for being its natural self. This does not free humans from responsibility for their being dry, fierce or treacherous. The Calvinist paradox is thus first formulated, as an attribute of the hero: not only are events decided by *Necessity*, fate and the gods, to the exclusion of human choice, but character is destiny, and unchosen though it be, for its violations we are responsible.

Compassion is not a heroic virtue. The hero in the full throb of his mission is, following Achilles, cold to pleas for mercy. This is an inevitable consequence of the nature of hierarchy. The teller of the story, and the listener, may be moved to pity, but what can they say, for instance, to the son of the Duke of Wellington when he utters his life-defining lament? His father was the Englishman closest ever perhaps to Achilles in heroic greatness — and more diverse in his talents and virtues. It was he who, among other glories, defeated Napoleon at Waterloo. That son, just before his father's death — on which he would inherit the title — is reported to have said: 'Think what it will be like when the Duke of Wellington is announced and only I come in.'[22]

In the aftermath of action, even within the circle of tragic pity there remains a certain aloofness. Fatalism inclines to a detachment from day-to-day life. This is an aristocratic view. Achilles is a man of honour, a big man who must suffer, his suffering commensurate with his size. With aloofness goes sobriety. Big human beings are unfazed, even by frightful events. Shock is sublimated into tragic witness. The hero never blushes, and the extraordinary thing is that in his or her case, this is a virtue.

Yet there is a strain of one type of judgement in *The Iliad*. Some acts do bring supernatural retribution, to balance the books. If you go too far, as does Achilles, and the gods disapprove, then you will be punished. The logic is unclear, its application fitful, and humans remain in fear more of the spite and caprice of the gods than of their sense of justice. Indeed, the gods seem more concerned with impropriety than with sin, and their language is never righteous. Achilles is punished less for his evil, the slaughter without mercy, than for his overweening pride, the impiety of his mocking of Hektor's corpse. His is a sort of impropriety in sacred order.

The hero is a tragic hero.[23] The determinateness of things broods over the action, its dark destiny playing the events one by one, as in a masterful chess game, steadily leading Achilles into battle, and in a way that will doom him. This greatest of all mortals approaches an end that will be so weighted by the time he has profaned the corpse of Hektor that his own death will be a mere going through the motions, unnecessary to describe. That is tragic predestination, when the end is so powerfully fated that it becomes almost superfluous. There is no need to waste time with death itself. The funerals have taken centre-stage, the living burying the dead, cursing and lamenting, but making sure the last rites are carried out to the letter. Propriety is all.

Once fate is inviolable, and everyone knows it, then choice, progress and happiness all go out the window, leaving Truth. The logic is, do what you have to do — the necessary retributions, the necessary excesses. Life must be dedicated to balancing the accounts of guilt and reparation, a mission that merges into a balancing for its own sake, as if balance is everything — poise on the tightrope of fate. There is the praying, too, not to die before the essential task is complete. Its lesson to the hero who manages to fulfil its terms is that the whole is set within the right Truth — an order to which he has been awakened by his own tragedy.

Happiness does not belong in the heroic order. Things are too grave for humans ever to let go and enjoy themselves. Even at the close of a successful day's battle, when the passion has ebbed and a quieter time of reflection is near, the mood is one of relief. The relief is that you did all right and survived with honour intact. There will be no dancing. You were fortunate just to keep going in tolerable good form — no blunders, no mess. This is an enervated pleasure, and it belongs to a twilight beyond cosy talk, one of exhausted sighs.[24]

Death, even for Achilles, is going to be a mere going through the motions. Important to him has been riding his fate, a strict rein on himself, doing what was necessary when it was necessary — waiting until the Greek leaders came to him on their knees, preparing Patroklos for battle, advising him, then himself going into battle to avenge his companion, the killing of Hektor, the grieving for Patroklos, the funeral games and, finally, the encounter with Priam. Judge the man by what he does. According to the hero archetype, we are what we do.

For Achilles, what is important is how he conducts another's funeral, not his own. In the vicinity of his own death, he knows he is under the wisdom of Ecclesiastes, for all these things, you will be brought into judgement — although the Greek sense of retribution was more shadowy, less sure. In part, his job now is moving to redeem the laws he has abused. In part, he does not care. His last two acts obey the heroic injunction: focus your life on doing properly and completely what you have to do. Achilles carries them out with an impeccable correctness. The goddess' comment behind the scenes to the hero is that you have achieved a lot, Achilles, almost enough, in terms of balance — apart, that is, from your own death, which hardly matters any more.

Tragedy's reward for the remarkable man who, like Achilles, can embrace it is the retreat of death. Not that the dark is expunged — as the terrible last battles attest. The actual death is slight beside the man. His abiding image is that of an immense figure standing alone on the plains of Troy in the dusk, a singular human form, its aura a thereness negating the physical surrounds. Homer's art paints a black background — the deep shadows of mortality, the capricious fury of *Necessity* — and onto it, in spite of all, this presence, of how it is to be a man, what he can make of his time on earth. We shall remember him.

Achilles by the end has had enough. His meditations on the woefulness of the human condition have detached him from his glory, which he knows will go unrewarded in the cold death that waits — one and all take the one-way descent into *Lethe*. If he is fortunate, he may hear, rising over the facts, the voice of the goddess, filled out with pathos, singing of the devastation that is life, his life, rising until it hovers over the action, a radiant screen on which the drama was projected. He has joined in death by grey water those for whom grace sighs through her eternal music or arrives in a silver flash.

What, then, is the inner condition of the hero? He is soul deeply rooted in doing. Yet while his life is geared to action, he does the deeds in order to *be*. But what does that 'in order to' actually mean? It has something to do with full occupancy of the self. By the end, the hero is complete *being* — his character, his mission, his story, everything complete. All restlessness to become someone — someone huge and splendid — is past. He is in want of nothing — no experience, no woman, no extra goodness and, certainly, no more glory. He is able to accept himself and his story, in a state of settled inwardness. So it is that Achilles can take the hand of the enemy king, address him reverently, with honour: 'aged, magnificent Sir', and weep with him as they reflect together on the sense of it all. In this, he is close to Magdalene, although her path is a different one. And as for us, the participant witnesses, we are left to stand back and admire him, as we do her, which is to say that in the deep Unknown, we are in the process of recognition.

4.

Soul-Mate Love

The story is so well known that it hardly needs telling. It is not even a story; rather, it is an icon, medieval in its simplicity, planted deep in every psyche, waiting to stamp itself on life as lived. Out of the Dreaming, out of the Unknown, overwhelming the imagination, is the Other, the fantasy print of him or her, of two souls joined forever. My wholeness, my only happiness and meaning, its popular language is that of 'Mr Right' and 'She's the one.' Almost every time a voice rises in a song of suffering, the theme will be: 'Oh, dear God, it must be him or I shall die' or 'I fall to pieces.'[1]

This fantasy has generated an intensity of energy unmatched in the last two centuries of the modern West. To fall 'in love' became the most charged and encompassing state of being — to fall out of normal existence, out of ordinary time. Even the simple English words, 'We just want to be together!' are pregnant with a grand philosophy of *I am* — of what it is to be.

Popular song became its lead vehicle, rising with a gale of yearning — the whole culture one of longing. Even the sceptical, world-anxious youth of the contemporary West are drawn to the familiar age-old lyrics. Their rational selves may have given up on belief in traditional marriage, fidelity until death do us part, living happily ever after and so on. The actuality may be a string of affairs and one-night stands, little enduring beyond the moment. Yet they remain captive to the spell of the archetype, still hoping for 'the one'. Here is yet another instance in which the Dreaming wave of fire and *pneuma* obliterates the rational understanding of ordinary experience.

All is in the Hollywood kiss — from its 'golden age', romance the second major cinema tributary to that of the hero. The vast silver screen is bathed in the pair of lovers' faces, they who are the whole world. The camera paints the icon as it dwells in close-up and slow motion on her eyelashes, the hint of a flutter, a meeting of eyes, which lose themselves in windows on eternity, then close.[2] Focus shifts to the lips, which part, move close. They almost touch — not urgently or greedily — for the flesh here is no longer its spotted and wrinkled, sweat-streaked self.

The cinema is merely doing what Athena did when she wanted Penelope, the wife of Odysseus, to recognise and love him after their twenty-year separation. She lends him beauty, from head to foot, making him taller and more massive, his hair red-golden like hyacinth, lavishing delight over his head and shoulders.[3] Thus it is that all humans in this moment are bathed in divinity.

The make-up counts, its mask hiding the particular behind an illusion of universal beauty, perfect and without blemish, its contours in harmony with arrival on the Olympic summit of universal love. The *I am* is thus both unique, with its one and only Other, and transcendent. Accordingly, the climax to the Hollywood kiss is not physical, but the first sigh of *pneuma*, like a spark leaping the lovers' almost-touching lips. Its breath becomes theirs, kindles, then spirits them away. A veil trembling with intoxication, the moment is fleeting yet timeless.

It was Plato who set the scene, with a fable told during that famed all-night carouse in ancient Athens — the *Symposium*. His small party of men passed the time by talking of love. 'In olden time,' Aristophanes opened his chronicle, 'we were nothing like we are now.' The human race was divided into three: the male, descended from the sun; the female, from the earth; and the hermaphrodite man-woman, descended from the moon. All were round in shape, like their parents, but with four arms and legs, and two faces and sets of privates. They had such strength, impetuosity and arrogance that they tried to storm heaven and assault the gods.

Zeus retaliated by weakening them. He cut them all in half, Apollo rearranging their bits to produce humans as we have known them ever since. Mortals were left with a desperate yearning for their missing half, to the point of apathy about anything else, flinging their arms around each other's necks, longing for complete oneness. So it is that the youngest of the gods, Eros, is always trying to reintegrate us, by restoring our former nature — including homosexual and lesbian natures.

Socrates takes up the *Symposium* story through Diotima, a woman versed in the mysteries, who had taught him all he knew about love. Eros, she had told, is a great demon spirit (*daimon megas*) plying between earth and heaven:

> As the son of Resource and Need, he is far from tender or fair as most suppose him. Rather he is hard and parched, barefoot and homeless. Always he lies on the naked earth with no bedding, sleeping in doorways or in the very streets beneath the heavens. True to his mother's nature he dwells in want. But he takes after his father in scheming for all that is beautiful and good. He is brave, impetuous and highly strung, a famous hunter, always inventing some stratagem. He is desirous of wisdom, and competent, throughout life seeking truth, while a master of sorcery, enchantment and seduction. By nature he is neither

mortal nor immortal. In the same day he is flourishing and alive
while his resources last, then dying, only reviving by force of his
father's nature. His resources are always ebbing away, so that
Love is at no time either totally impoverished or wealthy.
Furthermore, he stands midway between wisdom and ignorance.[4]

Diotima's final revelation is that only immature love focusses on
the beautiful body. The charms of the outer physical form are
nothing compared to those of the soul. Eros fulfils himself in
spiritual loveliness, seeing beauty even in an imperfect husk. He
enables us to seek our own personal god — our soul — in that of
the beloved, each needing the other to awaken it. His power is to
inspire 'divine madness', a state of reverent clarity in which the
soul sees once again all that the burdens of its mortal existence
have made it forget. Love in its erotic mode is the higher and
illuminated union with the kindred soul.

Soul-mate love was thus in origin a Greek conception, but it
remained a minor thread in Western culture until the
Middle Ages. Plutarch, for instance, the last of the great classical
Greek story-tellers, has his Antony besotted by Cleopatra — 'as
if he had been born part of her'. This echo from Plato, however,
is countered by the fact that Cleopatra is herself more controlled
and calculating — Shakespeare repeats the imbalance — and
that Antony's warrior 'virtue' is corrupted by his passion.

With the medieval tale *Tristan and Iseult*, the modern tradition
takes off, continued in such legends as Abelard and Heloise and
finding its most influential *midrash* in Shakespeare's *Romeo and
Juliet*.[5] Northern Europe here adds the theme of *Liebestod*, the
union of desire and death in a sort of holy wedlock. The lovers seek
immolation in passion, souls welded in eternity, the proximity to
death lifting the passion to a crescendo — evoked musically in

Wagner's opera *Tristan und Isolde* (1859). To live on after such a consummation would be banal and demeaning. Love is thus a sort of initiation out of the all-too-human into a higher, eternal sanctum. Romanticism's credo is born: I feel, therefore I am.

The leading stories of romantic love, from *Tristan* to *Anna Karenina* and on to Hollywood, often included the theme of adultery. The purity and sublimity of soul-mate love, of those who belong together in the sacred order, are contrasted with the pedestrian routines of marriage, in which the couple are together only because of social convenience — for reasons of status, wealth or power. In part, a social revolution was being mapped, the change away from pre-modern marriage, which followed much the same logic whether in tribe, traditional Europe or India and China. For most of the pre-modern world, economic necessity — with its handmaiden, strict social kin and caste regulation — ruled, making romance a leisurely and courtly luxury few could afford. In the English case, Jane Austen's novel *Pride and Prejudice* (1813) illustrates the turning point in the social elite, from people marrying out of family obligation to choosing a life partner they actually liked — even loved.

The sublimations and pathologies of soul-mate love follow. Implicit in popular forms of the archetype is that they lived happily ever after. The hope is for a *happy marriage*. As in fairy-tales, the story ends before the future reality unfolds. Indeed, major Western literature has been loath to portray this state. The two major novels of Tolstoy are an exception, the famous opening line to *Anna Karenina* (1876) acknowledging: 'All happy families are more or less like one another; every unhappy family is unhappy in its own particular way.'

Tolstoy does describe a happy family, that of Levin and Kitty. It is not, however, based on the intensity of soul-mate love. Kitty regards her husband as a 'good man', and Levin is more preoccupied with his own struggle for faith, occasionally seeing his wife and thinking how lucky he is to have her. Moreover, their story is a pallid and often tedious interruption to the main love tragedy.

Tolstoy had earlier tacked another happy marriage on to the end of *War and Peace* (1869), in the Epilogue — as if to indicate that it is post-story. The separation of soul-mate love is explicit. The wife, Natasha, lost the love of her life, and now marries a man with whom she hopes she can be tolerably happy — and is.

Kierkegaard, writing in the 1840s, philosophised the distinction. He took marriage to be the ideal and typical form of the *ethical* state, intermediary between the *aesthetical*, which is based on pleasure, and the *religious*, based on dread. A love affair belongs in the aesthetical. Marriage is in essence an oath, which is stuck to irrespective of the pleasures and the pains which follow. In its pure form, it is irrelevant whether the spouse is handsome, beautiful, interesting, clever — indeed, personality does not count. Marriage runs on universals — one marries husband or wife, not an individual.[6] It has its own binding power, which Kierkegaard epitomised in the story of Agnes and the merman. The merman is a seducer — purely of the aesthetic. Agnes is an innocent young woman who trusts the merman, abandoning herself to this stranger from the depths who woos her with smooth talk. The moment, however, that he feels her trust, he collapses, his lust melting away — his natural element unfaithful to him.[7] The true ethical supersedes the aesthetical. The 'happy' in Kierkegaard's marriage is thus rooted not in pleasure but in a sort of moral wellbeing. Just as *eros* is separated off and limited to the aesthetical, the soul, which belongs in the religious sphere, is also virtually absent.

Third Reformation art was sceptical of the 'happy marriage'. Even its two most obvious tributes fail. In Jan van Eyck's *Arnolfini Marriage* (1434), the couple are wooden, like sombre and lifeless dolls, more vitality in their dog, the artist displacing all his love into their costuming and surrounding objects. Rembrandt's portrait of the *Jewish Bride* (c.1666) centres on the husband's hand tenderly placed on his wife's clothed breast, hers gently touching his. Closer inspection, however, reveals a guilty calculation in his expression, discontented reverie in hers.[8]

That Western 'high culture' has been suspicious of the happy marriage needs placing in the wider context of its scepticism about love in most of its forms. All of its great realist psychologists, from the Duc de la Rochefoucauld to Freud, have insisted that the state of being in love is delusional, a form of mania. La Rochefoucauld's basic formula is that the condition is narcissistic, the lover intoxicated by his or her emotion. The beloved is merely a device for arousing passion — it is the passion itself that is exciting. One falls in love with one's own divine drunkenness. As one of his maxims puts it: 'Love, like fire, needs constant motion; when it ceases to hope, or to fear, love dies.'[9]

Freud makes the association with hypnosis, and derides romantic love as a form of infantile regression.[10] It fits that Romeo and Juliet are hardly more than children.

More explicit pathologies derive from the archetype. On the female side, there is the *femme fatale*, she who attracts men by her seductive combination of flirtation and frigid aloofness. Her man-terrifying variants include the Amazon, who conquers them; the vampire, who sucks their vitality; and the Medusa, who turns them to stone. In all cases, the man is rendered impotent — without power.

On the male side, there is the Don Juan figure, whose single interest is in the conquest. Once he has succeeded, his eternally restless nature drives him on to his next victim. Preoccupied by his own power — due to dread of lack of it — he is but one remove from the rapist. Yet the pathologies on both sides, through illustrating the dire consequences of the failure of the archetype, tend to reinforce it. They show its despotic grip. To come under its thrall, in circumstances in which *pneuma* does not preside, is to fall into a psychic abyss. Then, out of anguish and rage, a lust for power and control may rise as false redeemer.

Once again, the deeper recognition is: 'I am not', which unleashes the dark force of *pneumaphobia*. The social world is pervaded by its rancour. As much as the popular love song sails aloft with *pneuma*, it leaves in its wake a reeking flotsam. There is self-righteous moral law, there is bitchy gossip, and there are eyebrows raised in hopeful anticipation that they will get what they deserve — heartbreak and failure.

Third Reformation art projected soul-mate love obliquely. In the great works, there is never the immediacy and transparency of the Hollywood kiss. The lovers do not even appear together. The most direct representation is the male artist's celebration of his model.[11] He is the lover, the troubadour crooning under the window of his fantasy beloved. Or when Titian evokes *Danae* in a swoon during seduction by the Zeus shower of gold, it is the artist imaging himself as king of the gods.[12] Often, it was not all fantasy, Raphael for instance immortalising his mistresses in paintings of the Madonna — hence their earthiness.

In general, modern Western popular culture has plunged itself into the archetype without inhibition, while 'high culture' has remained at a curious but distrustful distance. Mozart restored some balance, above all in his perfect late work, the opera *Così Fan Tutte* (1790). His story accepts the doubting position, but takes it in a new direction.

Two young officers, Ferrando and Guglielmo, boast about the constancy of their respective fiancées, sisters Dorabella and Fiordiligi. An old cynic, Don Alfonso, wagers that he will prove the women are fickle, like all their kind. The officers accept, and agree to go along with whatever stratagem Don Alfonso devises. They feign being suddenly called off to war, then reappear disguised as wealthy Albanians, and immediately set to wooing each other's fiancée with brash gusto.

Failing to make progress, they pretend to be broken-hearted, and to poison themselves with arsenic. The sisters' maid, Despina, a young cynic in alliance with Don Alfonso, dresses up as a doctor and cures them. She urges the sisters to relax and enjoy the caprices of love. Dorabella is the first to give in. Fiordiligi resists until she, too, surrenders. The men are now furious with their fiancées, but Don Alfonso calms them down with his philosophy that all women are like that, and 'happy is he who is able to take the rough with the smooth'. The plot is revealed, forgiveness all round follows, and the couples prepare for marriage — the two men older and wiser.

That is the surface story. The music sets a quite different tone. To hear it without understanding the words would make any listener imagine that the opera is about the most sublime and eternal love. Fiordiligi, for instance, in the last stage of her resistance, sings the exquisite *rondo* '*Per pietà, ben io, perdona ...*', a love song which in its crystal intensity of feeling soars free of gravity out above the human plane. Yet it is carried not by yearning for the beloved, but by remorse — 'pardon, my love, this vain and ungrateful heart'.

One of the most beautiful love duets in the whole of Mozart's work follows soon after — '*Fra gli amplessi ...*' It opens with Fiordiligi longing to be in the arms of her fiancé, Guglielmo. Ferrando draws his sword and threatens to kill himself while singing of his undying love for her, his friend's beloved — it is unclear how much this is still a pretence. The two slowly move together, with her sighing: 'Do with me what you will' and them both joining in unison: 'Let us embrace, my darling.'

Mozart gives a *midrash* wrench to the archetype, binding the *mythos* in pathos. Grace rises not from faithful love but out of the lack of constancy, the light remorse, the spurts of jealousy and, finally, the forgiveness. From the waves of the fickle, the petty, the vanity and mistrust — that is, the living — breathes the sacred breath. *Pneuma* is restored to the individual, with the other an exchangeable vehicle, as are the emotions. Both sets, of their nature, lack fidelity.

What the music does capture is the swoon of *eros*, the rising out of self in a surge of sublime passion. Ego, with all its worldly cares, is shed for the moment, like a constraining dress slipping to the bedroom floor. Here is the erotic counterpoint — I am loved, therefore I am free to lose myself. The Mozart constellation is of each touching the other's hand, then soaring aloft in parallel jets of solitary ecstasy. It is divine madness, but not much to do with kindred souls.

Aged fifty-six, the widest-ranging and deepest of the modern West's philosophers, the one who approached the truth by means of story, not abstraction, put the question. Nicolas Poussin asked: 'Who am I? What do I know about the *I am*? What have I learnt — about destiny, about love, about glory and achievement, about life? Let me look at myself, including what I am not, for there is the key.'[13]

Poussin imagined himself dressed in authoritative black academic robes. Looking in the mirror of self-awareness, he saw a somewhat melancholy face, open, undefensive, matter-of-fact.[14] Refusing to pose for himself, he does not pretend or assert, nor search, Rembrandt-like, for intimations of soulful grace within. He tosses his head slightly back, the black hair a little unkempt, almost wild, the skin a touch puffy, yet a wincing softness, and great knowingness, emerging out of the battering of fate. I am steady in my recognitions, he may confidently assert, above the need to curse and to lament. Beyond that, there is little to observe. Indeed, to look at him directly is to observe very little.

What he most intimately knows is that he is not alone, in spite of the surface facts and the solitariness of his vocation — none of his contemporaries understands his work. There is a *she*. Without her, he reveals, I am not complete. Without her, there is no story. More, without her — and this is the extremity of the enigma — *I am not*! But who is this *she*? What does she look like; what does she do? His vision clears, as if he were his own Matthew visited by an angel, and he makes out distinctly this stranger, like some apparition, as in a dream, coming into focus behind his back.

A bright-eyed young woman she is, about thirty, with curly golden hair held by the gold tiara of a princess, a third eye set at its centre. Her face gleams. Her profile is sharp. She looks straight ahead. Her eyes are clear, her mouth opening slightly as if to suggest triumphal ruthlessness, unerring confidence, anticipation but also gravity — what she approaches is serious. He observes a pair of anonymous man's arms embracing her, the hands only lightly touching her shoulders, in part hesitant, in part in celebration of her. He knows they are his own, but at a distance from the time-bound, ordinary fifty-six-year-old self whom he observes here in the glass. In this woman's presence, he is propelled outside ordinary time.

But who is she? Who is it that hovers there invisibly just behind one, the presence occasionally sensed, like a fleeting ambrosial breath? Perhaps his muse?[15] Perhaps his *daimon*? There are precedents. There was Socrates' *daimon*, the divine voice that whispered *No* to him whenever he was inclined to do something against his interest. Or, perhaps, she is his patron goddess, like the ones who often materialised in Homer's battles near their favourite heroes, to give them advice or bathe them in glory?[16]

There is a thirteenth-century marble relief in the Procuratorio of the Basilica of San Marco in Venice, of St John the Evangelist with a woman positioned behind his right ear, pointing. She is probably Sophia, the personification of Divine Wisdom or Inspiration. From the High Renaissance, there was Vasari's portrait of Lorenzo, in which the Medici prince listens to a grotesque mask whispering to him, words of either temptation or counsel.

There are many examples. The seventeenth-century English Platonist Henry More spoke of 'something about us, that knows better often what we would be at than we ourselves.' And Shakespeare has a character address Antony:

> *Thy demon, that thy spirit which keeps thee, is noble, courageous, high, unmatchable, where Caesar's is not. But near him thy angel becomes a fear; as being o'erpowered.*

Perhaps Poussin, in this his most analytical reverie, is imagining the guardian angel, the figure made popular by the sixteenth-century Counter-Reformation, claimed to accompany people from birth, guiding them, deciding the important meetings and protecting them from death? But although this one looks to him, as he scrutinises her anxiously, like an angel, he knows otherwise. He who has always cringed at the rosy piety of the traditional Christian imagery has learnt that his own demon is not nice. She has little compassion. She is wilfully uncaring, at least towards him. Her single concern is Truth.

In the insistent clarity of his own dream state, he observes her emerging out of a shadowy landscape, the queen of the night. She is the light, shining like silver, contrasting with the sun, which has gone behind a hill. It is all happening behind his back, seen through the mirror on himself, a juxtaposition that serves simply to expose his vulnerability. Tiger or sphinx, she could be, springing onto his shoulders, the claws sunk deep into his flesh.

He broods that she might, alternatively, be his creation, under his power, a figure in one of his own paintings. After all, his vocation is to master his muse, his demon, by channelling her force through his work. But here, she glides out of her frame, out of her landscape, out of all limit. Vocation is much, especially his, but it is not all. Irrepressible she is, rendering him powerless.

He smiles wryly at the academic robes he has donned in order to give himself some aura of mastery, of authority. How feeble, and he a mature man in his prime, in nonchalant control of his destiny, dignified — or so he thought! The truth is that he is cramped and tense. His actual right hand, which would, ideally, like to seize control of her, steadies a portfolio he holds under his left arm. It does so, he notices, with an awkward bend at the wrist, breaking its strength. The papers he has stuffed inside the portfolio include theoretical texts on painting, diagrams of perspective, and his own preparatory drawings — even they are of her; that is how obsessed he has become. The rational, conscious self employs these intellectual and technical aids to his craft. But truth comes out of the dark, from behind. Only the third eye sees, and it belongs to her.

Yet he also knows that his other arms, which are bare, the ones bathed in divinity, embrace her. She is beautiful, she is all-seeing, and she is his — for better and for worse. There is intimacy. He tilts his head to cock an ear, to hear what she whispers to him. He loves her. He knows she sees through him, and for that, too, he loves her. From her, he can hide nothing. He fancies in her look, moreover, the seriousness of one in the act of being married. Indeed, he has to collect himself on the instant, lest he melt away.

Yet he can seem to embrace her only from the side, and from behind his back, as if *incognito*. Forget your name, forget your fame, forget your daily circumstances, including your wife, Anne-Marie, forget your maturity and your wisdom, she is saying, if you wish to approach me. It is his deeper being that embraces this stranger whom he seems to know better than he knows his own self.

A ribbon tying the portfolio of his own drawings wedged under his arm is red, the blood he has sweated in their creation, kin to a red scarf on the back of her head curbing her wildly abundant hair, and the blood dribbling down his back. Luther-like, this man strives to assert that here I stand. I have triumphed over that brute of a woman, sublimated her furious will into my work. While my imagined right hand cradles her shoulder, the other, the real one, is steady on my own personal contribution to the painstaking process of preparing one of my works. In spite of all, his consoling wisdom tells him, I am up to her, up to that marvellous quality of the ancient Greeks, their 'hair-raising cheerfulness'.[17]

The ring he wears is another sortie in search of composure — a diamond cut in the shape of a pyramid, in a square gold setting. My work, he is saying, which it will cap, is a priceless jewel, perfectly formed, and also set in a gilded frame, like his young woman's gold tiara. In my painting: 'I have overlooked nothing.'[18] The diamond is his third eye, the one that sees, through his canvasses.'

So who is she? We can be sure it is to her that he pledges fidelity, bowing in all-consuming devotion. She is, in Elizabeth Cropper's expression for her, his 'beautiful beloved'.[19] His stare at her through the mirror is intense, with him taken aback, hurt, irritated, perhaps even angry. It is as if he acknowledges her as his true self — which is little help to know, for it just displaces the mystery about the form of that true self.

But this cannot be the whole story. Who is he kidding? She is too vivid, too alive, too present, for her not to be in one persona a real body-and-spirit woman. He has known someone. Someone has known him. When that happens, the two are not alone, for seen from his perspective, a range of presences descend on her, become her — Aphrodite her very self, even Athena, shades from time past, and above all, eternal soul-mate images from within him anticipating her, awakened by her. They are her.

Perhaps the reality is that it was only a brief *Casablanca* encounter. He did, two years earlier, such are the facts of his life, curse Fortune as a 'blind madwoman'.[20] Maybe that blind madwoman had stripped him of his beautiful beloved. Is it, perhaps, not she whom he now remembers, the one who got away, and in adoring celebration, timeless as he finds her, without measure?

Henry James offered advice to Mrs Mahlon Sands on how to present herself to an artist she had commissioned to paint her portrait. He writes that her task:

> *is only to be as difficult for him as possible; and the more*
> *difficult you are the more the artist (worthy of the name,) will be*
> *condemned to worry over you, repainting, revolutionising, till he,*
> *in a rage of ambition and admiration, arrives at the thing that*
> *satisfies him and that enshrines and perpetuates you.*[21]

Yet Poussin, in his own rage of ambition and admiration, seems driven to harness her, whoever she is, to his art, asserting that it is through my vocation as painter that I have found my strength, and what I know. If we were to catch a glimpse of his face, we might make out pride and determination. It would also become clear that the brazen tyrant actually loves him. She embraces him, admiringly, gazing straight into his eyes. Her mouth is open with a tender, laughing joy. There is complete intimacy. Her face glows with passion. Even the third eye is now soft, its insight caressing. After a wild struggle, things are in balance. Harmony prevails. Nevertheless, it is her radiance that dominates this wonderful man.

Poussin has hereby returned the Western Dreaming to one of its foundation motifs — its locus in the reflective individual. Even soul-mate love may in good part serve as a chariot for the self — the *I am* — to ride in search of its own essence, its own spirit.[22] Mind, he has introduced the Emmaus enigma — in the form of a different type of stranger, who walks beside the one on the path of love — into any further serious consideration of the nature of being. Who is the He; who is the She; is there an independent We; to what degree is She a part of He, and He She?

But, as in the beginning, we are urged not to press too hard for precise answers, for there are personae and formed *pneumata*, even divinities beyond our normal understanding. With the awakening of the Dreaming, one and all of those surreal presences are blown hotly into the thick of the story, forming and reforming, dissolving and commingling. Indeed, to put the question again: Are there one, two or three on that journey of journeys?

So where do we find ourselves? In *Così Fan Tutte*, there is a moral. Mozart's story grows the protagonists — the men — up[23] from romantic love to adult prudence. Their puppy love was centred in ego infatuated by its fantasy beloved, intoxicated by its own surging passion, swooning at the story image over its head, in love with love transcending ego. The vanity extended into the self-indulgent rhetoric: 'I am betrayed; I betray. I am inconstant; I am constant.'

Mozart's 'sentimental education' teaches two things. It urges caution about human character and passion, accepting the flaws, the good with the bad, and striving to make the best of a capricious reality. It implies the need to grow up, out of the narcissism of youth, although it fails to indicate what a more mature love might look like.

It also teaches that it is psychic mayhem and suffering that may free the soul to wing aloft in song. Grace comes via anguish, feeding off it. It is the song that matters — not the particular words, but the spirit that breathes through them. To it, the soul responds.

Mozart is thus in direct line of descent from the Homeric *mythos* as pathos. Yet the critique of soul-mate love that he represents remains, on the whole, unconvincing. At the most, it establishes a conversation with the archetype, adding little itself to the story.

In the Hollywood kiss, she is, care of the make-up, universal; he being in love with the eternal female — that is, with Aphrodite, goddess of love and beauty, as incarnate in the particular woman. But he is none the less in love with the one and only, flesh-and-blood, character-and-soul incarnation — his beloved. In *Casablanca*, for instance, it is inconceivable that Rick could love another woman or she another man. The power of the film is in good part due to the presence of Humphrey Bogart and Ingrid Bergman, the singularity of the two principal individuals — those who in playing the parts become them. To recast the film, replacing either of them, would be to wreck it.

Similarly, the particular young woman conjured up by Poussin, through his third eye, as his 'beautiful beloved' is not to change — although we are unaware who she was. She, too, both plays the part and is it. We come to know her, nameless as she is, and would not tolerate a switch in identity. Indeed, she becomes planted in the Dreaming imagination — forever. She is, surely, not to deface.

Film and painting, in their visual immediacy, do not lie. She *is* the one! He *is* Mr Right! Yet Mozart is shrewd to stress the difference between romantic love, *in love with love*, and the grown-up union of kindred spirits that Plato sketched over two millennia earlier. Shakespeare had already filled out the contrast, in two stages. A few years after *Romeo and Juliet*, he wrote *The Taming of the Shrew* — that is the likely chronology — and then, after another pause, *Much Ado About Nothing*. Jane Austen was to retell the latter story in *Pride and Prejudice*.

Much Ado About Nothing centres on the slow coming together of Beatrice and Benedick, who spend most of the time sparring, making witty jibes at the other's expense. The other characters all recognise that these are two apart, different from themselves, and that they belong together. Indeed, they are the only ones with judgement and loyalty. The men are quick to assume that a fabricated story about the unfaithfulness of the Juliet character,

Hero, is true. Only Benedick is not persuaded, and he immediately trusts Beatrice's defence of Hero. When he talks in the abstract of the ideal woman, he does not gush about the colour of her eyes or the fullness of her lips but spells out thoughtfully how she must be fair, wise and virtuous.

The timing is crucial. We are informed that they have been together before — and it was too early, on that occasion Benedick proving unfaithful, hence her prickly, aggressive wit and her hinging her acceptance of him this time on strong proof of his fidelity, and hence his now grown-up reflections on the qualities of the ideal woman, and his slow recognition that it is Beatrice. The test centres on trust, and both now pass it.

In *Much Ado About Nothing* it is as if Shakespeare is rejecting the whole tradition of romantic love represented by *Romeo and Juliet*, just as Mozart would later satirise it. Shakespeare, however, returns to the Greek form articulated by Plato.

Beatrice and Benedick are, in the important matters, of the same being. They do belong together. Although their future marriage is not described, we are left in little doubt that it will be as Petruchio has pictured the general state, in the simpler work *The Taming of the Shrew* — boding what is 'sweet and happy' — that is, peace, love and a quiet life.[24]

While *The Taming of the Shrew* anticipates *Much Ado About Nothing*, it has its own integrity, supplying an image of the earthy vitality of love to complement the kindred-spirit emphasis of the later play. Taken together, the two works provide a picture that is closer to completeness. Shakespeare's dramatisation of the final relaxation of the shrew and her tamer into love for each other is beyond paraphrase:

Kate: *Husband let's follow, to see the end of this ado.*
Petruchio: *First kiss me Kate, and we will.*
Kate: *What in the midst of the street?*
Petruchio: *What art thou ashamed of me?*

Kate:*No sir, God forbid, but asham'd to kiss.*
Petruchio: *Why then let's home again: come sirrah let's away.*
Kate: *Nay, I will give thee a kiss, now pray thee love stay.*
Petruchio: *Is not this well? Come my sweet.*
Kate: *Better once than never, for never too late.*

So where do we find ourselves? In this province, the youth of today may be on the right track. Their paradox seems deceptively close to the facts, and thereby honest. In spite of disappointment and mess in the actual life experiences, the archetype of soul-mate love endures — commanding and true. But it fits the human reality with woeful imperfection, bringing on mainly suffering.

Usually, fragments meet, not wholes. Here is the principal problem. In a piece of music that is predominantly discordant, sublime strains occasionally break through, to be swamped. The grace notes are too rare and fleeting, exposing the pair to their own characters and their defects. A myriad tangled threads of insecurity are then free to take over — Does he still love me? What did you mean by that? Why were you talking to him? Nerves raw and exposed, each becomes preoccupied by self, thus self-centred and selfish — moaning Poor me and my fragility. I am nothing without you. If you were to leave me, I would be finished! So is love reduced to psychodrama, or apathy.

Compounding the problem is that once the Dreaming archetype is awakened, it projects itself in huge, brightly lit imagery on the wall in front of which the aspiring lovers struggle to dance — the cinema screen a perfect analogue to active Dreaming. They see the contrast with their own puny shadows jerking clumsily out of time, and the sense of failure may become overwhelming. She becomes irritated by the way he slurps his soup, he by the shape of her mouth.

At this point, Plato's image is damagingly false, implying that each is missing a part of itself, which the other supplies. The vision that he or she will be for me everything I lack — providing the absent pieces, the failed vitality and enterprise — indicates that it is not soul-mate love. Eros may be a god born of want, his character swinging from one extreme, of poverty, to the other, of abundance — the cup that floweth over — yet as such, he is an unstable companion to soul-mate love, which seeks constancy. In its truest form, love is assured and calm.

Hollywood has encouraged the delusion that love makes whole. Its tendency is to project an anxiety-charged fantasy of the other, lit up with syrup-and-tinsel *eros*, its invitation to step outside reality into the swooning dream, clamped to the other. It runs with the easy half of the truth, that erotic love is the most accessible path to the non-tragic escape from self in sublime transcendence, to join with the Oneness of existence. It ignores the soul animating the individual *I am*, that unless it acts as the dynamic agent, *eros* serves merely as an intoxicant, its passion a type of addiction, providing rapidly diminishing returns in pleasure.

Mozart's erotic caprice is the self-conscious exposure of this Hollywood delusion. Its lovers believe in the ideal of one true love, but are incapable of living it. They reach sublime heights by pitching themselves into the tense chasm between their ideal of constancy and the fickle narcissism that actually compels them. It is the tension itself that fuels love in love with love. There is not the slightest glimpse here of kindred spirit attachment. The marriages that follow will need a miracle to bring wellbeing.

Soul-mate love, to prevail, must begin from positions of strength and independence. The *pneuma* it inspires takes flight from two steady and balanced *I ams* — it must, that is, have its source in *being*. Otherwise, it is likely to blow away with the first turbulence. Freedom to embark on this testing journey depends on trust that the other will not fall over, that both she and he are their own centres of gravity. This love is alive, for example, in two friends who silently admire each other's presence and strength, instinctively at ease in their affinity with the way each moves separately in the world. The friendship itself sets up a field of force that contributes to poise. Indeed, it is worth recalling that classical Greek employed three words for love. As well as *eros*, there was *philia*, meaning friendship, a dispassionate commitment as in philo-sophy, the love of truth. Finally, there was *agape*, meaning selfless, brotherly, charitable love. Soul-mate love ideally requires a fusion of all three.

Poussin pictured the relationship as it is, and should be — in all its perplexity. His deeper self — which he does not know directly — saw his beautiful beloved face-on, bright-eyed, astute, although hovering spirit-like behind the back of his surface, worldly self, which he sees and knows all too well. Her entire being focussed lovingly on him, she is yet merciless — in her clarity and directness, ruthless to his flaws, challenging: Are you up to me and my hair-raising vitality? If you are not, then your life is hardly worth living. She dares him to *be*. She is, care of the third eye set in the middle of her forehead, wisdom. She is his own Unknown seeing. She is his commanding enigma. When she exists, and manifests herself, guide to everything that matters, herself the confluence of all significant female personae, human and divine, all in one, she is his own soul-steady kindred self. And yet this woman whom he loves as never before or after, through whom he has come to understand love, if fitfully, his Diotima, she is, it has to be remembered, unlike him — she is a woman. In her own separate self, she traces her own distinct path.[25]

More straightforwardly, in the deepest Unknown, everyone knows there exist pairs like Beatrice and Benedick, and that their story is not just a fairy-tale. They are glimpsed in every bankrupt romance, in every Hollywood love story. It is their shadow that brings untold misery whenever this Dreaming truth is awakened then thwarted. And the aftermath of recognition through failure is *pneumaphobia*. For in no other human state does the soul so let down its defences, opening itself to the heavens and to hurt. No *mythos* is so gravely identified by its pathos, and in that word's full Greek range of meaning — experience, passion, suffering. Mozart provides the antidote to this *pneumaphobia*, his music born out of the same discord but transforming the suffering into a sublime breath.

What is known is that, magically, a *he* somewhere, some time, does manage to find the *she* whom the glass slipper fits. And she may glide her foot into it. They are the chosen ones. They have found themselves on their Emmaus road, with the stranger who has appeared from nowhere and now accompanies them the rest of their way, till dusk, when they shall find the tiny roadside inn with a supper table set for two. In his presence, the heart does burn within, and suddenly, their eyes are opened.

Magdalene belongs here, too, and as usual, she brings her own difficult inflexion. Her final intimacy is with her beloved's Emmaus self, their story the ultimate in soul-mate love. Her own encounter on the road she knows not whither occurs when he reappears in the form of the gardener, addressing her intimately by name but immediately cautioning: 'Touch me not!' In part, he is urging her to detachment, explaining that the one you truly love is not the man you knew. Let me go. Cease from clinging, for you no longer need me, my flesh-and-blood self. What we share is beyond human togetherness.

The Western way of reading his words has at the same time moved contrapuntally, urging her to embrace him, to love him intimately and personally, as he does her. Our soul-mate love is detachment through engagement, engagement through detachment. Your and my distinct being inspires the deepest tenderness, me always there beside you, whether you see me or not. From that base, you are freed to carry your love to the world. Yet, once he has gone forever, she gradually, in a kind of tragic after-life state, becomes him, takes on his form — his face, his eyes, his suffering, his presence. In this last phase of the archetype, it is her suffering that makes her beautiful.

Stranger fits. This holds whether it is the extraordinary Magdalene story or any other. For it is not the garments of the person, neither physical attribute nor character trait, nor even name, that identifies the charisma of the companion. Indeed, there is nothing to learn about him or her. A hallmark of soul-mate love is that any enquiry about who you are, what you have done or where you have been is entirely superfluous. It is the *I am* in the other, hardly needing to speak, but to acknowledge with gratitude and awe: I am known. Someone walks beside me. Then each to each on their journey of journeys, they may repeat: Courage. *I am*. Don't fear!

5.

The Mother

The modern West has grown awkward about the mother, out of sorts with the archetype. Fewer women become mothers, and if they do, it will be delayed, even until their middle to late thirties, and there will probably be only one child. The public feeds on negative imagery, of an ever-increasing number of single-mother families in need, or of bored housewives with low self-esteem imprisoned at home with the kids. Children are seen as expensive and a nuisance, demanding too much commitment. The countering ideal, supplied by magazine features and advertising, is that of the *supermum*, chief executive of the family, running the home with a pleasant, unflappable smoothness while pursuing her own career. But her lofty success intimidates most, who see it as unrealistic — that is, unattainable for themselves.

It is as if the entire culture has turned its back on one of its richest Dreaming sources. Other times and other societies take it so seriously that they gear much of their community life to protecting, supporting and celebrating the mother in what she does. They regard the family as the key to human wellbeing, with the mother as its heart and its soul. They follow this principle in planning their houses, their villages and suburbs, their kinship laws and codes of honour and worship, their intimacy customs, even their opportunities for labour and income.

That sometimes cosy, communal world came at a high cost to individual freedom, and the modern West has gained irreversibly from opening more diverse life paths up to its women. But in the process, it lost touch with the archetype and, as if to excuse its own bad conscience, descended into lower-order truths about the mother. A vast literature, ranging from the files of psychotherapy through films and novels to biography, has blamed the mother for unhappiness, stress and anxiety — for the woes of the profane self. On the one hand, she has been portrayed as overwhelming, her love total, jealously possessive, daily on the telephone, or just the ghost presence letting son or daughter know she languishes for their call. On the other, she is accused of having not been there when it mattered, preferring a brother, caught up in herself or in her work, or lavishing all her deep affection on her husband. Either way, her presence is read as casting a shadow over the entire life, offspring never seeming to cut the psychic umbilical cord.

Modern psychology is merely recognising, if dispiritingly, the singular, extraordinary influence of she who creates and nurtures new life. Fairy-tales do the same in their own different way, polarising the good mother and her feared inverse, the wicked witch. On another front, tribal initiations have been interpreted as an attempt by male elders to free boys from their mothers.[1] Here is an example of the general male fear of the power of women, that they know more about the things that matter, that they are more grounded, and that it is they, in fact, anchored in their own centres of gravity, who rule.

Signs are thus — in myths, dreams, fantasies, inhibitions and compulsions — that mothers are universally both the source of perfect, unconditional love and a problem. There was the golden age of infancy and childhood, when you could always run to her, bury your face in her lap, the one secure place in the big, threatening world, assured you would be bathed in warmth, whatever you had done. There, you were not a miserable, tiny, scared weakling, but the greatest treasure on earth — indeed, you experienced yourself, within her loving orbit, as everything. That paradise of tenderness without limit has now gone forever, and it may be hard to stand the loss. Perhaps that is the reason the very old become child-like, only memories of their earliest years of any remaining interest.

She is never just the particular — my mother. Here is the crux. She belongs to an ancient tribe, reborn every generation, drawing on a deep instinct in the blood experience, memory on hoarded memory, of the superhuman power of creation, transcending rational mortal knowing. The archetype speaks through her, its primordial charisma resonating through each particular case, weighting her with its authority.[2] Thus each and every poor and blessed child is cradled by a giant sorceress persona rearing out of the Dreaming. Little wonder the experience is overwhelming. But 'persona' is not quite accurate, for it is the sacred story she inhabits that charges her sanctuary, the archetype, as it manifests through her.

In the Western tradition, the mother archetype is given a full *mythos* oddly late in the day. The Greeks, in their fear of women, had demonised the mother as rancorous, perverse or wicked — Hera, Clytemnestra, Jocasta, Medea, Phaedra, Agave — as well as projecting her into devouring or paralysing monsters, like Scylla and Medusa.[3]

The mother archetype did finally crack its way through the repressions and impel itself into form, in a story drawing, almost casually, on two of the *Lives of Jesus*.[4] Its first idiom was primitive, that of the melancholy medieval icon, exemplified in the stiffly simple, distant, other-worldly Madonnas of Duccio — a culture that survived right through to modern times in such figures as Mother Teresa. The Third Reformation then transformed the imagery beyond recognition, painting for the first time in the West a complete and sympathetic portrait of the mother, deepened by tragedy.[5] According to it, no vocation is higher. And every woman, once she crosses this threshold, is of Mary, even if she had been, up to this moment, no-one, vegetating in embryonic being.

The Mary we first meet is an artless young woman, not knowing what to do with her life, which has been narrow, lacking experience. The future is a blur, without shape, of hope or apprehension. Yet she is neither girlish nor hesitant, but ready for the moment that will fatefully change her. Sitting on a cushion on the floor, she simply looks up from a book at an angel who stands before her.

This angel is terrible. With red hair, full lips, mouth slightly open, chunky arms, he leans nonchalantly on one knee into Mary's space, outstretched right arm pointing straight at her breast. While his robe is white, his wings are thick and tactile, coloured in sections. Their top is crimson-orange — an aggressively earthy colour, mixing blood and terracotta. The middle colour is also rich, a royal blue, magisterial, kingly — this angel comes to rule. The bottom plumage is white, but a compromised off-white. The wings are those of an eagle, suggesting pride and victory, and the pagan god of Greeks and Romans.

His bare feet are fleshy, with grubby nails, and the left knee is itself far from angelic, jutting forward towards her. The slow, purposeful rhythm of his body moves with loaded intent, reaching its climax in mouth, eyes and coercive hands. Now the angel stares at Mary's midriff, his look straight into her womb. There is a hint of a wicked smile.

But who or what is an angel, and one like this? Is she lost in fantasy, this her dream lover? Or has Mary, naive girl that she was, just seen with fresh eyes the man who is everyday husband or boyfriend — some Joseph — now arriving in a blast of wind, his ordinary self metamorphosed into a fiery magnificence, as if what he has achieved, and he and she together, has been touched by divinity — well, not completely touched? The condition she has entered these last few hours, of pregnancy, has worked its miracle — vision through the mists into the sacred essence. She sees before her what *it* really means.[6]

Mary does not question. In an instant, she has emerged from sheltered childhood into full female pathos. Sitting cross-legged on the floor, she is dressed in dusty pink. She rocks back, throwing her arms out wide, fingers extended, palms open to the world — no kneeling, bowed submission here. Her head tips back, eyes closed, surrendering her defenceless face to the moment. Her lap is wide open, as is her mouth, expressing a silent groan. She is in a swoon.

Her feet, too, are bare, the soles and the underneath of the toes exposed. They pair in one direction with her open hands, delicate in shape, as are the wrists, elegant fingers and fine skin. But there is a coarseness to her upper lip. Mary's feet seem to pair in the other direction with those of the angel, in shape and position, his more assertive, hers more passively receptive. It is as if all four dance to the music of time. Now is for pleasure; the tragedy will be on her soon enough.[7]

Already, a wisp of shadow mist drifts in. Even with the feet, all is not earth. The bared soles link back to the open palms, and their vulnerability is that of the source from which the forgiving rays will stream. Through these sensitive spots, the nails will be hammered. So the sensuality of hands and feet is at the same time the sober, tragic earthiness of mortality. What Mary's visitor announces is martyrdom.

A demon-angel does not consult. There is no alternative door for Mary, no choice. One woman, called from within, one way! So why should he bother to speak? Indeed, why is he here at all? There seems little point. She is born into what she must bear. Things happen as they do, his arrival announcing: This is what you are — accept it, for now it begins. You are mother, any mother, every mother, except in that you have me, and my presence tells of how extraordinary will be he to whom you give birth. But as I am here for you, I will be there for all the others, and for all time, if they, too, are ready.

Mary had known all this as a five-year-old girl, when she strode alone before a huge crowd up the steps of the Temple, her entire head and body encased in a flaring aura.[8] She did not need an angel to tell her. How she had glided up those steps, innocent, face to the light. Then, in her teenage years, she had become distracted, forgetting. Now it rushes back.

Her sphere is not syrup religion, one of sweet music, soft pastels, veils of white lace, charming cherubs, peace and harmony — the cares of the world left far behind. Who would wish to be Mary? Her condition is dreadful. Yet this is her story, and *mythos* is pathos. Her eyes are closed, and were they to open, she would find herself confronted by his gleaming stare, the orange-crimson rearing up behind and bearing down on her, driving the remorseless, nonchalant precision of his assault. She would see his arms like a pair of godly dividers poised over her life, the right one directed at her, striking her heart, the left effortlessly pointing upwards, to the other and higher source of his power. He is destiny and Truth.

Grace here means seizure, body and soul, freeing her from the horror of seeing, full on. Knowledge is sedated by rapture, so she closes her eyes, as if to say, Yes, I know what is to come. I accept it; it will not crush me. I can bear it, for my strength is in who I am, and its radiance is forever. I am not going to flee. She can give herself so fully because of her dread, burning off any illusions.[9]

Mary balances in herself, sitting lightly pivoted on the cushion, the head eased back in equilibrium with the forward set of her feet, and in the sideways plane, the outstretched hands and knees acting as stabilisers, as in a tightrope-walker's pole. Balance is everything. In a sudden reversal, the fright is transferred to the angel.

That it is Mary who has abandoned herself to the moment signifies little. The angel's arrival had been in a rush. He hurtled into the scene, imagining that he could take it over. The wickedness in his face has something of Cupid, the imp whose erotic arrows play havoc with human passion. But this angel came to a sudden halt. Frozen in his headlong motion, his resolve collapses.

He imagined he had power, but now under her spell, he finds himself helpless, pulled irresistibly towards her. The crimson-orange of the wings turns against him. It is he who will bleed. The blue in his plumage is changed from royal authority to an echo of the blue of a shawl she wears, not forward veiling her forehead — as in piety and chasteness — but tossed casually onto the back of her crown, revealing her own reddish-golden hair. Thus the two strong colours in the wings pick up those in Mary's hair and shawl. It is as if the wings are her agents, closing off the angel's escape backwards — indeed, a magnet passion planted in the middle of his back.

As she releases herself, she draws him to her lap. His kneeling in the vertical plane is unsteady. Her arms, stretching wide with open palms, encompass him, setting up a field of force which, like an invisible net, has him trapped, and with him the entire precariousness of male being. He is her pawn.

Seated by herself, on a wooden floor in a modest room, in a house and a place nowhere in particular, she is queen, on her green cushion of fecundity. The angel is helper, under her power, easing her way, merely husband, at best security guard. This *is* virgin conception, but not in the usual sense. She is alone with the seed.

She had been reading a book, perhaps as a meditative means of tuning in to her conscience, so as to be ready. Conscience tells of Truth, her destiny within it, and saves her from plunging into Fall. How quickly she has come of age. Different will be Magdalene's fusion of flesh and *pneuma* — the two elemental forces, each depending on the other's vitality — Magdalene ultra-feminine but not motherly. This Mary's blue cloaking dusty pink is trust, for the angel comes from above, and what might have been lust is transformed into love — including, later, *agape* — the beastly into the human, on earth under higher law.

Yet her moment of grace is not free from Fallenness. All is weighted.[10] Such is earthly vocation, even hers. Mary has the burden of Cassandra,[11] foreseeing the future — the terrible fate that awaits her son and her own final act. Additionally, she is herself flesh and blood, and in that is liability. In her swoon, she can already feel the pressure of nails on hands and feet. There is already an austerity to her, a *Touch me not!* distance from others, they who are of the world. Not for her the excessive weeping and kissing of Magdalene.

Mary launches her entire being forward, trusting, like a high-trapeze artist propelling herself into thin air, sure she will be caught. Here is valour, and energy, her own type of sacred rage that will not be inhibited by what she knows. She does see too much, and closes her eyes, so as freely to embrace her forward momentum. She believes, and *it* is there, waiting to catch her.

Her wounds are not just allusion. The form of her body in flight — arms out wide, lap open, feet crossed, head tilted back, forehead bare — is that of female Crucifixion. She is woman identified with Jesus, her son — but in her own quite different way. The sacred foci shift from the spear wound in the side to the womb and its potent seed, from the tragic pain in the face, looking down and back, to the anticipatory knowledge and uplifted openness to the living moment, eyes closed. The wounds in the palms are implicit, receptive to both nails and *pneuma*, in hands that take in only to fortify her capacity to give.[12]

All of this, the angel witnesses. A sadness overcomes him. His arms become gentle in their directing, his look tender, helpless and sorrowful. Strangely now, his wings evoke the brilliance of her son-to-be.

All is weighted. It is Act Two, and dread searches in eyes that see forwards into her own fate. She steps out from behind green curtains, a young mother cradling the boy infant. She is entering the world, presenting him to it, her gift, but so reluctantly, she can hardly move.

Motherhood is joy. Tucked in against her right side, he sits on her supporting left hand, she quarter-turned to him, his baby-flesh shoulder leaning into her breast, her right hand firmly stabilising him under his chubby outer arm. His head tilts, nuzzling against her neck, but faces forward. They are one, the boundaries of her self dissolving and reforming around him, as if he were still in her womb, but not, for he was an alien there, an embryo body guzzling strength, while here, he is himself, already concentrated *I am*. It is no longer physical, the bond, but her entire mental being, *pneuma* formed to her person including him, indeed focussed on him, he the nucleus, she the surrounding fluid. Thus he is naked, cradled in a voluminous shawl that begins as a crown on her head, billows out behind, and sweeps under her left arm then up under him, the whole a rounded cocooning swirl, an idyllic dream of oneness.

He floats weightless, the intimacy of this union never to be recaptured. It is the opening counterpart to what Magdalene will achieve thirty or so years on with his dead hand — she with utmost difficulty. For the mother, it is easy, merely natural. Such is the first movement of selfless love, its archetype known across the stretch of the human world and back into primeval time. The mother has already sacrificed herself out of existence.

That is only surface, for her deeper wish here is to retreat back behind the green curtains, turn him to her, and hug him tight and forever. Motherhood's second movement is greedy, its temptation to clutch in timeless possessiveness, praying that he never grow up, that this moment be frozen. It is he, already ruthless, who will have none of that.

If the announcing angel was demonic, what of him, this infant boy, here eye to eye with the world? It is he who will, in a couple of years' time, be holding the candle to Light his father's work. Already his fine, reddish-auburn locks flame out, long and wild. He tucks his right leg nonchalantly up, in lotus position, to rest on his mother's supporting wrist. He dangles his other foot down, while drawing his right arm back, bent at the elbow, the hand firmly gripping the shawl that sweeps under it. This hand is cocked, ready for action. Imperial, he sits. Alert, he purses his lips, a slight downturn of bitterness showing, but there is also patience and resolve. For he who was born old — is anything left Unknown?

It is the eyes that compel. Deep-set, a slight furrow to the brows, they pierce, timeless, seizing what is before them. They have just widened at what he has seen, his life to be, the shade of fearfulness soon eclipsed by a recessed sacred rage, barely held back. He will do what he has to do, and it will be almost everything. Moreover, the toes of the dangling foot flex. He is itching to be off, to begin his mission.

This is a huge and formidable, lion ego, Greek in its grandeur. It eclipses the serving mother — already, he no longer needs her, as if whispering cruelly in her ear: 'Woman what have I to do with thee!' All this she sees. It is how she would want it — at least, the strong, Stoical part of her would — and, in any case, for the moment she can relax back into the present, where this bravado of his remains just for show. He will rush back to the security of her lap at the slightest setback. She still has to hold his hand, restrain that exorbitant urge to throw himself, helter-skelter, into his destiny. In fact, he is pleased to be held back. But how few will be the years — remorseless time, marching heartlessly onwards, her enemy.

For her, it is not to be the high drama of teaching, redirecting those wayward in spirit, the feeble and the confused, everybody, then the climax on the Cross — but day-by-day anxiety. Her role is not to build monuments — indeed, not really to do anything at all, in terms of action in the world. Stepping out from behind the green curtains, she voyages on clouds, but not airily. Her feet are skew to the ground, never firmly based, prone to stumbling, her centre of gravity in the circle of caring love, the fire glowing in the hearth at the centre of the home, her crux, others drawn to it, wanting to be around it. Roundness is her logic, as when she sat, queenly, on her floor-cushion and welcomed the angel. Her body discloses her destiny, the flesh soft, easy to bruise, quick to lose its shape.

Her expression speaks of resignation, tinged with pride: Here he is, what I have made for you, my creation out of nothing, and you will take him, mistreat him, leaving me alone with the pain of knowing how beautifully perfect he was, how great, in me, of me, from me. Look at him, all of you — take in the poise with which he lounges in my cradling arms; take in that mouth, those eyes. Shrink back, for you can already see how powerful he is, already with such a frightening lion presence.[13]

Her eyes are wide, facing the world, yet inwards, almost the entire look turned back, onto what was and what will be, looking into the well of her own tragedy. She has power, to be sure, the godly power of creation, but unlike men, she gets little pleasure from parading it. It is as if everything in her that matters faces inwards, away from the public, backwards into her sanctuary behind the green curtains. Her realm was in there, where with a piercing triumphal scream, she delivered him.

She feels utterly helpless as her whole reason for being drifts into the impersonal yonder, already as good as gone. She will, it is true, be able to follow his doings, and take pride in them, from a distance, him embarrassed by her, telling her to stay away. As far as he is concerned, she has done her job, and that is it, finished — and, of course, he is right. What does she expect? But she herself, what will be left of her, what more than the exhausted, used-up, sagging, puffy flesh of a woman alone with her memories? Who would wish to be me?

And as if this were not enough, *angels* are back — demon-angels, this time two of them, in the form of impish little boys, chubby-limbed, with round cherub faces just like that of her son, and perky coloured wings popping out of their shoulder-blades. Directly beneath her, they slouch against a rail. They look up and roll their eyes, these brats, bored by all that tragic stuff going on in the scene above, as if she were their mother, and mothers are killjoys, reigning in playtime. If you get too serious, ponder too much, they seem to say, you won't be able to move. Their eyes twinkling, they are eager to be off on their next prank.

She is thus mocked by the male principle, taunting: Don't nag — what's the fuss? That's just soppy chatter making you depressed — why don't you get up and do something? These two naughty boys are all rush and purpose, too busy with their games to feel in the flesh, their biology untroubled by pity. She will have to admire the empires they build, even encourage them, but again it will be her giving, always giving, then waiting for the broken spirit, which will surely return one day, beaten down by the world, when once again she will be needed.

Fecundity and nurture are not her only strengths. In her own sphere, she is not passive. So it was with Joseph, she, of course, choosing him. He was far from her ideal man, too lumbering and slow-witted, lacking charm or flair. Indeed, as the legend would unreliably convey, it was a miracle she became pregnant. But she knew he would be stalwart, her chosen man, so she could rely on him, like the donkey he would lead, regally carrying mother and child into exile in Egypt — and who would want to be exiled into the discomfort of the Egyptian wilderness.[14] He will always worship at her feet, and that means something. Knowing what is required of her, she can move decisively, sacrificing girlish dreams to fulfil the reality. Few men would have the nerve, and the resignation, to act with such resolve, then accept what she accepts — which means live with it, make the best of it — and she will, largely for the sake of her child.

The angel boys are blithely incapable of putting themselves in her position, and even if they could, would shy away from the embarrassment.[15] Here is a courage they do not have, will never have, the unflinching concentrated look straight at oneself and one's fate, at the whole sombre, imperfect truth. She is again more selfless, able to admire their irrepressible vitality, join with them for an hour in their fun, warm with unself-conscious pleasure that they are happy. And they remind her that there is the good life, other ways of being, less harsh than her own. She envies them — her lot would be so much easier if she, too, could lose herself in activity.

As she has observed, boys remain boys, boyishness usually resilient into old age. Yet these two and their heirs will not be able to stop themselves filling the world with images of her. From a safe distance, with sweet longing, they will daydream away. In their churches, they will lodge statues of her idealised form, backed by stained-glass windows glistening with Madonna blue, alongside altars in sentimental fidelity to the heart of the human world. Then there will often be some wall — in home or office or gallery — on which hangs a crudely painted or photographed image of a particular woman as instance of her, and it will be her eyes, always her eyes, looking out through the blurred and distant face.

Whenever they are afflicted, dispirited or oppressed, they come seeking her out, stumbling into her Church in one or other of its many forms, on their knees before her, pleading for her warming embrace. When in need, most of them prefer her to her son. That church may be almost anywhere, even a lonely beach under the summer sun, wriggling the naked body into the sand to feel the heat of her form, envision it in rounded sand dunes, seaweed by the water, translucent rock-pools. Opulent and generous is Nature's maternal order, like her.

And when they fail to do that, honour her, their existence becomes cursed. Women turn frigid and hysterical. Men work with obsessed frenzy to build things — cities, palaces, churches, theories — to an abstract intellectual plan, their rigorous geometrical orders and mechanical perfections a tactic to shut out feeling. Some take to ranting fundamentalisms; others are submerged by depression, careless and slovenly in what they make. In that world on Monday morning at seven-fourteen, everyone drinks coffee.

They are in awe of her, women and men alike, for she and her son are singular, they themselves inimitable in their greatness. Yet all those ordinary mortals recognise a bit of themselves, for every mother is of Mary, believing on the day she is visited by her angel that her child will be — in what he or she is and will do — of the boy Jesus.[16]

A ct One — she discovered that she was with child and met her first angel, the terrible one, and joined him in flight. Act Two — she emerged from behind green curtains to present her infant to the world, he who already scarcely needed her, and she was mocked by two impish angels, looking suspiciously like her own son. Throughout, she was weighed down by the knowledge of her condition.

Act Three, her finale — she is needed once more. This moment is called *Pietá*, from the Italian meaning 'devotion, mercy, piety, pity'. Her son is dead. She has outlived him. They have just taken his body down from the Cross. She has two selves, one collapsing onto the ground where her story began, this time uncushioned but once again in a swoon.[17] With her son breathing his last, her own spirit has drained away — leaving blank eyes and ghost face, no sense of human presence animating her evacuated form. Three young women, tested on entry into their own mission of care, support her, try to bring her back to consciousness. They talk to her. They will talk on and on for days, hoping to build a web of communion to hold together she who is so miserably sorry for herself.

Her other self is strong, alert, and on its feet. It insists once again on taking him in her arms, this flesh of skeletal brokenness, emptied of being, which is somehow still in the vertical, propped up against a marble bench with the help of the beloved disciple. One arm around the shoulders, she uses the other hand to firmly grip the right wrist and bring the hand up against his chest, exposing the wound to the world — displaying her creation afresh but this time grimacing, without pride. His left arm has flopped down onto the marble, as his head lists against hers, cold cheek to her now grey, sunken, wrinkled cheek, her heavy-lidded eyes staring dolefully at his closed lids, their mouths close enough to kiss, but her lips sagging open in anguished sympathy.

Here is the essence of care, which will be misunderstood as her son's vocation. It is her own. What began in conception and continued in motherly nurture finds its fulfilment here in embracing the dead body. Her message is to all mothers: Do not think you have finished when your children have grown up. It is for you to know they will die, and in death need your consoling love again, from that other side from whence you first brought them. Don't fear; this is not as absurd as it seems, especially for you, who of all people have always known that nothing important is rational.

Deny this, she continues, the final chapter, and your later life will drift into sick futility. Most of you will deny it, not prove up to it, particularly those who imagine motherhood as just another task, much like any other, nothing special. Then will come your evil. As ever, it is Law, vengeful, demanding retribution, that the sacred stories be fulfilled.

The appointed yoke is strapped tight around her neck, *Necessity's* ultimate curse on the universal mother, she just another beast of burden, with one last load to haul. Great gifts come at a high price. What is given is taken away. What she ushers into the world she will have to usher out. So it is determined. Circle and cycle are her pattern. By making new life, she felt herself immortal — such exhilaration could mean only that, eclipsing every other human experience. And she believed that she had broken free, for it is gods who create out of nothing.[18] Vanity of vanities, for everything born onto this earth will die. Even Achilles — and *his* mother was herself immortal — had to perish, and in the arena of battle, his own field of strength, shocking to see, crashing down from the back of his chariot like the sacred and ancient oak, felled, dust to return to dust.[19] Even the great Achilles — he, too, was born out of the ether from behind her green curtain — was to die into oblivion.

Vanity it is also for her, outrageous and impious vanity, to imagine she was more than midwife. The crucible of being — conception followed nine months later by first breath — is fired from beyond, not by a mere mortal mother. Who does she think she is?

This Act, scripted without pity, has hard *Necessity*, who never blinks, murmur in Mary's ear: The season for you to relinquish hope has come. Done is your reason for being — it is dead in your arms. As you lost yourself in the grander existence of the infant lion, lose yourself again. I, and my three beautiful daughters, who spin the thread that may be neither cut nor loosened, we know just how dark it is, your closing act. You must plunge down into the underworld shadows and lie with the corpse of your own child — hugging it to your breast, death to death.

Little wonder, then, that the mother in her pure type, instinctively aware of her full condition, lives as in a dream, captive to ever-narrowing circles of haunted imagination. How extraordinary, then, is the woman who knows all this in advance, yet still decides: Yes! I shall do it. I shall put on the yoke — I shall become a mother! The Western Dreaming casts her as peerless example of what, in terms of obligation to being, is demanded of the complete human. It pictures no greater courage.

As the boys notice, she never seems to do very much. It is as if she is permanently shrouded in reflections on her fate. She is too engaged to console herself with the wisdom of the human cycle: that for every time, there is a season, dust returning to dust as it was in the beginning. Nor does her love save her from full-on confrontation with the Deluge, for she has every reason to identify with the mother whose family is about to drown. The debilitating thought hovers around, too, that her domain has merely switched from the helplessness of the baby to that of the dying, nothing much in between, and that her hopes for him were futile. Indeed, for her, there is one truth: that he who was all is dead, beyond caring, beyond her love. All it seems left for her to do is tear her hair out, shave her head, try to scratch herself out of existence! Only detachment may save her.

In response, Mary the mother, now faceless, cloaked and hooded in black, merges with all those other impersonal spectres — ravens, Furies, witches — that gather throughout the human world to wail around the anointed and masked body. They who bridge the great divide sing the departed spirit on its way, and back to them, in a mysterious communing with it and the primal Oneness. And on and on they go, crooning of their affliction, this sacred community of women, for hours and days, beyond all normal sense of time and place. Nor are any angels present to listen in on the collective requiem of mother shades.

6.

Vocation

Work has become, more than anything else in the modern world apart from intimacy and family, what gives purpose to a life. It does so because it has been freed from *Necessity*. Its primary motive is no longer the profane business of earning a living — to put bread on the table, clothes on the back and a roof over the head. In the West, it has found a higher and universal law to frame it, that of *vocation*.

Consider again the waitress who throws herself body and soul into what she does. In her own mind, she is an artist. She makes sure she places the fork down *just right*, without any jerk to her motion, noiselessly, in the exact spot in which it belongs — and which her inner eye sees precisely, to the nearest millimetre — in relation to plates, serviette and other utensils. When she stoops down to pick up a fallen roll, she knows she is on stage, being observed for the slightest mistake. So she moves with grace, that the whole be harmonious, the potential discord smoothed by her professionalism. She strives to be as perfect as the gleaming crystal wine glass into which she has just poured immaculate burgundy liquid. By the end of the evening, she is exhausted. She loves her work.[1]

This waitress would be ashamed to do a slapdash job. Shame is her commanding emotion, with its impulse to bow head, lower eyes, flush the neck and exposed ears, and force her down on her knees — its presence suggesting that she feels judged from above. She works under higher law, to do the job *justice*. Moreover, she touches all who are served by her. They know unconsciously that she is pointing the finger at them, her presence asserting: If you in your own central life tasks do not take them as seriously as I do, everything at stake, then you are breaking an eternal law, and you will be struck down with guilt. To observe her is to know she is right. The fact that her job attracts little social prestige, nor is well paid, adds to the authenticity of her message and the sting of its coercion. She is one of the great moral educators of the modern world, teaching universal law. She has the power to mobilise *the* sacred passion — shame.

She believes that when she puts the fork down 'just right', the act is somehow bigger than the facts. She is in effect striving for a sort of form, a contemplative means, through action in the world, enabling her to rise to meet a universal truth. It is as if that truth hovers in the beyond, invisibly framing what she does, just as surely determined by law as the exact spot in which the fork belongs. She is metamorphosed out of her puny individual self through her act, rising to become that truth. This is part of what is meant when someone says: I lose myself in my work. Hers is not just a job, done for the pay, but her religion, guided by a faith that may not be rational but that it is how it is. She works in the hope of silver lightning spearing through the grey ether towards her.

The modern world knows her well, as its steadily and quietly achieving, exemplary star. She could just as easily be an Olympic sportswoman, a carpenter, a tax accountant. She is there wherever individuals throw themselves with relentless dedication into what they do, desperate to carry it out to the best of their ability, beyond the call of duty, and train themselves, worry about their performance, feel guilty that they could have done better and betrayed when their work does not give them this opportunity to prove themselves.

How may we understand the waitress? Is there any depth to her, or is she merely duped about her prosaic tasks, living under what Nietzsche deemed a 'redemptive illusion'?[2] From where, in other words, do these secular vocations draw their strength, if anywhere? The Sixth Story is their beginning.

The waitress' godparent is Matthew. His story is that of a young man who finds his mission. He could be a car salesman, a security guard, a courier. In fact, he is, in his own beginning, a lowly tax collector, hated for what he does. One day we find him sitting at the end of a table in a dingy, undecorated room, a dirty window above him letting in no light. Pen and ink lie on the table next to his account book. One of three men seated with him counts out coins, which he puts down with slow deliberation. Matthew watches morosely, tightly clasping his money pouch. An old man standing next to him stoops over the table, and scrutinises the money through a pair of glasses perched on the end of his nose. This is a lethargic, squalid and ludicrous scene, burdened with mortality, everybody just going through the necessary motions.

A stranger enters the room. He looks at the five around the table, a broad shaft of light from behind him picking up bits of each figure in lurid chiaroscuro. He remains in shadow, especially the eyes, as he stretches his right arm casually forward to full extension and the light parades his hand, which points at one of the men as if to announce: You! It is unclear which one.

There is confusion about who is being singled out. All five seem to fathom the gravity of the moment, sharing the instinctive reaction: Please, not me! The old man with the glasses keeps his gaze immovably fixed on the money, pretending not to notice — If I don't see him, he will overlook me. Two finely dressed young dandies sitting at the end of the table nearest the stranger both sway back from his line of sight, their eyes glued to him, like a pair of deer knowing that to elude the lion, they must keep his every move in sight. They are pretty sure they are safe, assuming that this business is too serious for the fickle likes of them. But they remain anxious. A flicker across their stupefied faces acknowledges that whatever is going on here is enough to make them change their ways, if they could only understand what it meant.

The central figure in the group counts out his money. He is an imposing middle-aged man rakishly sporting a black velvet cap. When he notices the new presence, however, he swivels off-balance in his chair, lurching up from the table. Wide-eyed with fear, he looks at the pointing hand, his lips weakly sealed, trembling behind a profuse disguising beard. His right hand props on the table, thumb and forefinger tightly clasping a gold coin. His left rises across his chest in imitation of the pointing gesture, echoing it, hoping that it will continue on past him to settle on the old man or the young tax collector. It is as if he is saying: 'I know nothing, I want nothing, I am nothing. Surely not me! In any case I have paid my dues, in gold pieces, Look! — here on the table.'[3] He could serve as Danae's gaoler.

Only Matthew and the stranger know who is the target, and he himself is not entirely sure. Matthew is not yet Matthew. He just collects taxes, moving in a human world of money, chicanery, and people trying to deceive him, slandering him behind his back as a money-grubbing traitor. He works in this distant Jewish province of a great empire for a huge and alien bureaucratic order, which he begrudges, his labour serving to make Rome fat. But at least gold is gold, bringing him security and funding his pleasures.

Feeling the assault, he hunches over, dropping his head, trying to concentrate on a coin, with which he fiddles. Instinctively, he hides the hand clutching the money pouch, already ashamed of his work. The line from the stranger's eyes through the pointing finger burns into the crown of Matthew's head.

A swarthy youth, heavy-jowled, with no mark of refinement, he is dressed like a lacklustre clown, a mop of dark hair covering forehead and temples as if to provide maximum camouflage for a blurred, uncertain identity: This is too big for ordinary little me — why not someone else? He can just manage a last fancy of escape, of joining the boys as usual tonight at the tavern.

The stranger remains calm. From the shadows, his eyes seem to incline in pity towards the assembled five, his mouth opening with concern, as if surprised by this intersection with common humanity. Simply doing what he knows he has to do, it is with some reluctance that he has extended his right arm. The light catches a deep incandescence of rich red burgundy sleeve ringing the pale skin of his wrist. His pointing hand just hangs there, nonchalantly propelling its vector towards Matthew, in itself so casual that he might be mistaken for one of the dandies. His power is such that he holds back, slightly crooking his index finger to take the edge off his charisma, veil it, lest they be blinded.[4]

Matthew is right to hide himself, singled out unjustly early, in his youth, before he has had time to enjoy it. This is no place for the dewy-eyed, the half-hearted or those who are after pleasure. What he is being called to is toil and hardship, decade upon bitter decade of it, with little human warmth or recognition to oil his passage. The intrusive stranger likes his reticence, a sign of sensing what is involved — that he may be up to his calling.

The silent monologue continues, directed through the hand at the sunken head. From this moment, here and now in this dingy room, you will feel rising within a pressure like insatiable hunger. Any success will merely gnaw with its inadequacy. It will propel you onwards, this demon *pneuma*, ever onwards, hurtling you through winter storms of the rancour you arouse, slogging you through summer languor of the resistance of those you try to budge. Home and family will not be yours, worldly ease being out of rhythm with your hounded spirit. Your only constant companion will be what bloweth, temperamentally — for days, a chilling whirlwind that forces you off course, dizzy and dispirited, then perversely fills your sails, before turning mild, caressing the throbbing temples. You will gain little recognition, and have to comfort yourself with: Well at least I did what I had to — if the wayfarers passed by, then that was their loss. Bewildered, you will come to curse the one who started it all, who aroused the sacred rage.

Nor will there be any external sign. That stuff about the shepherds following a star in the night sky was a sweet fable for children. Here, all is inward and invisible — Truth. No-one else is party to what is going on, who is being addressed, and by what. And so it will continue, on and forever on. At rare moments, you will know. I know, but I will soon be gone. Nor will you be able to speak of your trials. Yearning to be understood, you will remain silent. Although joining a large company, its membership is secret, known only to itself. Occasionally, you will sense its existence, and that will provide some solace on this, my lonely path.

No wonder the outstretched right hand inclined towards Matthew moves in its charged intent with sorrowful hesitation. Yet it has given the tax collector the greatest gift of all. He can move. He is standard-bearer to the perfect form, revealing the inner story of every vocation. The waitress, while lesser, like everyone, is of him, knowing the size of what she does. This is why she cannot be swayed.

Vocation is light and dark. Failure is its shadow half, an ever-present sword hanging over those born on earth under the alternating majesty of sun and moon. Failed vocation is represented by its own lunar archetype. Michelangelo gave it form in his sculptural masterpiece *Moses*, carved over thirty years — and with a virtuosity that breathed into brute marble spirit and feeling as vital as that found in any real human flesh. The Renaissance sculptor introduced, in a work that is transparently autobiographical, a complex modern psychological dimension into the stories.

Freud was haunted by this *Moses* for much of his adult life. He devoted his last five years, on and off, to the Moses question. When he visited Rome in 1901, he went every day to the Basilica of San Pietro in Vincoli and spent hours staring at Michelangelo's creation. Ernest Jones comments: 'What fascinated Freud about this statue was just that, the riddle of why it affected him so deeply.'[5] Yet in 1914, when Freud came to write 'The Moses of Michelangelo', he became sidetracked in petty detail. The essay reads like a furious rationalisation for his own compelling interest, with him determined to suppress its true unconscious life. In his own terminology, there is strong resistance at work.

Michelangelo's *Moses* has a range of moods and personae contained within its one form. In outward shape, he is massive. Although seated, his physique is that of a modern body-builder — Herculean shoulders, barrel torso, titanic bared right knee and lower leg, the neck of a stallion, the head itself square and heavy like an antique Zeus, and biceps polished and hugely muscular. The hands and the feet are those of a giant. The moustache and beard are like rampant vines in a tropical jungle, cascading down to the waist. This is the Judeo-Christian Achilles, God's warrior, proud and stubborn prophet, chin-jutting leader of his people.[6]

The inward shape is opposite: effeminate and indecisive. Moses looks upward to his left, recoiling from what he sees — and what, we can only imagine — his right shoulder tipping back, his left arm slightly raised as if to ward off attack. His seat is unsteady, some critics misreading it as him being about to stand. Off-balance, his hold on the two stone tablets of the law given to him on Mount Sinai by God himself is awkward, with them jammed by his right elbow against his side. The hand is bent over the top of the tablets, perpendicular at the wrist, limply fondling the beard, like a woman toying with the strands of her long hair.

The left hand is cupped awkwardly in his lap, to catch the lowest pair of strands of the beard but also there to protect the lower abdomen. It is as if the beard is sensitive and exposed, its nerve ends needing cover. At the same time, it is like a gushing torrent, the left hand blocking the end trickle, stopping it dripping to the ground.

The titanic right leg, knee protruding forward, has the hollow presence of a cardboard theatre prop. Michelangelo has covered it in voluminous folds of material, quite out of keeping with the rest of Moses' dress. It alludes to the heavy shawl, conventionally used in European art, to cover the Madonna's head and shoulders. The leg then doubles as a ghostly maternal face — the sculptor is building in a psychobiography, of himself turned to stone by the cold anti-Madonna mother.[7]

The actual face reveals more. The eyes are wide open, with pupils dilated. There is astonishment and fear at what he sees. Under darkly tense brows, the eyes glare, but blankly, with neither the assertion of command nor the balance of inward reflection. In their fearful astonishment, the eyes have retreated, gazing nowhere, close to madness.

The viewer's eye is drawn upwards from beard to pouting mouth, eyes, and then on up to incongruous horns perched on the top front of the head, bedded in clumped curls of hair —

what Freud completely ignores in his analysis. This is a horned Moses! But these are not the horns of a noble Viking warrior, touched by rays from the divinity. They are demonic, alluding to the grotesque figure of Pan, with his goat's legs, pointed ears and horns. The bacchanalian Greek demigod of the twilight woods embodies bestial lust. Then there is Satan, the Judeo-Christian reworking of Pan into a different breed of seducer, leading humans into temptation and sin and thus ensuring their damnation. A third possible projection is literal: they are the thick, stunted horns of a castrated bull.[8]

But why is Moses demonic? As with Pan, the horns are displaced testicles. Michelangelo underscores the association by having the beard spilling into the genital region. However, this is not aggressive, phallic masculinity, but Pan emasculated — the castrated bull. The right hand fondles the beard as in an enfeebled, passive narcissism. The lower beard trickles into the left hand. Not with a bang but a whimper! The first message of the statue, cued by the horns, is thus one of psychopathology, and self-condemnation: I am loathsome.[9]

The right hand resting on the tablets of the law simultaneously pulls the beard aside, as if Moses is exposing a wound. The primary coordinates governing the work as a whole centre on the point in the midriff uncovered by the drawing aside of the beard. The hands gesture passively through their horizontals to this point, as do beard strands and horns through their verticals. It is a matrix with all of Moses' shame, and his need to tell his private story, concentrated centripetally on this one still point, the wound.

The great leader, ambassador of God, has exposed himself — hence his agitated, awkward seat, his sideward cringing, and his wide-eyed stare. This work is a confession. It is an elaborate and ruthless story about its maker, his story: of the demon that drives him, of the dread of women that gave it its black, distorted, horned form, and of the empty wreck that he has become.

Freud's fascination was in part with a work that outpointed him at his own psychoanalytical vocation.[10]

Michelangelo, however, is not limited to the lower, psychological plane. The cause of this Fall lies in sacred order. The Hebrew prophet is looking directly up at a black, vengeful God who is fuming. What Moses sees is rejection. This is indeed the moment of revelation — but in negation, the horror of *not* being chosen.[11] His movement is that of anti-call. The contrast with Matthew could not be greater — that callow youth, undistinguished nobody, even worse, a despised tax collector, but he the one visited by a saving divinity.

Moses recoils in dispirited reflection, muttering to his God:

> *You chose me above all other men, calling me to the greatest of human vocations, and I obeyed you. I, Moses, have done immense deeds for you, dedicated my life to your ends, accomplishing everything that you asked of me. Now you turn away in scorn, indicating that it was all for nothing. Why was my path to the stone tablets of the law the wrong way, my mission false?[12]*

So the Jewish hero swivels away, unbalanced, the despondent terror in his eyes protesting: How can this be! I do not understand! A vast ruin of a man is left to cry out: 'Look on my works ye mighty and despair.'[13]

Moses becomes angry, enraged at his fate, and at the god who has betrayed him — wilful, fickle and unjust like the Greek divinities, like Sophocles' 'savage god who burns me'.[14] 'I who was given leadership, and not just mundane political leadership, but that of bringing the moral law to my people, and leading them to the Promised Land, I have been deceived.' Then, as the anger quickly cools, he withdraws bitterly into himself, tired and old.

The synthesis follows. In the hopelessness of Moses' despair — powerless and defeated — energy drains out of him, as symbolised by the cascading beard. Once the rage exhausts itself, the rays of light that illuminated his sacred head turn into horns. His God has cuckolded him, swindling him of his *pneuma* and reducing him to his sexual, animal self. The beard of his wisdom is also metamorphosed, into the chaos of one ultimate truth: life is absurd and horrible.

Once vocation fails, then any individual is at risk of being submerged in his or her own character, sunk in psychopathology. Then the temptation is to seek analysis of self and its discontents, in order to relieve the pain, but this is yet another pursuit of the wrong knowledge. Even Michelangelo succumbed momentarily. Indeed, successful vocation — alone, silent, head bowed over the work — may itself prove to be the one meditative means of disentangling the threads of a difficult personal life.[15]

In old age, Michelangelo the magnificent, whose own Herculean achievements stand as the artistic counterpart to Moses' deeds, would write: 'Oh, wretched man that I am! Who shall deliver me from the body of this death?'[16] He had used his own *Moses* as his finest redemptive stratagem. Opening with a ruthlessly honest self-portrait, thinly disguised, he proceeds in search of understanding. But he is not a Freudian patient, trying to relieve his guilt through analysis.

Michelangelo's first insight is into his psychological self — driven by fear of women and impotency to inflate his body with protest masculinity and to join the dissolute ranks of Pan. He then confesses, exposing his wound to his God, and in a state of total vulnerability and humiliation, pleads for forgiveness. The hand that exposes the wound also rests on top of the stone tablets of the law — the outlaw wants to restore himself. But he is rejected, left cowering before an unforgiving God, no longer sure that the disowning judgement was capricious. Perhaps, he whimpers, God was right to curse me, his wrath justified, wretch that I am.

Moses' attempted way out follows the same two paths. Psychologically, he identifies himself with the aggressor, with the power, and turns himself into a woman.[17] This is a dead end, as his current state reveals. The other way is the religious one, to work towards some restored relationship in sacred order. The active Catholic path, of confessing to his God and begging for mercy, is futile — he has just tried that and failed. What remains is to come to terms with his own nature, which disgusts him, and resign himself to his fate — however outrageously unjust it has proved. And there are signs that at this, the moment of his failure, his wasted life flashing before him, he is gaining a quiet, inaccessible dignity. Nothing more can be done to him, for there is nothing left to take. Yet he has not been crushed. Moses begins to grow into his physical size.

This statue serves as a further indicator that the West has reached its critical metaphysical turning point, the one at which the just and merciful Christian God is in the process of being banished from the Dreaming. Michelangelo finds himself driven back into the territory of the classical Greek vision.

There is also tragic vocation. Captain Vere is in charge of a British warship, the *Bellipotent*, during the Napoleonic Wars.[18] A new arrival on board ship is immediately loved by the rest of the crew, who soon want to do his washing, mend his clothes, make him a chest of drawers. Billy Budd is twenty-one, golden-haired, beautifully handsome and strong. He is guileless, a character whose simple goodness is without taint — 'Adam before the Fall'. Billy has no perception or comprehension of evil. He walks with a charisma that is pure *charis* — grace — lightening the spirits of others. A mark of his not-quite-human, angel nature is a speech defect. He sometimes stutters. Yet Baby Budd, as he is nicknamed, sings like a nightingale.

Not all love him. The master-at-arms, one John Claggart, eaten up by monomaniacal envy of the 'handsome sailor', schemes to destroy him. He reports to Captain Vere that Billy is plotting mutiny. Vere instinctively mistrusts Claggart, repelled by his presence, and recognises Billy's virtue. He gets Claggart to repeat his accusation to Billy's face. Billy, so shocked that his words choke, in reflex punches Claggart in the middle of the forehead. The master-at-arms drops dead.

The captain's first words, muttered in reflection, are 'fated boy', followed by 'Struck dead by the angel of God! Yet the angel must hang!' He calls a drumhead court of three other officers. As the sole witness, he recounts the sequence of events. Billy defends himself, protesting that he has always been a loyal subject of the king, and held no malice against the master-at-arms. It was only because he could not speak that he struck out, not intending to kill the man who 'foully lied to my face and in presence of my captain'. Vere has already interjected, paternally: 'I believe you, my man.'

Some members of the court are inclined to lock Billy up for a few days and leave the case to the admiral of the fleet. Vere argues that Billy must hang, and now. Sailors take their oath to the king, and as such they are ruled by the Mutiny Act. According to that Act, a sailor who kills an officer superior in rank, whatever the motive, is guilty of murder. The death sentence is mandatory.

Vere adds a practical argument. They are at war and, at any moment, may find themselves under fire. Their country is threatened. Recently, there has been a serious mutiny in the British Navy, followed by a general unease through all ships. Revolution is in the air. Sailors are a simple and superstitious breed, tightly wedded to ship forms and rituals. They know what has happened and they know the king's laws — if Billy is not hung, they will take it as a sign of weakness in the captain. The danger of mutiny is too high to take this risk.

He sums up his case: 'with mankind forms, measured forms, are everything.' The court defers to its captain. Billy is hung at dawn, with all due ceremony, the entire crew watching on. He speaks his last words in a clear, unimpeded melody: 'God bless Captain Vere!' Not long after, the *Bellipotent* enters an engagement with a French warship, the *Athée* (the *Atheist*), and the captain is wounded. He dies on shore, murmuring the parting words: 'Billy Budd. Billy Budd.'

This story captures the essence of politics, the nature of that public duty and its responsibilities which are vital to the wellbeing of every human community. Machiavelli put the same case uncompromisingly, that any man who is not willing to sacrifice his soul for the good of the State should not enter politics. In public life, there will always come a day when a decision has to be made involving the sacrifice of some for the greater good. In peace, this may mean economic decisions that undermine some industries, destroying the livelihoods of whole regions. In war, it may mean sacrificing one regiment — the lives of many of its young men — in the interest of the overall battle strategy. Such is the crux of the cold and pitiless business that is politics. As Shakespeare's King Henry IV laments: 'Uneasy lies the head that wears a crown.' To be worthy of high office, the mere mortal who wears the crown has to be willing to bear in full conscience the consequences of his or her acts.

Vere is the perfect, Platonic form of captain — that is, of political leader. He embodies all the necessary talents and virtues. He is considered, selfless and courageous. He has reflected wisely on human nature and is endowed with a large measure of both rational and intuitive insight into individual character. He rises to the challenges of mastering his ship in time of war. He has a high level of practical intelligence and can stand back to take in the larger picture. He loves his ship, his crew, his job — and Billy — all in the warm yet detached avuncular mode of vocation at its finest. He is not a narrow man, circumscribed by nautical matters. He knows that he condemns an innocent being, and for that, he will be judged before some higher court. In spite of the full gravity of his understanding, he can still act. As he might put it, given the circumstances, if I am not willing to sacrifice my own peace of mind to the needs of my office, I am not fit to be captain. I should resign my commission, and join a religious movement or withdraw to cultivate my own garden.[19] As captain, my oath is to the king, not to God.

Billy instinctively understands, and that Vere has made the only possible decision. He sleeps soundly before his execution, calm in the knowledge that his captain trusts him. Indeed, Billy, who regards the king's laws as highly as does Vere, would be horrified if he were let off — he, too, loves and respects right order. Hence 'God bless Captain Vere', Billy's recognition that only he has the power to forgive the doomed master. The story leaves open the captain's condition at death. That he is killed by 'unbelief' is not a good sign. His first, unconscious words after the master-at-arms' death should have been, rather: 'Fated man!'

Captain Vere, named 'truth', is a *midrash* of elements of Achilles, Matthew and Moses. He, too, is a warrior, but fits vocation better than the hero archetype. He, too, is visited by an angel, but while clear about his calling, finds that its demands turn horrible. He, too, both leads his people and is himself doomed but not a failure. His story is that of a man acting with the impeccable correctness of an Achilles, a good man moving in harmony with his destiny, yet a man who in doing what he has to do, and doing it with courage and honour, ruins his life. According to the Western view, the high path of politics is both necessary and tragic. When vocation is involved, this may deepen into a Dreaming truth.

Captain Vere is left with the Deluge, murmuring 'Billy Budd. Billy Budd', hands aloft in prayer, as the sheets of grey close in. That he has been the best of captains is of little comfort now. His last hope is that the silver javelin will flash its welcoming sign.

Failure, and fear of failure, preside over so much of the modern West, and predominantly in relation to vocation. If many find meaning through what they do, the reverse side is anxiety that what I do does not matter. It is arbitrary, a speck of passing indifference in the cosmos. Or, I do not do anything very much. Or, unlike the waitress, I refuse to take my job seriously, lest I fail. Here, the shadowing presence out of the Dreaming is that of Michelangelo's Moses, huge and darkly intimidating.

We have already indirectly met the failed mother. For some reason, the god of her vocation has abandoned her, just as did that of Moses. She does not have it in her to love the whole person — child, teenager, adult. She has not been able to take them as they are, respecting their own *I am*. Full and unconditional love is not hers, such is her curse. Only then would she be up to taking the dead body in her arms — to cradle and care for it. Her own self has intruded. She is lost in herself and in the self-pity that follows. She fails for want of vocation.

There is the middle-aged lawyer who daydreams of early retirement. His work has become routine to him, disenchanting. It crushes his spirit, or so he believes. He belongs to a large company who imagine that, on retirement, they will be freed to live — playing golf, fishing, touring, taking it easy. They all could learn from the waitress, who teaches that it is the spirit that leads, the task that follows. That was Christ's lesson to Simon the Pharisee: Magdalene is recognised because her love came first.

There are those who pretend, principally to themselves. The priest may belong here, the one who clings to the ritual or loses himself in social work to conceal his loss of belief. So may those teachers who project their own lack of inspiration onto their students, blaming them for the dullness of the classroom. The banking executive is not different, who hides himself behind the imperative to increase profit when he sacks half his staff — protesting that his hands are tied, that he is not responsible. How weak *he* looks next to Captain Vere!

There is the editor of health-care literature, lowered by her work. She puts it:

> *I think most of us are looking for a calling, not a job ... Jobs are not big enough for people. It's not just the assembly line worker whose job is too small for his spirit, you know? A job like mine, if you really put your spirit into it, you would sabotage immediately. You don't dare. So you absent your spirit from it ... It's so demeaning to be there and not be challenged. It makes you not at home with yourself ... It's possible for me to sit here and read my books. But then you walk out with no sense of satisfaction, with no sense of legitimacy.*

In the same study of Americans at work, a receptionist laments: 'A monkey could do what I do.'[20]

The editor is close to giving up. Dreaming just remains present in her, driving her to resist, and keep alive the flame of her dignity as someone who is more than ordinary human. She would give everything to be Captain Vere. Yet she is turning into the doomed Moses, on the brink of *pneumaphobia*.

The outpouring from failed vocation releases the *pneumaphobic* repertoire — bitterness, complaint, pessimism, enclosure in self-pity, and a blanketing low cloud of rancour. It also imposes its particular colouring. It seizes with riveted fascination on those who have found their vocation — the star athlete, the prime minister, the great actress — above all, those in the subject's own line of work who take it with waitress seriousness. Rancour sits on the edge of its seat in anticipation of disappointment and downfall. Its pleasure is in destruction, wallowing in the oblivion and nothingness in which it discovers a perverse self-vindication.

The active life exemplified by vocation is a liferaft floating atop the slick of passivity and detachment coursing through the modern West. The vast pseudo-culture of consumerism encourages the buying, the eating, the gorging on television, the overdosing, the drinking, to coat the essential *I am* in a restless, distracting, soothing variety of brand-spanking newness. Or it promises to fill the dead inside, the void in the stomach, with sweet-tasting chocolate. Not what I do but what I eat! And so to dream of winning the lottery, metamorphosed into a multi-millionaire, for then I shall truly be freed from my lacklustre, low-spirited, ordinary self, to become somebody. The rich have power and style, ease and luxury. What I, who am not, might be!

It goes without saying that the lottery is the wrong magic. It contrasts with the true fortune, beyond all reason, of young Arthur when he came upon the sword Excalibur. He found it fixed in a stone from which the strongest and noblest warriors in the land could not budge it. Arthur merely had to grip the haft for the sword to slip free and become a part of him, indicating his call, that he would become king, to found and lead the Knights of the Round Table. Vocation opens with a miraculous happening upon the sacred instrument for the carrying out of its particular tasks.

The shadow of Michelangelo's *Moses* is long precisely because vocation is so unsure and obscure. Its failures just as much as its successes elude precise charting. Even Matthew, whose call is clear and direct, will lose his way, his call appearing wasted, until years later, when he sits down beside a river to write the story and is visited by an angel. Furthermore, in the eyes of others, some may appear like a Michelangelo, uniquely successful, what they have accomplished a celebration of the best that is human. Yet to themselves, they are an embarrassment, their every move plagued by hesitation and doubt.

There is the architect. The precariousness of vocation, and the momentousness of the consequences of either success or failure, are clear in this calling. Its story is rehearsed whenever we create fixed spaces in which to dwell. Any vocation requires form. To be in form means to realise *the form*, to draw on Plato's timeless notion. Every species of thing has its ideal form. The human world is cluttered with buildings that are amiss, designed by out-of-form architects, ones who do not see. They look wrong, the shapes and planes somehow failing to fit; the materials and colours do not harmonise — they are at odds with the terrain, its slopes, its trees, the light, their neighbouring buildings. They clash, these crooked forms. They are restless and disturbed — deformed — and, as such, contagious.

Architects who fail condemn those who inhabit their buildings to a state of perpetual distress. It is worse in that the victims will most likely not know their deprivation, its source or its effects. In out-of-form conditions, we are usually not aware of the fact, at most registering an extra sluggishness, a slightly out-of-sorts indifference to things, a blurred and clogged mode of being — dis-eased.

A bad room teaches the consequences of lack of form, the supreme concrete symptom of failed vocation. Those who enter experience vague irritant qualms that make them pace around, or sit rigidly, fidgeting, squirming, shifting from a straight upright posture to a sprawl in order to settle the ache in the joints, the tension in the muscles, that just materialises from nowhere. Try as they might, they cannot slip into that easy state of feeling at home that comes in a space amongst objects where things, including oneself, are 'in their place'. A bad room chases out. It is not a place anyone wants to be. Just so are all out-of-form states — cast out from *being*, a condition of homelessness, of nowhere to dwell.

The architect who succeeds — given the site, the materials and the requested functions — in designing the perfect building enters the Matthew condition. There is only one perfect building for each particular situation, where the form is right, where they who dwell feel at one with its presence. The *own-ers* must themselves find form, in order to belong, to make it their *own*, but that is another story. This architect has for once been able to obey absolute law, to build in harmony with its rules. Obligation has been fulfilled, by doing the job justice. However, as all true architects know, it was not they, as great creative genius or whatever self-aggrandisement the world encourages them to use. The inspiration came from beyond. They were the tool. They held Excalibur, and like the samurai warrior in form, for an instant, became their sword. This was their grace note.

The better the architects, the clearer their recognition of how many buildings they have bungled. To experience, at least once, what it is like to be in form is to know how out of form they usually are. The satisfaction from this building is rare and pure. It is not, however, in the logic of the completion of the task to congratulate oneself. What follows is, rather, the dusk exhaustion of the Homeric hero, and gratitude for having been allowed, for a moment, to be an instrument of justice. Work done rightly has a chance of becoming sacred, itself the prayer that brings the blessing, head bowed in recognition of the higher order that it is everyone's life mission to obey. Thus speaks the Western Dreaming. As Matthew was to discover, vocation is an honour, as if bestowed by a divinity. It is a lesson in humility.

Architecture has a further teaching. In the West, it has been founded upon the five classical orders, beginning with the Greeks, developed by the Romans, and passed on by example and through the writings of Vitruvius. The Gothic style radically reworked the theory, then the Renaissance re-established a *midrash* of the original. An underlying vertical principle is stipulated, orchestrated through a range of rectangular planes to generate spatial harmony.[21] The creations of this tradition represent enduring human projections of the essence of any culture, that it establish the vertical over the horizontal — life against death.[22] They are physical manifestations, within which humans dwell, of the structure of things, securing in their solidity, reassuring in their timeless proportions. Through admiring a great classical building, we are reminded that all is right with the world.

That great classical building stands as an image of vocation. Its Dreaming form shadows the hunched-over Matthew, as he begs, 'Please not me!' — then looks up at the hand that has singled him out. He calms down, and finally is able to rise and begin work. It is there, too, framing Captain Vere as he paces the deck of the *Bellipotent*, deep in thought, steering the ship of his fate. The countermovement is Michelangelo's Moses, for whom the form departs, leaving his own huge frame to sag, slumping downwards.

This is a story about being at home on the earth. To abide requires an abode — where one fits.[23] Vocation is right dwelling, a way of possessing the here and now as a place in which I abide. It has taken over in a modern West in which other homelands, the more traditional ones, have been left to run down, or abandoned — tribe, community, town and suburb, church, and even family. Ever present, in the near vicinity of *I am*, it is that trustworthy intimate who is also portable, like a favourite light coat. Snug in that homely coat, the *I am* may speak through the act of doing the work, speak the grace note. Vocation informs being.

7.

Fate

The modern understanding is that vocation is a calling to a type of work. It concerns the particular life activity to which each and every person is fitted. Calvin and the Second Reformation established this usage. Yet the grey eminence directing the Calvinist spirit was that of Oedipus. In his story, the call is somewhat different. It is to fate.

Oedipus the King (c.430BC), told by Sophocles, is high poetry in the genre of tragic drama.[1] Oedipus grows up in Corinth, son of the king and queen. He hears an oracle telling that he will kill his father and marry his mother, so he immediately leaves home. On the very journey on which he thinks he is eluding his destiny, he meets his real father, Laius, at a crossroads in the Phocian plains under Mount Parnassus, on the side of which, high above, overlooking the Gulf of Corinth, sits Delphi, from where Apollo's oracle has spoken. Laius, with five henchmen, tries to force the young man, who is alone on foot, off the road. Oedipus strikes one of them, then his father hits him over the head from his passing chariot with a heavy stick. Oedipus loses his temper and kills all but one of the strangers.

Continuing on his journey, he arrives in Thebes, not far away, where he saves the town from an ancient curse by solving a riddle posed by the Sphinx, 'hook-taloned maid, cruel singer' — part woman, part lioness, part bird of prey. He is rewarded with the kingship, and marries the widowed queen, his own real mother, Jocasta, with whom he sires four children. Years later, a terrible pestilence strikes Thebes, blighting plants, cattle and women — a black death over the land. The king, troubled by his responsibility, seeks advice from the Delphic Oracle. He is told the plague is due to unavenged blood guilt for his murdered predecessor.

Oedipus dedicates himself to finding the killer, and Sophocles' story, opening with pestilence, takes the form of the king's slow discovery, clue by clue and with mounting horror, that the criminal is he himself. When the full truth is revealed, Jocasta hangs herself, and Oedipus stabs his own eyes out with his wife/mother's gold brooches. He then banishes himself to the slopes of Mount Cithaeron, where he had been abandoned as a baby to die — by parents who were responding to the same prophecy. Immediate death would be too good for him, given the unspeakable acts of which he is culpable.

In the twentieth century, Oedipus once again became a principal imaginary companion to the West, due in significant part to Freud, who held this legend to be archetypal of family drama. It brings to the surface the compelling attractions and murderous hatreds that inevitably and always exist between parents and their children. Those drives are normally repressed, re-emerging in disguise in dreams and in art, and in adult psychopathology. Freud takes his cue from Jocasta:

Before this, in dreams too, as well as oracles,
many a man has lain with his own mother.[2]

The explanation, then, for the timeless interest in this story is its universality, revealing the secret drama at the centre of every life. Oedipus is psychological everyman.

Freud's reading is partial, and diminishes the play. *Oedipus the King* is, first and foremost, the archetype of Greek tragedy. Aristotle based his whole poetic theory on it, arguing that tragedy works by arousing the emotions of pity and fear in the audience. It then provides them with catharsis. The pity is at the hero's unmerited suffering, the fear out of identification with him and his plight. The feeling that is left over after the emotional catharsis is that of tragic wonder.[3]

The most persuasive modern theory of tragedy, that of Nietzsche, is also based on Oedipus. It extends Aristotle by arguing that tragedy arouses in the audience a strange exhilaration, feelings of 'primordial joy' and 'metaphysical solace'.[4] This comes from identifying with the hero, feeling with increasing anxiety and horror his impending doom — which takes the final form of the annihilation of his normal human self. Out of crushing suffering, and the end of any hope of worldly happiness, he is freed from the bonds of individualised ego to join the cosmic Oneness of existence — Oedipus old and blind, alone in the foothills. Greek tragedy, for Nietzsche, is culture at its truest and most powerful. Its quintessence is *Oedipus the King*.

The uncanny paradoxical force of tragedy, however, and spectacularly that of Oedipus, derives from elsewhere. It is predicated on a simple and absolute vision of an order within which all human events are set. In that order, fate rules.[5] Forces from beyond decide things — a grand, implacable, predestining order, its ways incomprehensible to mortals and within which there is negligible human freedom. Homer had already painted the scene, this aspect of the story of his Achilles, however, finding its full realisation only later, in Oedipus. Sophocles differentiates two types of supernatural force, the *moirai* — or the Fates — who weave the thread determining the path of individual destiny, and the *keres* — or the Dooms — who make sure that it is fulfilled.[6]

Oedipus is repeatedly referred to by the citizens of Thebes as the greatest of men, singular above all others in knowledge — only he could solve the riddle of the Sphinx, a riddle, by the way, about human identity, and one probably set by Apollo himself.[7] Oedipus is well born, intelligent, confident, responsible, loves his daughters, and is willing to take on anything — he is, in short, an admirable and courageous man, apart from one character flaw: his short temper. He does everything possible to evade his fate, believing that we humans have free will, that we, at our best, are in charge of our own destinies — this oracle stuff, his rational self tells him, is mere superstition, for those who are a bit backward. I shall teach the hysterical virgin priestesses of Delphi who is boss.

The story singles out Oedipus' assurance in order to mock it — disdainfully, categorically. On his very journey of self-determination, he meets his real father and unwittingly sets off the doomed chain of events. He walks, blindly, straight into the arms of his fate, a human lamb to sacred slaughter. The murder is done at the foot of the mountain housing Apollo's oracle, at a meeting of three roads, one of them directly from Delphi, the second indirectly, and the third leading to Thebes. What choice is there here? In effect, the story commands: Look up, proud mortal, and remember you have just come from the sacred site. Didn't you take in the motto carved over the entrance to my Temple: 'Know thyself!' Look up, foolish mortal, and know thy place![8]

When fate rules, justice and morality both slink away into the wings. Oedipus does not deserve his misfortune, his character flaw tiny next to his punishment. Nor is he culpable in a modern legal sense. He did not have a 'guilty mind',[9] for he acted unwittingly — if he had known that it was his father at the crossroads, he would have restrained himself; and that his mother was Queen of Thebes, he would have been paralysed by the very thought of sleeping with her. Yet he feels as wretched as if he had acted in full knowledge; and the audience, identifying with him, knows his despair. It knows that it would be wrong, even shameful, for anyone to walk in the shoes of Oedipus and then protest innocence on the grounds of ignorance. So much for moral equations and legal reasoning! The audience finds itself unconsciously affirming the Calvinist paradox, that we are not free in what we do, yet are responsible.[10] Indeed, the Oedipal equation holds that the less free, the more responsible!

Yet indiscriminate fatedness is not what moves here. Predestination is set squarely within a given and timeless higher order framing the human condition. One dimension of that order is a collection of absolute laws, which include, as this story teaches, 'Thou shalt not murder your father!' and 'Thou shalt not marry your mother and sire four children with her!' Oedipus has unwittingly violated sacred order, and he must suffer appropriate retribution, if balance is to be restored — for things to return to their rightful place. This play is at odds with any modern relativism, any view that serious moral laws are human creations and, thus, arbitrary, belonging merely to one time and one society. To come under the thrall of *Oedipus the King* is to be reminded that Law is absolute. Every individual breaks it at his or her peril.

Further, Oedipus mocks the modern creed that knowledge is good, that its pursuit will make its pilgrims better and happier people. He was the smartest of men, with insight into mysteries, his surface self a Humanist hero, yet about the one thing that mattered — the nature of his own *I am* — he had no idea. Finding himself inwardly compelled to pursue his truth, the nature of being, his own being, he discovered his identity — that it is an abomination, a crime against nature. Maniacally stabbing his eyes to pulpy gore was to scream out that his knowledge had been based on false seeing, and not only had it done him no good, it had proved a handicap, distracting him from true vision.

Oedipus' daughter, Antigone, suffers a fate even worse than that of her father. Kierkegaard, her deepest interpreter, speculated in his *midrash* that Antigone's curse is that she is the only one to know the truth about her parents, a secret that ruins any possibility of her relating to the living.[11] Her written tragedy, *Antigone*, again composed by Sophocles, turns aside from the full horror of who she is. It concentrates on the more manageable duty of her breaking the social law — committing treason — in order to bury the body of her dead brother. The story makes it clear that she is driven to appease the nether-gods, those that rule the underworld, deliberately bringing on herself the climax of being buried alive. She who was born the daughter/sister of Oedipus is the last of the line courageous enough to bring the story to a fitting close, with due rites of honour. She thus lives so as to fulfil her fate, which is, equally, her family's fate.

Oedipus himself is life as vocation. His story is commanded by a simple and single axiom: each individual is called to his or her fate. Try to elude it and see what happens! The Stoic philosopher Epictetus would rephrase it: Let your will be that things happen as they do!

This axiom is scripted into the archetypal stories of the West, holding for all the principal figures. Magdalene and the mother play Oedipus, as do Danae and Matthew, all four in their different ways called to their fate. So, too, was Achilles. Poussin was chosen by his mysterious companion. Captain Vere's revelation about himself is: 'Fated man!' The Western Dreaming is faithfully, fatefully shadowed.[12]

The Oedipus legend is thus pitched diametrically against the Humanist beliefs that the modern West thinks it holds true: all individuals are free to make themselves and choose their ways, responsible for their conscious actions, aided by reason and knowledge. A deep unease about any notion of fate has pervaded this consciousness.

Freedom is the ethic of our civilisation — both sustenance and guide. Or so we have come to believe. If there is a new faith, this is it. Our common sense tells us that we have freedom of choice — we choose our careers, our husbands and wives, our motor cars and what we eat for breakfast. As robust sceptics, we rely more on our practical wisdom in evaluating the truth than on more abstract authorities, and rightly so. In short, free will comes with the best modern credentials.

Once we pause, however, to differentiate our experiences across a spectrum, with the passing and trivial at one extreme and the important at the other, then we find that the closer to the trivial we move, the more plausible our freedom. That we choose when we drink our morning coffee is not worth contesting. By contrast, we have no influence over what will no doubt prove the most important material moment in our lives, that of conception, the instant at which the genetic roulette wheel stops, determining some of our character and our physical disposition. We do not choose our parents, or the times and fortunes into which we are born. We have little choice over the other people who will become significant to us in our lives, or how and why paths cross, stay together or diverge. The serious diseases we may suffer, the time and manner of our death, and other profound crises are usually completely beyond our foresight and control. Those who 'chose' to go to war in 1914 would typically refer to their own end with a stark fatalism: 'if your number is on the bullet'... Primo Levi, a non-religious sceptic if ever there was one, wrote of who survived Auschwitz and who did not: we were 'totally helpless in the hands of fate'.[13]

If freedom is the modern value, then Oedipus is its most deadly enemy. Yet the modern world has worshipped at the feet of Oedipus. How can that be?

Oedipus is the modern world's secret self. We are all Oedipus — but not because of dread of incest. On the surface, we imagine ourselves positive and intelligent, loudly proclaiming our freedom of will. Underneath, our life's path is obscure, and we suspect that our belief in ourselves as free is a conceit, that our significant encounters and doings are somehow scripted. What is more, the script may be the key to the meaning of it all — that it has meaning. Our further Oedipal paradox is that we do not rest easily in powerlessness. At some level — how much we do not know — we are responsible.

Outrageous misfortune was Oedipus' teacher. It obliterated the mix of ego, will and spirit that the West has valued as identity. The truth that this man learnt was to bow down in awe before the higher and hidden order that frames each individual destiny.

The ancient Greeks sometimes doubted the existence of the gods, but never that of *Anagke* — *Necessity*. Parmenides held that Being is trapped in the net of *Necessity*. Even the powerful sun god, Apollo, would admit that he could merely influence the surplus left over by *Anagke*, and it is petty. *Necessity* makes sure that everyone plays their given part, so there is no deviation or excess. But all of Greek life was an excess, over its determining element, death.

Before Plato arrived to stress the *good*, *Necessity* had ruled, with some assistance from the vain and capricious gods, and some from her underworld kin, the dark Furies, spirits of vengeance and retribution. Humans did not need to concern themselves much about morality, as long as they revered the upper divinities and kept some check on their passions — their lust and sadism, their infatuation and hatred, their jealousy and despair. This, of course, was impossible, given their intemperate natures and the frequency with which the spirits of *Anagke* clouded their minds.

So the Greeks gave pride of powerful place to *Necessity*. Fate, or destiny, was also there, sometimes linked, sometimes subordinate, sometimes independent. There was good and bad fortune, and other agents, too, such as the force or demon given to a person at birth to guide destiny. These conceptions were imprecise and mobile, with *daimon*, for instance, depending on time and context, meaning any of demon, god — the *daimonia* were a lower race of divinities — fate, and even the human soul. All in all, the Greek religious view subjected the human condition to an awful vulnerability, one that we might expect would crush the spirit and induce a prevailing mood of self-pity and complaint against the obscure higher powers. Rather, the works surviving from ancient Greece suggest an intoxication with life, a gratitude in spite of all.

It has been protested that the ancient Greeks were emotionally and morally primitive compared with us. Indeed, some scholars argue that in Homer and Sophocles, there is a crude picture of motivation, little character development and no sense of inwardness. We have progressed far beyond this, the argument might continue, in the ethics of Kant, the psychology of Freud, the literary sensibility of Henry James. The countercase is that Homer's 'archaic' portrayal of human action includes the basic notions of intention, will and responsibility, and is not in its fundamentals different from our own rather fuzzy understandings.[14]

Aeschylus' *Agamemnon*, the first play in the Oresteian Trilogy, from 458BC, is seventeen hundred lines of searing lyric incantation questing Truth. It works with few events, opening with fire, the chain of beacons across most of the known world bringing the sign to the Greek citadel at Mycenae that Troy had fallen. This is to be advance warning to the proud, aristocratic queen Clytemnestra that the worst had happened — her husband, Agamemnon, had proved victorious after ten years and would soon be home. The play is half over when the king does finally arrive. He is accompanied by his slave concubine, Cassandra, King Priam of Troy's beautiful daughter, who had been punished for betraying the god Apollo in his advances to her by being given the gift of foreseeing the future accompanied by the curse that no-one would believe her. Agamemnon succumbs readily to his wife's flattery, and steps down from his chariot onto fine purple fabric that has been laid out for him. Once inside the citadel, he is murdered in his bath by Clytemnestra, assisted by her lover, Aegisthus.

This is not tragedy in the sense of a noble character or characters being trapped by terrible choices. Neither of the principal figures is admirable. Of the secondary ones, Aegisthus is low, Cassandra to be pitied rather than identified with. If the audience stands in anyone's shoes, it is those of the Chorus of town elders, who observe and comment and through whom Aeschylus pitches his questions. They have no individuality. In fact, the main band driving through the work, the one on which the audience seizes, in rapt identification, is the hymn of metaphysical query itself, both exhilarating and foreboding, as it wrestles to make sense of human destiny.

Aeschylus tries different explanations. There is Zeus, king of the gods, as first cause — of the Trojan War itself, predetermining its result, acting in his role as guest-god, incensed at Paris having betrayed his obligations as a guest in the house of Menelaos, seducing his host's wife, Helen, then fleeing with her. There are many references to Zeus, who even:

drives late to its mark the Fury upon the transgressors.[15]

However, the various postulations of Zeus are speculative and unsure. The Chorus exclaims: 'Zeus: whatever he may be.'

Artemis, the chaste goddess of earth and its creatures, and of the hunt — Diana in her later, Roman persona — also plays a role. She becalms the Greek ships on the way to Troy, at Aulis, and her oracle decrees that the winds will not blow unless the leader, Agamemnon, sacrifices his innocent and beloved daughter, Iphigenia.

There is Justice, too, sometimes acting as an agent of Zeus, at other times seemingly independent. Crime brings retribution:

And Righteousness is a shining in the smoke of mean houses. Her blessing is on the just man.[16]

Disaster inevitably follows from pride or excess, what Aeschylus calls 'sinful Daring'. Impiety, too, brings justice, as Agamemnon himself knows when he still chooses to walk on the precious purple:

Discordant is the murmur at such treading down of lovely things.[17]

Then there are the Furies, spirits of the vengeful dead, or something like that, black forces from the underworld working their own form of justice. And death is all around. Of major significance, and linked with the Furies, is the bloodguilt on the House of Atreus. Atreus, Agamemnon's father, served his brother pieces of two of his own children in a pie for dinner. Aegisthus was the third, surviving child. Thus, one cause of the events here may be the sins of the fathers vested upon the sons, setting off another cycle of retribution.

There is some allowance for human agency. Excess and impiety are the two great sins. Humans get carried away, so they are punished. Agamemnon is proud. Clytemnestra exceeds all justified revenge for the death of her daughter and for the ten-year absence of her husband fighting to retrieve her fickle sister,

Helen. She is jealous of Cassandra. None of this justifies murder. Indeed, it is hard to fathom Justice, and the many references to her through the play sound more like an anxiety at her absence or, at least, her fitful presence, the instability of her scales. Doubt pervades. The Chorus is so insecure about transgression that it proves unable to welcome its victorious king back after a decade of battle with any spontaneous warmth, worrying, rather, about what is appropriate behaviour.

Aeschylus is shocked by the incomprehensible balance sheet — a ten-year war, the flower of Greek manhood dead, Troy and all its civilisation extinguished, the sacrifice of Iphigenia, all ships but one lost on the voyage home, a fearful foreboding of what might happen next — and all for 'some strange woman'. In particular, the murder of Agamemnon does not weigh up, out of all proportion to his trampling of the carpet, even taking that sacrilege as a metaphor for his barbaric sacking of Troy and its temples.

Aeschylus is unsure of the strength of any explanation: 'I have pondered everything yet I cannot find a way.' He weaves his imagined causes together loosely. Justice is postulated more in hope than with confidence. The role of Zeus is unclear. Humans act, but given the puniness of their figures in the grander scheme of things — not that we see that scheme with any clarity — they are hardly blamed. Aeschylus does not moralise. The Furies, too, are there, but often no more than as some dark force needed to explain why a course of events seems to conspire so malevolently against those subject to it. They do make sure that nobody escapes:

The black Furies stalking the man fortunate beyond all right wrench back again the set of his life and drop him to darkness.[18]

Then there is *Necessity*. She has her petty modes in everyday life, in the brute struggle for survival that has weighed down most of human life in most human societies. There is the need to gain food, clothing and shelter, the relentless tedium of labour, the inescapable biological cycle of birth, growth, disease and death, and the recurring threat of war. All conspire to turn the human condition into that of a slave, an animal chained by existence.

Aeschylus is not concerned with this basic order of *Necessity*. He focusses on her metaphysical, Dreaming powers. The *Agamemnon* is crosshatched with the image of her yoke being put around the neck. All humans suffer from this harness, as does the city of Troy, Cassandra being different merely in that she sees the slave's yoke around her own neck. Another image is the binding net woven by the Fates. It covers Troy, and is used by Clytemnestra in the guise of the folds of a cloak, to trap Agamemnon in his bath, so she can stab him.

Scholars have much discussed the case of Agamemnon, as recounted by the Chorus, when he found himself at Aulis having to choose between two evils: sacrificing his beautiful and innocent daughter or ruining his army and its cause, the pride of Greece and his own warrior-king honour. Either choice presages disaster. Aeschylus frames the resolution in one line, having Agamemnon 'put on the yoke of *Necessity*'.

How freely does Agamemnon act? In fact, he has no choice, and realises it.[19] Yet he is not passive in relation to *Necessity*. It is he who places the yoke around his own neck — the precise Greek reference is to the strap that attaches the yoke to the body.[20] One modern reading likens the act to that of putting on armour.[21] Battle is imminent, so the soldier automatically arms himself, although here, it is strapping on the bronze plates of inevitable doom. The sliver of free choice that might be claimed for Agamemnon is over the timing, whether today or tomorrow — a minor discrimination, given the grandeur of the Aeschylean landscape.

Aeschylus seems to be saying that humans confronted by *Necessity*, and aware of the fact, may, as it were, go forwards to meet their destiny, accepting it with eyes open — not resisting, weeping, complaining. There is dignity here. Accounts of those who face murder, execution or some other great personal tragedy disclose widespread interest in how the victims take it, with universal admiration for the courage of those who do so calmly, not losing their poise. They are putting on the yoke. The expressions 'to take it like a man' and 'to take it on the chin' draw upon the same judgement. It is the slave who is completely passive under the onslaught of *Necessity*, but not because of the absence of freedom.

The word 'freedom' is quite inadequate. Cassandra has no meaningful freedom, being captive booty, yet as she walks into the palace to meet her death, she can decisively assert: 'I will take my fate.' Human dignity is here identified with presence of soul — not mind — aloof from the slings and arrows of a brute destiny, accepting of them as a part of life, accepting them with courage. It involves a type of valour. Cassandra is a hero.

The Stoic view, and in many cultures, holds that the good life depends on living in harmony with fate — being willing, in the terms of Aeschylus, to harness oneself to it. There is some sort of tacit compact that while the binding knot of *Necessity* is inviolable, we humans may accept it willingly, with a 'So be it!' By that acceptance, we establish a gravity of being, a thereness, that we are more than some infinitesimal speck of matter tossed in the gale of eternity. It is out of this harsh contradiction at the heart of the Greek view of things — nothing cosy, nothing logical, nothing sublime — that arose the extraordinary buoyancy of spirit that breathes through their creations. It launched the Western Dreaming.

The tragic song of the *Agamemnon* does not reach its highest pitch in the Chorus, but with two figures, very different from each other: Cassandra and the Watchman. Cassandra screams out her prophecies, foreseeing her own imminent murder. She is the one who knows. She fathoms the deepest truths, but what are they? She sees a 'drunken rout of ingrown vengeful spirits' swarming around the humans. She sees her own fate, which she likens to 'the sheer edge of the tearing iron'.[22] Better not to know, better to be blind, better to be lost in the all-too-human hopes and confusions of everyday life — such is the message of Cassandra. There is no salvation through knowledge, no happiness, no consoling wisdom. If Oedipus yearns for true knowledge, Cassandra warns against it. Grace comes somehow violent, if it comes.

Cassandra envies the nightingale its fate, its sweet life free from lamentation. We humans are not birds, able to soar. Earthbound anguish is our lot. One dimension of transcendence is possible, in a voice pealing out over the action, wailing the truth about events, in purity of sight struggling to detach itself from the absorbing rough and tumble below, tracing the soul's hurt, the dread. This is the song not of the nightingale but of tragedy. Who would choose voluntarily to enter Cassandra's door? It is necessary.

A more bearable image of how to live is that of the Watchman, who opens the play. And whose life, in its essence, is better than his? His lot is to lie awake, sprawled out like a dog, night after night, on the roof of the palace, through summer heat and winter chill, in eternal vigilance, in fear that he might fall asleep and miss the sign. He pleads respite from the weariness of his watch, redemption from the tedium of his earthly discomfort. When, finally, the light flares, he leaps up with joy, only to relapse into his gloomy thoughts once he begins to reflect on what may happen now. His human tragedy is in the wrestling between sacred hope and bitter reality. His beacon rises out of the darkness of the terror at what humans do, his life in the watchful wait.

How might this ancient Greek view translate for the modern world? There is the feeling that sometimes comes after having made an important decision: that it was somehow right. One may have all sorts of reasons for doubt, and not be able to sleep. The decision's links with the present and with sensible speculations about the future are entirely obscure. Its implications for this work or that intimacy, or for as yet unmet events, are unknown. One is entirely in the dark. Yet, somehow, it fits. An inner voice is saying *Yes*. That voice is aware of a grand design. The sense is of something like one's predetermined fate, and this belonging to it. One has responded to an illuminated turn-off on the night highway, although there was no signpost, one had no map, and there are no welcoming lights ahead. This does not happen often, and it is most likely to occur in difficult times. It separates off moments of inner confidence, in spite of the sleepless nights, from other decisions, in which one has to use one's wits, one's practical sense, and is left having to hope for the best.[23]

The feeling continues in the modern West that we are the helpless victims of grand forces which are indifferent to our well-being, aloof to any appeal or prayer, at times there to grind us down. *Necessity* is out to inflict pain and crush the spirit, and once unleashed, nothing shall sway her from her determined goal. She is remorseless and unforgiving, with cold eyes and a set mouth.

She is there when a certain course of events has been initiated — it may be a love affair, a business venture, a war. It is as if that heedless, casual first step set a time bomb ticking, and events take over, obeying some inner logic, moving from bad to worse whatever willpower, resourcefulness, brilliance of strategic calculation, and perseverance those who are subject to its workings bring to bear. The most capable and virtuous in the world are as stick insects crunched under the wheels of the juggernaut of *Necessity*.

The Greek instinct was to start with *Anagke*, recognise her as the determining reality, with Being trapped in her net, and from there go on to enquire how it might be possible to live. One answer was the Homeric hero, fighting as if a *daimon* breathed through him or a goddess moved by his side. He was able to give himself to the moment, without backward glance or anticipatory anxiety. He knew that what will be will be, and whatever he did could not influence his allotted fate. His message was that *Necessity* liberates while freedom paralyses.

That *Necessity* liberates is provisional. It depends on good fortune, and finding form. In the underworld, the shade of Agamemnon laments that to die in one's bath, murdered by one's wife, is not that. In form, it is easy to put on the yoke, as easy as Matthew visited by an angel found it. Out of form, it takes courage, that described by Aeschylus in the earlier episode in the life of Agamemnon, when he straps himself to it, knowing full well that the consequences will be unbearable, starting with the slaughter by his own hand of his beloved daughter. Captain Vere will prove one of the Greek king's noblest offspring. These men remind us that our fulfilment may depend on how we bear up to what we have to do.

The wilfulness of *Necessity*, that her yoke may not be resisted, is qualified by the existence of the higher, sacred domain within which human affairs are set. There is nothing arbitrary about what Oedipus has done. He has no doubt that the two laws he has broken are absolute, that he is guilty, and deserves the most extreme punishment of which he can conceive. He stabs his own eyes out; he exiles himself. Thus he takes active responsibility for restoring the order he has unwittingly violated. Even he finds a steadiness in knowing that he lives and acts within a set domain, which he has come to understand through breaking some of its laws. Tragedy is fatedness within higher and eternal order.

The wilfulness of *Necessity* is also qualified by the hope, underwritten by the Greeks, that the gods, once engaged, at times show some care for their protégés. To take the leading example, there were classical Athenian interpretations in sculpture of the characteristic gesture of Athena towards those whom she favours. It is led by the right hand, which she raises aloft in nonchalant command, deliberate and precise — as if to announce: I have arrived, and this I decree, this is what will be. The left, loosely by her side, is to allay, the lower arm moving up and forward into the horizontal, palm open towards whomever she is addressing, generous. She offers her indulgence, her help — I am with you, she seems to say, and as long as I remain, just accept that *I am*, so don't fear![24]

If there were no *Necessity*, then there would be no tragedy, no dignity, leaving us humans condemned to the eternal frivolity of the Greek gods, for nothing can be serious to those who do not die. What a demeaning sort of life that would be! It is thus out of not just fascinated dread that we identify with tragic fortitude but also a sense that this is what makes us human. Mortals are left to hope that the three beautiful Fates have etched out a destiny closer to that of Matthew for them, the age-old human hope that *Necessity* be gentle.

The Dreaming stories are by now gathering together to form a collective vision, and starting to mobilise their cumulative force as they move towards their climax. Much of the modern West is little more than an image of Christ etched over the Oedipus blueprint. It is then translated into the four Protestant principles of faith alone, individual conscience, vocation, and no free will — that is, fate.[25] All are Oedipal.

The wind that bloweth has turned into a sacred gale whistling down from Delphi. May it not be that Jesus, on the donkey track passing through Emmaus, travelling west-northwest, was bound one stop further than distant Athens, eventually on the very road that Oedipus had trod, for Apollo's sacred site?

Vocation as fate is Christ etched over the Oedipus blueprint. What this means is that when the waitress places the fork down just right, she is building the Cross. The mainstream current of the Western Dreaming carries her onwards, sweeping her buoyantly along, determining her every gesture, her story now that of Joseph the Carpenter.

The call requires one and all to listen to their conscience, learn what they know. Nevertheless, they may be quite unaware of their vocation, even when they execute it to the full, even when it is fated. They may be doing what is right, under the most afflicting circumstances, and yet, unlike Matthew, Moses or Captain Vere, not have the foggiest idea what they do.

Let us consider the father of Jesus, Joseph the Carpenter. At the decisive moment in his life, he is bent double at his task. It is night. Standing over a beam lying flat on the ground, he drills into it with a gimlet. His five-year-old son is in front of him, holding a candle to illuminate the work. The flame is gigantic. The man's head is down, like the young Matthew's. He stares at the beam with an obsessed and troubled concentration. The hands that turn the boring tool are stiff and tense, themselves shaped as if excrescences of the wooden handle. The old man has no idea what he does. He is no writer of sacred texts, no lawgiver and, certainly, no leader of his people out of captivity. Nor does he know that he is in the act of putting on his yoke.

What is being constructed in the obscure shadows on the ground is a cross. Joseph works, driven by hidden knowledge, at his one true task, to meditate on the terrible destiny that awaits the boy, his son. Nothing else matters. And even now, in early childhood, it is the son who helps his father bear the future path that he cannot know. The boy, with bright innocent face, luminous near the flare, raises his other hand to shield the candle flame from any draught, so his father can make out his work. The man toils, on the brink of despair. If he actually knew what he knows, he would be paralysed. He represents all those humans who are unconsciously driven to make preparation for their own impending, though unforeseen, death — in Joseph's case, it is his son's, not his own.

The gimlet turning in Joseph's hands is itself in the form of a cross. His whole life is here, a complete biography. It is awfully sad. In his love for his son, which is all he is, that love, he pours everything he has into his vocation, as carpenter, to make real and concrete what will be, years later, the finale to the boy's tragic life. So he meditates on the cross. The son helps him — holds his hand, so to speak — and guides him, that poor father. Without the flame, the man would be in the dark, his work impossible. The son is calm and joyful, pleased just to be close. But he worries for his father, that he may falter under the strain. In the intimacy, together, it is as if the boy whispers words of encouragement.

Work is one human tool for the job of the sacred. The call is to such work. Joseph the Carpenter is the human extension of the gimlet that bores a hole in the beam. Just as that beam will be transformed from a dressed fragment of a dead tree into the Cross, from lifeless matter into the most sacred object of the West, so too will the mere carpenter find himself as a man executing the higher mission. Whether it is the actual Cross, on which his son will be crucified thirty years later, is of little account. Joseph's call, like anyone's, is to meditate on his own fate, to live it through with his hands on the wheel, the gimlet, thereby doing what is right. He is not under any delusion that he is the driver, that he has any control over direction. He holds the gimlet to steady himself, eyes open and ahead, wondering, praying, like Oedipus on the tail of the dreadful truth that he cannot leave alone, in spite of his wife's plea: Better to be ignorant.[26]

Joseph could not be on more intimate terms with his fate. There is no evasion, sipping coffee, chatting away the hours. He is not at a loose end. A candle flame is all that is between him and his son. The man who was called to be father has no other life. Bent over, head down, he is at work. He yokes himself to two vocations, those of carpenter and father, each with its own law. It turns out that the former is necessary to enable the latter, and together, they make him human. Joseph, moreover, can manage it only because his son is by his side, holding the light.

It is as if he is born bending down, on all fours, animal-like, face to the earth.[27] So the waitress bends down to pick up a bread roll. The wood lies on the ground — the living tree has been felled. It will rise once more, in the form of the Cross — the tree of Western culture — re-establishing the vertical, hence the fundamental principles of architecture. The gimlet, the tool of his trade, ties him to the beam, forming it, but also supports him. It is the potential means for reversing his descent, the sinking feeling that is not just in the pit of his stomach. He exemplifies the key to being human — that is, dedicating his life to stay vertical, suspended between the up and the down. Only then may he become higher. The horizontal has neither roots nor upward-reaching branches. It has neither weight nor loftiness. It is as a corpse.

Joseph is not entirely oriented down. The boy gazes diagonally up at his father's downturned face, halts the plunging motion, connects *pneuma* with flame, and imposes a simple verticality. The boy momentarily relieves Joseph of his tragic burden, frees him to turn the gimlet, almost deftly, which now appears like a steering wheel. He charts his destiny, a man in form, his touch precise, Joseph's strength because his wheel is the Cross. The final motion may be up, him rising through obedience to his call — work that, while it rules that he remain down, hunched over the earth, connects him with his son.

The bits of felled tree are at everybody's feet. The call, if it comes, will be in the form of the boy holding the light that enables work to start. That work will, in effect, be the same for one and all, building out of mere matter the Cross, that it may become vertical, that it may teach destiny. This timeless rebuilding is their life task, for themselves and their children, whether they know it or not, the knowledge itself incidental.

Only a few will be carpenters. It is not the content that counts. As the waitress teaches: If the work is flawed, I am flawed, for it is not that something useful has been made, but something right.

Yet there is little joy in the scene. Poor Joseph, the father! Poor boy, innocent as an ordinary child! Both are helpless victims to the savagery of fate. It is only because of his vocation that Joseph can bear it. A vocation is founded on dread, any vocation. Here is a reason why Luther stressed the darkness of faith, why the Greeks cast their seer Teiresias as old and blind — the one who tells Oedipus who he is. Here is why Joseph works at night, not daring to look at the flaming candle, certainly not daring to look into the eyes of his son. If the waitress were to look, the invisible flame that lights up her life would blind her. Fate rules.

Even the father finds his own son's presence dreadful. It is the seeing, not to see, so as to steer by an unconscious light — to travel and bear witness, but not become a seer. Aeschylus warned for all time against that ambition, having his prophetess wail out the terrible consequences of knowing the future — in her case, foreseeing a fate, her own sheer edge of the tearing iron.

Joseph, like Oedipus, cannot see the sheerest edge of his tearing iron. The exposed five-year-old hand, shielding the flame, has its palm open and bared to the light, the flesh transparent crimson. It will receive the wound, just as his mother had during her ecstasy, when the angel visited to announce that she was with child. The boring of the beam, the steel biting into wood, gouging it out, is the same steel as the nail that will pierce the soft centre of that hand. The hammering into the nerves to violate sacred authority is the source of Joseph's vocation. Little wonder that he struggles to continue drilling the cross, in spite of its necessity to the fulfilment of his son's life. The onlooker can only wince as the gimlet turns, and hope to be steadied by the gigantic flame that is already fed by the agony to come.

Witnesses to this story can take it for an instant, can for a second at most stand in the sandals of Joseph, gimlet in hand, dimly aware of the son close by. Perhaps, in the obscure shadows across the ground, what the carpenter works on is not a cross. Perhaps the boy is just a boy. After all, Oedipus mistook the man he killed in the chariot at the crossroads, for just some malevolent old fogey.

Anybody may deny the call, that it is a mission — attempt, like Oedipus, to deny their fate, and believe they are free. At the key moment, one and all may hesitate, as Matthew does, hunching up, not see what they see, take cover, bury their one talent, attempt to forget, then drift away with their lives. Even within the call, what is being worked on is hazy enough for doubt. Joseph himself does not realise what it is — so his strength may prevail, keeping him at his task, accepting that his very life hangs by this slender thread. Unlike Captain Vere, unlike Oedipus, unlike Agamemnon, he is not big enough for conscious knowledge.

Those torn out of the oblivion of being — and this *Lethe* here is heavy with obscurity — they who make out what truth it is in the lower shadows, the Truth of Truths, may now understand the reason for Joseph's half-crazed, compulsive concentration on his work, his being on the edge of despair, and the boy's joyful and wonderstruck aid to his father. They should find themselves bolt alert, shaken to the heart of their conscience. Joseph the Carpenter calls, calls into the deep mainstream of a fate, that a person know what to do. Thus speaks the Western Dreaming.

8.

The Genesis of Evil

S o what happened *en arche* — in the beginning? The Western Dreaming opens on the plains of Troy, valiant souls of heroes dispatched to Hades, their warrior bodies abandoned to feasting dogs and birds. It opens with Homer's three-word invocation: 'Wrath sing, goddess'... It is the wrath of this huge and brilliant man, Achilles, at being slighted, and later, his berserk grieving rage, which will soak the plains in blood, to be sung, as only a goddess can, her song pitched at the Olympian heavens.

So what happened *in the beginning*? The Western Dreaming opens somewhere away to the southeast, in a garden laid out by the very hand of God. The story is called *Genesis*, which means birth, and concerns the first man, Adam, formed from the dust of the ground, God breathing into his nostrils the breath of life. Homer, at the other site, records heroes spraying blood from their nostrils as death's dark mist closes in about them. Then came a wife for Adam, formed from his rib, whom he named Eve — meaning *living* — 'bone of my bones, flesh of my flesh'. And the two first humans disobeyed their God.

At one place, the goddess sings of mortals, of those who become great, bring to fulfilment their own doom, then gain a sober, tragic wisdom in the twilight hour between battle and death. At the other, Adam and Eve wake from the first oblivion, that of not being, to find themselves in Paradise, the golden garden of timeless happiness, free from *Necessity*. Then they do something, and are cast out. Their Fall is into shame, into labour — pain of childbirth, drudgery of eking out a living. It is Fall into knowledge and into mortality.

Cast out, east of Eden, stripped of immortality, clothed in shame! Was this a calamity or not? The Greeks understood immortality as its own curse. To be free from the fear of death made their gods unable to take anything seriously, reduced to passing the days in bickering, petty pranks, bursts of lust, vanity and jealousy, and caprice — the tedium of the idle rich. Yet, down on earth, human life had to be lived to the full, for it was all that was given — the departed soul subject to its own curse, an infinity of another sort of tedium, in Hades. *Mythos* was for humans, and it was pathos.

Why, then, in the beginning, did the primal ancestors disobey God? The Hebrew text blames the snake. Devious and cunning, it tempted Eve with beautiful fruit hanging on a tree in the midst of the garden, that eating it her eyes would be opened, gaining the knowledge of good and evil, and she would be wise — become like the gods. It was the very fruit that God had forbidden. So she ate of the fruit, gave it to her mate, and he ate also. Adam trusted, or feared, Eve more than he feared God, who had threatened him with death if he even so much as touched what was forbidden.

This is the first version of the story, the cryptic primordial text. In fact, it is so condensed that it would need a rift, a sort of amnesia of two millennia, before its fuller truth would be brought to light.

Reconsider the Garden of Eden. It is the state of Nature where there are no human creations. Adam and Eve are naked,

Adam sitting on the ground, looking at Eve with a wide-eyed and naive trust. It is as if man has not yet stood up. Eve is on one knee, in the transition to the two-legged *homo erectus*. She places her right hand on Adam's arm, to alert and reassure him, as she points straight upwards at apples overhead. However, there is no snake. Humanity did not need an outside agent to be tempted.

What, then, is the temptation? This is the springtime of creation, but in reality, it has none of the frolic, fecundity and airy optimism of the paradise garden as it would come to be imagined. There are no flowers, and the pervasive green is dull. Humanity is born in the dark, naked, close to the ground. The temptation is to escape from the wooded undergrowth, its night terrors and the thicket boredom of the animal condition. This is not even a temptation, merely intelligent.

The escape required that we humans stand up — achieving the vertical, free from the square-to-the-earth animal state. It is Eve who is eager to move, to rise. But to stand up depended on access to the saving truth — pull from above as much as thrust from beneath. There are material and metaphysical dimensions. The means is knowledge. It is the fruit of the Tree of Knowledge to which Eve points. Next to it, also in the midst of the garden, is the other tree, that of life. Larger than apples, its fruits are mysterious unripe pomegranates, belonging to Proserpine, Queen of the Underworld, who returned every spring to regenerate the earth.[1]

The temptation is thus that of knowledge, the means for metamorphosis out of brute existence. It is not linked, in the first instance, with good and evil. The simple fact is that Nature is not a comfortable condition for humans — tedious, claustrophobic, fit only for creatures governed by instinct, creatures without dreams, without stories. Eve is bored and restless.[2]

Her form snakes up, slithering in defiance of gravity and, thereby, Nature, to seek the vertical. The upward pointing hand hints at a tongued head. She carries the fallen state within, a condition of her being, which includes curiosity, ambition, calculated thinking to the point of intelligence, daring and potential solitariness — but not evil. Her fallen condition separates her from Adam, the innocent animal contented with his four-legged state close to the ground. Moreover, it is only because of the reptilian, its source in the underworld, that she has the strength, the mobility and the dream to thrust herself upwards.

So, alone in a chill, mindless Nature in which she does not belong — does not feel at home — Eve struggles to her feet and plucks the apple. As her teeth sink into taboo juice, she sets the clock ticking, once and for all time. This is the moment at which time begins. Inchoate story triggers history.

But let us — we who have inherited history — leave Eve in her blighted garden and move on. Ages come and go before we arrive at the summer of the human race. A prosperous and flourishing human order — civilisation — has been built. The fruits of knowledge have been realised. This is the earthly paradise, the best that may be achieved on the human plane. Nature has been harnessed, the oppressive cold and dark glade into which Adam and Eve were born transformed into a field of wheat and a vineyard. There is abundance, a city has been built, people are clothed, work is organised, and there is clean and running water, drainage, hygiene and medicine. There is time for leisure — and music and plentiful wine with which to enjoy it. Horses have been tamed to ease the burden of labour. There is not only agriculture to grow wheat but industry to make it into bread, and weave baskets to carry the plentiful loaves, casks to hold the wine, glasses from which to drink. There is philosophy.

All depends on a human hierarchy, led by an elite presiding over a just politics. Here is order, but not the natural order. It is the human creation, at its summer zenith, made possible by eating of the fruit of the Tree of Knowledge. The result is prosperity — indeed, just like the fabled land of milk and honey, bridling the potential abundance of the earth to a rational and benevolent political will. Humanity has reason to feel pleased with itself.

But it doesn't. Eve was restless with the state of Nature; her heirs are restless with material plenty. Many who inhabit the civilised world are bad-tempered or frustrated. They who have never had it so good turn sour. They who should be on their knees in gratitude complain: Is this all? Having achieved comfort, they discover that what they really want is the Light, but the path opened by choosing knowledge does not lead there. Eve chose the wrong fruit, and with the passage of time and the focus on human creation, the Light has become even more distant than in the state of Nature. The civilised order is one vast, impassable barrier to the true 'promised land' over the horizon.

This summer resting place, which is still not home, completes the logic of having chosen knowledge, indicating how Western civilisation would both gain and lose from moving along this path. It is the Humanist domain, to be revisited after 1500AD, in which free will works and, in combination with reason, engineers progress. Equally, it harbours the discontent that would forever accompany material abundance, and prepares the way to the next stage. *Is this all?* sows the seed of evil.

Let us move on again, to the autumn of the human race, the season of Fall. It took time to unfold, this story — generations, in fact — once having chosen the wrong fruit, the wrong knowledge. Old Testament history is subjected to radical *midrash*. Moses is dying. Civilisation lies behind. His people did once experience it, in Egypt, but for them, it was captivity — symbolic of its stifling effect on *pneuma*. Moreover, it is ages since Moses received the stone tablets of the law, the foundation of moral civilisation. At last, and in chronic old age, he has led his people to within sight of the Promised Land.[3] So he sends two scouts ahead to reconnoitre.

It has proven a long journey, detour after wayward detour, from the state of Nature, but finally, a way has opened to the Light in the distance. The landscape is now rocky, arid and forbidding, the prevailing tone browny-grey, the rich burnt reds and fiery yellows of autumn entirely missing. Humanity has to eke out its subsistence from scarcity, from a withholding nature, from the Wasteland. The age of comfort has passed, and with it the soothing illusion of knowledge, giving way to austerity. After forty days, the two scouts return with figs, pomegranates and, carrying between them on a thick staff, a huge bunch of first-ripened grapes. Two men, blind to the workings of destiny, are being fitted to the number forty — ominously — for it is the count of punishment.

The scouts have taken the journey of all journeys, destination unknown, having been chosen by their great leader, saviour of his people. Generous he was to them, trusting, his instruction simply to follow their initiative, find what they might, for he knew it was somewhere out there, what they all sought. We meet the scouts returning from the Promised Land, trudging along a boulder-strewn, rutted track very much like the one that leads to Emmaus. They have not found the Light.

The grapes are gigantic, ten times normal size, a grotesque profanity mocking the men — brute matter, inflated, an unendurable burden. The tail scout also lugs pomegranates, but they, too, are gargantuan. He has to brace himself just to support the load. He can hardly force another step. Hair matted and windblown, face weatherbeaten and craggy, his expression is that of unimaginable horror, as if he has just seen what no human can bear to witness. It brings him to a jolting halt. What he faces is himself. He is haunted by what is ahead, in time rather than place, what in fact he himself will do now the hopelessness of his own path has been revealed.

Fallenness is failure to find the Light. For humans, it is a metaphysical condition. It leads inexorably into evil. The front scout, pulled to a halt, looks back at his companion and astutely reads his thoughts. Seized by the same horror, his mouth drops open. He clasps his sword and slowly, deliberately draws it from its scabbard. What evil will do is slash at the grapes they carry on the pole between them. Wine-red blood will drip. Allegorically, these are the men who crucify Christ. The burden they haul doubles as the Cross.[4]

Men out of hell, with brown, sinewy, stocky limbs; large, misshapen feet; dark, hideous faces; their thick hair is devilish, plastered to their heads in curls simulating the snakes that adorned Medusa's head. The serpent has risen out of the underworld. What these men are about to do will turn any onlooker to stone. Yet they are not exceptions.

Their potential for evil recurs in the human world in many disguises, often appearing normal and innocuous. They are there in twitches of insecurity followed by malice — at her beauty and success, at his presence and generosity — in every swallowed taste of envy, in every self-censored smile at the discomfort or misfortune of others. They also lurk in any grand metaphysical resentment against the Fates, or whatever it is that a person feels has dealt such a poor hand with which to play life.

The scouts are caricatured in order to protect the everyday individual from being traumatised by his or her darker self. In fairy-tales, for instance, their presence is central: the wicked witch, driven by envy of maternal goodness and child innocence, kidnaps children, cooks them in her oven — symbolic of her own blighted womb — and eats them. The witch is just another Moses scout, too hideous for direct identification, but alive in the nightmare Unknown.

The fruit the scouts bear, like that Eve chose, is wrong. Unlike her, they know it. Knowledge that the Light exists marks the end of innocence. *Truth* may be worse than lethal. The door to hell on earth now opens for the first time, inviting in those who have awoken, stood up, taken the journey and then been denied. Once humans are attracted by the Light and set out in search, the practical reality is that some will fail. Failed truth drops like a lead sinker of futility, setting in train a history of negation. 'I am not', as coward Peter will put it. 'I am not what I am', as Shakespearean Iago, prince of envy, will put it. 'Nothing is but what is not', as Macbeth's evil will put it.

Thus, the way to the Light is equally that to the domain of negated Being. Evil did not enter the world with Adam and Eve. It enters with what is, in effect, the second Fall. Eve's first rise, aiming for height, had opened up the possibility of drop, which is now.

Rancour enters creation, and with it, envy, the malicious drive to destroy anyone who has eaten of the Tree of Life, on the grounds that if I cannot have the saving fruit, no-one else shall. Evil is thus not born out of either temptation or disobedience, but is an inevitable consequence of the human impatience with comfort and knowledge, once that discontent focusses into a search for the Light. It is 'original', which means constitutive. In the earlier summer condition, of material plenty, there had been bickering over shares, spite that another might have more, preoccupation with 'me' and 'mine'. Without the metaphysical catalyst, however, this is like the egoism of children: mean and petty but not wicked.

The specifically Christian dimension is that evil is necessary to snuff out the wind that bloweth, and at that point, the pomegranates metamorphose into sacred fruit.[5] Slashed grapes will ferment into wine, the liquid that induces, in this now dualistic world, either divine drunkenness or oblivion. The long road the scouts have trodden winds away into the distance. It is suddenly open, unlike any Greek road. Eve is at last able to take it.

The human world is now complete, and polarised. Gone is the dream of the Paradise garden, state of innocent Nature, playground of eternal childhood. Gone, too, is the fantasy that civilisation and its comforts might soothe the distraught soul.

The landscape is severe, but charged with the ethereal lightness of the autumn sky, in its narrow range of light blues through to lavender. It has become imaginable to breathe in an austere beauty made possible by the entrance of evil. An aura of brooding horror cloaks the two scouts and their grotesque grapes, as they stumble back along the rutted track to report their nothing to the expiring leader. Their black mission sends out contaminating waves, a slight bend in the front section of the pole indicating that their motion is downwards. Simultaneously, Eve travels the other way along the same track, gliding away into the distance, drawn by the Light. Creation has become interesting, thick with Story, but harsh and unforgiving — Fallen.

That is the history — not linear, but cyclical like the seasons themselves, with at most a rare spiral forwards, soon countered by a reverse. Now for the story. The scouts are Judas. Only for Judas, the Light has become man.

He used, in his younger days, to be handsome, a spring in his walk, lean, straight in stance, with clean-cut features, smooth skin, fine long brown hair, one who took care with his dress.[6] Perhaps he even came close to grace. However, once he sees the sacred rage in the other's eyes, the simplicity of step, the mission, Judas lowers his head, deep in thoughts that quickly turn to malevolent brooding. Thenceforth, he will not be able to help himself, glued to this presence, stalking, watching, scrutinising its every move as if to detect some flaw, hoping with every waking minute and many a sleeping one. It is as if he has become addicted to his own destruction.

The presence before him is so charged with *pneuma*. He is formidable and masterly, yet at ease in himself. He is the complete human being. Judas observes the enchantment coming over those drawn to him, lifting their spirits, lighting up their faces. They all want to be near him, to bathe in his golden aura. And I, I am nothing. Nobody seeks me out. Nobody breaks out into a shy smile when they see me coming through the door. What he calls the wind that bloweth has never dwelt with me. Judas starts to hate its very existence, to curse a world in which there is such breath. His unsacred rage boils. I shall drive it into oblivion. *Pneumaphobia* enters creation.

It is not the doing that has seized him, eating him up, every cell in his body bloated by obsession. It is the presence, the force, of that *I am*.[7] Judas' unbearable cry is: 'Why am I who I am? Why am I not he?' Visceral unchosenness is his story — 'I am not.'

And Judas knows all this, as he knows himself. He is close enough, like an older brother, to read the other. He is not a brute, blind to any scrap of light. Nor is he without conscience, an Iago who never suffers inwardly for the evil he does, a machine of shrewd, plotting intelligence.[8] Judas is as intimate with Jesus as is Magdalene, they the two who understand him. Only *his* knowing confronts him with how much lesser, irretrievably lesser, he himself is. Cursed to walk in the shadow, cursed with the monomaniacal ambition to be the one and only one himself, he is thus cursed to fail as no-one else in the Western story fails — but not to just fade away with a whimper![9] The Master will pay for my misery, and how he will pay.

If Judas' fate had cast him among the ordinary, living out his life in coffee-time, he might have got through. But what a futile *if*, more ludicrous than Oedipus' lament: '*If* only I had never been born!' And the fate of Judas is worse than that of Oedipus. Visceral unchosenness does not allow him the tragic composure of acknowledging fate and taking responsibility for himself.

Indeed, the wisdom of fate in relation to the good may equally apply here. It holds that it is not the doing of good works that makes a person good but the reverse — that a good person does good works. Magdalene, born the one who will love much, of her nature always loves, and as a result, there is never anything to forgive. So fate decrees simply, clinically, that an evil person does evil.[10]

We are never told how Judas became a disciple, one of the twelve. What a mystery! Is he set up, a scapegoat to be wheeled on stage, a teaching expedient? Is it to mock him, and by association, the tribal Judaism that he bears in his name? Or did a hopeful Jesus expect more?[11] All we know is that Judas was driven to betray his teacher, and to do so by means of the most brazen and deliberate act of duplicity — a kiss. He is paid thirty silver pieces, and according to one account, soon after gives back the money and hangs himself.[12]

We have already met him, at the villa of Simon the Pharisee, where he displayed his character plainly, for all to see. There, he wore his second identity inscribed across his forehead: 'Mine eyes are ever toward the letter of the law of the Lord.' There, he ranted against Magdalene, and her waste of precious oil, worth three hundred silver pieces, a year's wages — and lavished on *Him*.[13]

It had already happened. Judas has had his fateful encounter at the place where the three ways meet under the sacred mountain, and from there, set out decisively on the road to his Thebes — all of this some time before the encounter with Magdalene. Almost everything can be deduced from our first observation of him, at the villa.

Raging against her is, for him, the easy strategy in defence of his pride, inverting his humiliation into a virtue. Look at me, he is bragging, the single follower with compassion for the poor, disgusted by this extravagance. I am the holy one.

The texts have provided him with the excuse, identifying him as the bagman, the treasurer, the one who looks after the purse for the disciples. The others think, according to John's account of the Last Supper, that when Judas leaves abruptly, it is to go off on Jesus' instruction to buy supplies, or a gift for the poor.[14] It is an excuse with sinister undertones, Judas' every move as reported in the *Lives of Jesus* linked with money, setting up the association that will become central to the long, satanic history of Christian anti-Semitism.[15]

Judas employs the common tactic in self-inadequacy of 'blame the other'. And the other, Magdalene, is like him, almost an *alter ego*, also having lost her way, and extravagantly, so the identification is automatic. Both respond with kisses, his prefigured as a bitter inversion of hers, the one leading to restoration, the other evil. Indeed, once he has taken in her central act, pressing her lips to Jesus' dusty feet, his script is written, leading inexorably to his own intimate and deliberate violation of *Touch me not!* Point by point, their stories correlate. He can thus blame Magdalene with a good conscience, for she is obliquely he.

In Judas, intelligence is fed by psychological complexity — shorthand for a demonic concoction of inner conflict, embarrassment and fox cunning. He contrasts with Achilles, in whom intelligence is located in a straightforward, open character and grows into wisdom. Indeed, Judas becomes one of the Western paradigms of corrupt reason.

Reading the negation takes us to the first level of unconscious truth, that Judas' real lament is: Why am I not loved? He cannot comprehend how she — the lowest, the most untouchable — is the chosen one. That sumptuously robed, bejewelled slut is preferred over a good man who has kept the Commandments, and even spoken out for the poor! And I am one of the inner circle of twelve, the elect.

This Judas is Cain, the first-born son of Adam and Eve, who turned against his brother, Abel, and killed him, for the crime of having been favoured by God. Judas and Cain are both men of action. Not for them the black swamp of depression, the retreat into a cocoon of self-pity, nor a lifestyle of carping and complaint, projecting onto the world their own rejection. Neither are they among those frozen in their seats, too self-conscious to move, perhaps even attached to their own failure. Judas and Cain let their malice talk, and in what they do, represent all those others — the passive ones who only dream of vengeance.

Judas was not the first. Whenever and wherever humanity began its autumn journey after the Light, his ancestors were to be found, as have been his descendants ever since. There was Cain, at the start, providing one psychological blueprint for the origins of evil. Many families bear the imprint of his story, exposing a raw nerve in those who dwell there. It may well overwhelm them with its curse. The modern West, due largely to Freud, has made much of this theme.

Usually, the key figure is the mother, not the father — in modern as in earlier times. It is a tragic inevitability that she will prefer one child ahead of her others — occasionally, her husband will be the chosen one, or herself. All will unconsciously know the pecking order, however much care she devotes to compensating, with attention, presents and favours, those who are not. When she acts out of a sense of justice, compounded by her own guilt, or even out of compassion, all ears are alert to the undertone that it is not primal and total love which is speaking. Likely, the favoured one will be buoyed through life by a sense of inviolable assurance. The others may carry the mark of Cain, having suffered an insuperable blow, doubling them up in a state of permanently winded being, afflicting them with self-doubt. On earth, this is one of the primordial injustices, unwanted by all, especially the mother, at work even when her love is multiple and diffuse.[16]

Yet parents and ancestors hardly ever act as first cause. To concentrate on them, and expend psychic energy in seeking to understand childhood malaise, is usually futile — in terms of making the subject any happier. While the family scene, and its primal competition for love and recognition, taps into the archetype, it voices rather than forms it.[17] Likewise, the story of a son who fails to gain his divine father's blessing and displaces his patricidal hatred onto his envied brother falls short of the heart of the matter — which is to do with the essence of being. Indeed, the very turn to psychology, to the analysis of character and its formation in childhood, may be a deliberate if unconscious ploy in turning away from the unbearable truth about *I am* — that it is irredeemably cursed, its way irretrievably lost. For access to that truth, we need the Dreaming story.

Judas' envy of she against whom he rants, Magdalene, is itself another means of deception, serving as a further decoy. He would prefer us to believe this of him — for the one who walks the earth bearing the mark of Cain, while alone and outcast, retains some dignity.[18] To probe further would risk arriving at the deeper truth, which is just too dark.

The climax to the Judas story is the Last Supper. It is recounted by John with a concentrated dramatic intensity unsurpassed in the New Testament narratives. The scene opens with Jesus knowing that his hour has come. He has assembled his disciples in an upper room in Jerusalem the evening before the Crucifixion, to share their last meal together. He strips, girds himself in a towel and proceeds to wash their feet, ending by pointing out that not all among them are clean. As they settle down, lounging on the couches in a close circle around the table, preparing to eat, he explains briefly the meaning of service. By the dim, flickering light of an oil-lamp hanging low overhead, he concludes: 'I speak not of you all: I know whom I have chosen.'

With pregnant, abrupt aphorisms, he hammers repeatedly away at the central theme of his Last Supper — betrayal. First, he equates it with pollution, then unchosenness. Becoming deeply agitated, he states explicitly that one of them will betray him. The twelve are petrified, each pitched into the midst of his own insecurity. Peter speaks for them all in urging the beloved disciple, John, who reclines close to his Master, leaning against him, to ask whom it is. John receives the whispered reply that it is the one to whom Jesus will give the piece of bread after he has dipped it. He dips it, in another cup, again of destiny, and this time, he himself sets the fated events in motion, presenting the betrayer with his portion, dripping blood-red wine. 'I know whom I have chosen.'

Jesus gives the soaked morsel to Judas, addressing him: 'That thou doest, do quickly!' No-one at the table knows what the words mean, except John and Judas, both in their different ways, obscurely. John is too lost in horror to remember to pass on what he has just heard, leaving the other disciples stranded in doubt about their own condition. Soon to be proved cowards, they are, one and all, incipient Judases. Judas takes the bread and exits. It is all over in a minute. The narrative closes with three words: *en de nux* — 'and it was night.'[19]

Judas walks out into the most bleak and hopeless nothingness in the Western Dreaming.[20] The black Furies have got him, his demon now completely possessed by evil. He leaves behind the upper room, the lamp-lit table strewn with broken fragments of bread and half-drunk goblets of wine, surrounded by ten bewildered men, two others deeply troubled in spirit, the younger the one who decades later will write the story. That final, terse: 'Do quickly!' singles out the executioner, the black-hooded hangman, only it is he, the one with the cold lips, who will hang.

His metamorphosis is into deliverer of the icy kiss of death, the one who brings to fulfilment torture on the Cross, and relishes the prospect. He smiles. Yet at the same time, he is dimly conscious of his own self, of the horror of what he is about to do and that he himself is that horror. So he moves like a sleepwalker stepping to the tune of the nightmare chosen for him, blind automaton descending into his own *Lethe*, tragic victim to a destiny that renders him helpless. His fate is another 'sheer edge of the tearing iron'. Who would wish to be him? Judas suffers, and by the end, he too is to be pitied.

'What thou doest' is evil beyond human reckoning, so dark that the victim himself winces, wanting to hasten it, get it over. He shies away from this presence, more forbidding than the six-hour torture awaiting him on the morrow — shies away from this being, so tormented in its howling discord as to shake his own *pneuma*. 'Do quickly' serves also to propel Judas, 'whom I have chosen', onwards, lest he now hesitate, to shove him out into the gloom from which he will not emerge. The evil person does evil. In front of Judas, through the door, is the blackness of endless night. *En de nux*.[21]

I n the beginning, there was also *wrath*, sung by the goddess:

> *As inhuman fire sweeps on in fury through the deep angles of a drywood mountain and sets ablaze the depth of the timber and the blustering wind lashes the flame along, so Achilles swept everywhere with his spear like something more than a mortal harrying them as they died, and the black earth ran blood. Or as when a man yokes male broad-foreheaded oxen to crush white barley on a strong-laid threshing floor, and rapidly the barley is stripped beneath the feet of the bellowing oxen, so before great-hearted Achilles the single-foot horses trampled alike dead men and shields, and the axle under the chariot was all splashed with blood and the rails which encircled the chariot, struck by flying drops from the feet of the horses, from the running rims of the wheels. The son of Peleus was straining to win glory, his invincible hands spattered with bloody filth.[22]*

It is as if Eden is not the only primordial garden. There is also a garden of the other Nature — fang and claw. Again, in the first instance, it is not a garden of evil, nor for humans, of merely struggling to survive.[23] Here dwells *will to power*. Within its perimeter, power is the one and only pleasure. Its principle, elemental to the human condition, is: I hate and I destroy, therefore I am. Power makes its possessor feel big, feel somebody. Even the great Achilles was once such a brute.

Many taste of the fruit from this garden. Sweet little boys do who stamp ants' nests into mass graves of tiny corpses. Iago did, who hated Othello, not even out of envy, just gut loathing — so he devoted his formidable intelligence to destroying the other man. The pair of youths do who stand in a valley beating each other over the head with cudgels — as if to pulp.[24] Blood streaming down their faces, both semiconscious, they and their male tendency will keep on remorselessly slogging away until one drops. They cannot help themselves, and nor can all those whom they represent in all times — they featured once again in the modern film *Fight Club* (1999).

The will to destruction moves deep in every character — even Jesus himself tasted of its sap as he stood hungry before the innocent fig tree. And he annihilated it. Perhaps it is what Freud was groping towards when he introduced his most enigmatic notion, that of the 'death instinct', the notion that none of his followers has wanted to touch.[25] William Hazlitt wrote of Iago's ruling passion — his incorrigible love of power and mischief, without hint of moral scruple — as merely an extreme instance of a natural human principle.[26] The tree growing in the second garden is that of death and devastation, and of sadistic pleasure.

Phalaris tasted of its fruit, too, the ancient Greek tyrant who locked his victims inside a hollow bronze bull, lit a fire underneath, and relaxed to the music that their screams made when transformed by a reed set in the bull's mouth. His pleasure was the more sublime for imagining the intensity of the agony inside. This story is writ everywhere in the human domain, although strenuously denied by civilisation precisely because it drives at the core of its saving hypocrisies.

There was Marsyas the satyr — half man, half beast, like Adam — who found the oboe that Athena had discarded because playing it distorted her face. He masters the instrument and then, fool to vanity, challenges Apollo to a musical contest, with the agreement that the winner can do as he will with the loser. Naturally, Apollo, the god of music, triumphs. His fancy is to have Marsyas strung upside down by his goat legs to a horizontal bough, head swaying just above the ground, arms hanging down, looped under it, with wrists tied. Apollo then kneels and, with the delicacy and precision of a painter, or surgeon, scalpel in hand, cherishing his craft, proceeds to skin the satyr alive. A large feather in his left hand, he simultaneously tickles his victim under the ribs. The scene is accompanied by one of Apollo's beautiful muses playing the lyre, instrument of Marsyas' undoing. Such is the god's Phalaris pleasure, and he the divinity that presides over the sacred mountain.

Once history was under way, some time much later, around the Fall and in parallel epochs, things human began to develop complexities. Rancour was born. Hatred of those who succeed, who possess power, was progressively swallowed and became diffused. Openly black acts condensed into a grey mist of malice — to 'smile, and smile, and be a villain'. Where there is power, there must, equally, and oppositely, be lack of power — impotency. Rancour becomes the civilised means for making do with *I am not*, solace for those who feel ineffectual, and who appear in an ever-increasing diversity of personae, and segments of personae. With history, moreover, the stumbling block becomes less the capacity of the resented other to use physical force or display wealth — tyranny and moneyed power. It becomes, more, his or her character — the intangible presence, the *pneuma*.[27]

The insecurities spread. There is fear of failure, which may even stop a person getting started. There is fear of rejection — that I am clumsy or ugly or stupid, in some way misbegotten — a fear that tends to bring on its own fulfilment. Inhibition becomes a way of life, lest in asserting myself, parading myself before others as someone of stature or presence or beauty, I become deflated.

Embarrassment becomes the governing psychological condition, its deeper reflex an anxiety over humiliation. Judas is raw with embarrassment at himself. In his deflation, all lightness of *pneuma* gone, the *I am* is exposed, naked to the world in all its deformity and lack. And the presence of Jesus was the mirror that showed him up. Judas vows to never let this happen to him again. *My will is to negate.*

One of the central achievements of culture — the checking of sadistic impulses by blanketing them in bad conscience and displacing their energy into guilt — comes at high cost. All that inhibited lifeforce is itself liable to conversion into rancour. While Phalaris enjoys himself, those who fear him burn inwardly, smoulder impotently — like those inside his bull, except rancour is unmusical.

The parallel with male baboons is instructive: when two fight over a female, both experience huge surges in testosterone. To the victor goes not only the prize, but also hormonal levels that remain expansively high, while in the vanquished they plummet so low that within a couple of days, he is likely to fade away and die. This comparison is also false. The dying baboon's human counterpart, while just as dispirited, lives on to spread his fog of discontent and to picture revenge.

Evil thus has twin sources — unchosenness in relation to the Light, and failed *will to power*. Both drive Judas as he steps out through the door of the upper Jerusalem room into that endless night. Failure to the Light, to *pneuma* — failure of *I am* — chills his character. A lust for power enters the inner void, it alone able to arouse any feeling, his last remaining pleasure and goal.[28]

He has one power — to deliver his nemesis into the hands of the executioners, and to luxuriate in the public act of betrayal. *History will remember me.*

The crisp air quickly brings him back to his senses, and he recalls words that sear into his flesh: 'That thou doest, do quickly!' Now, he smokes with fury. The presumption! Who does he think he is to so condescend to me? If he thinks he knows what I shall do and still wants to control me, as if I am some nobody — then I shall show him.

Judas speeds through the dark streets to the house of Caiaphas, the high priest. Composing himself outside the door, he coolly walks in on a meeting of the Jewish elite — upper ranks of the religious hierarchy, Jerusalem elders, lawyers and intellectuals — gathered to plot what to do about Jesus of Nazareth. He introduces himself as one of the chosen twelve, the one who has realised that his Master is a charlatan troublemaker. He knows where he will be later in the evening. He is prepared to lead them there, with whomever they see fit. They will need that, for Jerusalem is packed with visitors for the festival of Passover. They listen carefully, then, in their desperation, simply nod to each other, and without further discussion, Caiaphas pays Judas thirty pieces of silver.

Judas returns at the appointed hour, towards midnight, and leads out an assembled gang of Caiaphas' circle, hangers-on, hired thugs, and a Roman centurion with a few soldiers. They walk through the pitch-black streets and out of the city, descending down a steep narrow path, across the Kedron brook, then back a short way up the west slope of the Mount of Olives, to the Garden of Gethsemane.[29] Judas has never moved in his whole life with such surety of purpose. Moreover, he is swept along by a buoyant tide of collective steel-eyed hatred behind him, resolved to exterminate the One.

He knows the secluded clearing in the garden where Jesus liked to withdraw to be alone. Close by, he sees the shadowy forms of a dozen or so men congregating around a central figure. It must be them — it must be him. Judas accelerates, his eyes narrowing to the glint of a beast of prey about to pounce, and glides across the uneven terrain as if it were clear daylight, leading on his stumbling mob. The disciples, uneasy as they are, willingly part to admit this force coming at them out of the dark.

Looking Jesus straight in the eye, Judas walks up to face him, close enough to touch. But even now, while absorbed in this final act, the memory of Magdalene's kiss hounds him, the warmth of the one who 'loved much' forcing itself back into his mind — taunting him, mocking him. Blinking away the distracting thoughts, he regains his focus, only to see his former Master go white and look down. He leers with delight at the weakness and suffering he senses in this man he hates, hates with a passion greater than any love he has ever felt. So Judas embraces the tensing frame, and feels the other body shudder violently as he puts his lips to the death-cold cheek. *And it was night.*

9.

'Courage. *I am.*
Don't Fear!'

I t began one Jerusalem Friday in early spring, at around nine in
the morning. His exhausted body slumps down, guided onto
the Cross lying flat on the ground, the torso red-wealed from
flogging, bruised puffy green, dirty sweat and blood caked in his
hair and congealed in waves down his brow from the crown of
thorns. Raging against his soul, they target his body. His right
hand is yanked over towards the end of the crossbeam, forced
open, palm exposed. Licking its lips, evil hammers steel into the
soft flesh at the heart, nailing down his authority, for here was a
centre of power, the source from where, this hand raised, the
forgiving rays streamed. They would murder the saving touch.

The hand convulses as he sinks beneath a crimson scorching
tide into momentary unconsciousness, the fingers clenching
around the nail as if to embrace it, caress it into mercy, that it
might relent. They have pierced the vital spot. Hand is claw,
locked that it not move, not even to flinch, lest it set off the
screaming pain. What futility, for they have placed the end of

the long beam in the hole chiselled in the Calvary rock and hauled him into the vertical. That hand, with the other Magdalene will kiss, has to steady the whole weight.

It takes until noon for him to gain a certain composure, three hours for the numbness to spread, and for him to surrender, give up his all-too-human resistance to the *Necessity* that his hour has come. The bulging vein slashing down the centre of his forehead tells of the will required, the cheeks sunk in rigid defence, mouth set slightly open, wheezing for breath, fighting to stay conscious, grimacing, wincing — almost a tremble, but that he cannot risk, lest everything dissolve. And those eyes, which did still the raging storm on the Sea of Galilee, which in a one-second glance did embrace Magdalene, stopped Matthew in his life tracks, they are but a slit, just resisting the reflex to clamp shut.

This is a man, like any man. He is suffering the worst death. The moment is not eased by thoughts of Paradise awaiting him, a next and joyful life to compensate for this world's ordeal. He does not long, Hamlet-like, for death as release, as itself the ultimate earthly happiness. This is a man enclosed in utter despair. He feels forsaken by everyone and everything, above and below. For him, God is dead. The dull ache drumming through his body is as if in sympathy with his wretchedness of being.[1]

At this Friday noon, the sun is eclipsed. The darkness over the Holy Land will last the three more hours he has to live. Now, he looks down. He surveys it all: his life, his mission, his disciples, the women and what will be. Is this what it has come to?

He sees his young mother there below, sitting in the shadow of the Cross, holding himself as an infant tenderly to her breast, everything she is and was and will be devoted to him, the intimacy so complete that he floats weightless on her cradling arm.[2] Looking down, he melts at the memory of it, that once-upon-a-time bliss when he, even he, was bathed in a mother's love. Then the clarity returns — she remembers what she knows, the horror fulfilment to his life, her life, suspended above her head, on the cord that may be neither cut nor even loosened. She lunges forward, in a mother's instinctive hope to save her baby son, thrusting him clear of the shadow, that shadow which is himself, his own life, fulfilled this Friday. She was merely another Oedipus in flight from Corinth, just as surely running straight into the arms of predetermined fate. Yet she had to try, acting as if everything was staked on her success, saving him from his own destiny, all the time knowing that what will be will be — or, as he put it, 'My hour has come.'

The frightful shadow hanging over her is her strength. She senses him with her, steadying her, whispering: Yes, it is all right. I am here. We are in this together. And he, high above, in the awful consummation of his mission, knows she is with him, always with him. In this moment of his greatest trial, he is not alone.

Never once had he really needed her — just another sign of how dreadful it was to be Mary, mother to a son who from birth went his own way. He remembers that cruel incident during the marriage at Cana when there was no wine and she badgered him. He turned on her: 'Woman, what have I to do with thee!'[3] This was his first act in public after being baptised and choosing his disciples. He had to make clear that while she still clung to him, he was already out in the world. What he had to do in the next two years — two years was all it was to be — did not allow him to pity she who without him was nothing. 'Woman' might just as well have been anybody, or nobody. How he crushed her.

From his high distance, he sees his disciples, too. He took such pains in choosing them, gave them nicknames, hoping beyond all reasonable hope that they were special, that they would hear and understand, come to share his burden, even be able to take over from him. Not always, he hoped, will I be so unspeakably alone. Of course, he also knew he had chosen ordinary men like any other men, and deliberately — whether they stood up would tell of the future, and it would be a story of failure.

People by the thousand flocked to him because of his miracles. Such was only natural, but how he loathed it all the same, to be taken for a vaudeville holy man showing off his petty tricks, a healing or two here and there. The twelve disciples were no better, one minute on edge, the next agog at his most vulgar powers. Early on, he was already snapping at them: 'If you don't understand this, you won't understand anything.'[4]

There was that time after feeding the huge crowd that had come to hear him, towards dusk, when he ordered the twelve across the sea so that he could withdraw to the hills.[5] He needed to be alone, away from all those who were grasping, clamouring and jostling him for more, always more. But even there, he had no peace, for in the thick of the night, he saw them, troubled as usual, this time by having to row into a rising wind, getting nowhere, so although they were not in danger, he strode across the water, intending to pass them by, not wanting their dispiriting company, except they saw him, and taking him for a phantasm — unsurprisingly — they were even more terrified. So he swept over to the boat, cruising across the waves like a graceful dancer,[6] and spoke five carefully chosen words: 'Courage. I am. Don't fear!'[7] That final *Don't fear!* had its intended effect, as if to say: You should be scared witless. And they were.

It was as if he had two selves. There was the ordinary Jesus, blind to the future, and thus free to forget and to hope: forget who he was, hope that his disciples prove special, hope that the Cross would not come to be. This self was so disappointed by them all — 'groaning deep in his spirit'.[8] Always expecting them to be better, it was moody, hurt by his own failure. And just as his Jesus self was foundering, struggling even with its miracles, he went up the mountain and underwent his second baptism — by fire.

This was his metamorphosis,[9] when his robe glowed white with radiance, as if struck by a lightning spear of that mega-voltage fire through which the king of the Greek gods spoke, and he met his ancestor spirits, Elijah and Moses. The ancestors were being superseded. Whilst Moses had gone up his mountain to receive from his God the stone tablets of the moral law, Jesus had been invested with fire. And out of this crucible, scorching off the skin of mundane being, his other self strode forth, Christ the newly initiated one. Water had been merely the preliminary, as in washing the hands.[10]

Again he was teaching by example, but only one understood. At the moment of his own metamorphosis by fire, a mad boy, foaming at the mouth, down on the plain of ordinary earthly existence far below, the other disciples striving futilely to cure him, looks up. Seeing what no-one else can look upon without being blinded, he is set free.[11] The father provided the clue to the mystery of this story, recounting how the boy's raving spirit used to throw him into convulsions, and then into water and into fire, trying to destroy him.[12] The spirit yearns for death by water and by fire, in order to be reborn, in order to pass initiated into the upright — for just as water finds its natural state flat out in the horizontal, fire's principle is flickering, roaring straight upwards.

Meanwhile, up on the mountain, the one thrown into convulsions had been Peter — who had accompanied Jesus. Blinded by white radiance, he rushes around in fear, wanting to set up three tents — already building temples, as if programmed from birth — and to shelter the three holy men, misreading the glowering divinity overhead as a dark raincloud. Thus he mistakes fire for water, an omen that his Church will be constituted of the element that extinguishes light.

The episode with Martha, Mary and Lazarus had been the last straw — well, not in fact, for there was worse to come.[13] They were good friends; Jesus had always been welcome in their house in Bethany, just over the Mount of Olives, an hour southeast from

Jerusalem. It was earlier this very same year that the two sisters had sent a message saying their brother, Lazarus, was seriously ill. Instead of setting off immediately to help, Jesus waited two days, deliberately, making it plain that his motive for what would happen next was not that of compassion for the dying. He tells his disciples that their friend is sleeping, 'but I shall go to wake him.' They take him literally, so he has to snap out the truth: 'Lazarus is dead!' Moreover, he tells them that the reason *he* is going to Bethany is not to save Lazarus but so they, the chosen ones, might actually learn something. At this, Thomas boasts of his faith, urging the other disciples: 'Let us also go, that we may die with him.' Yet Thomas is not one to have any claim to courage, the courage of truth, for like all the others apart from John, he will flee from the Crucifixion and then declare his doubt.

He remembers, too, how he had to reprimand Martha for her conventional and empty beliefs, wearily instructing her to forget about resurrections after death or God and his interventions. She, too, in her vacant piety, understood nothing. To her, he spoke the simple two-word central truth: *ego eimi — I am*! It is me, my living presence. *I am the life*. Do not look elsewhere; it is in your midst, here and now, what you seek. I am at hand. Still Martha did not understand, nor would she. It reminds him of when he cleansed the Temple, throwing out everything profane — the next day, it was back.

Nor did her sister, Mary, understand, the one with the big and spontaneous heart, weeping for her dead brother. He reacted to her grief with an angry snort, for he had hoped for more, at least from her.[14] Where was her instinctive sense, which should have checked her, drawing her to his presence, not her brother's absence? She had been startled out of all normal comprehension by him. And her grief was human, yes, empathy for another's suffering, and here it was suffering unto death, her brother's. Yes, his demand that she deny her heart was pitiless. But it was just so that they would know.

They all wanted him to be the healer, 'meek and mild', 'sweetness and light', the comforter putting his arms around those who suffer — and for two millennia, his Churches would usually prefer him that way. It would have been easy to take this path — others can do that — Mary of Bethany, for instance, now she has been initiated. He himself, however, had come, Christ the Lion, padding into the scene with a low rumbling growl.[15] He had come, smouldering with a wild Dionysiac rage — forged anew on the mountain — to disrupt and unsettle, to scare out the old, and then point the way. Bitter in his experience with the disciples, it had impressed upon him that to teach, he must first shock out of ordinary time. So, taking a slow breath, he set out systematically to terrify and humiliate them. Fear became his agent. Only then would they find out what they were made of — if anything survived to rise from their charred old selves. 'Courage. *I am*. Don't fear!'

Finally in Bethany, with a great warrior cry — loaded with smoking fury at the deafness that surrounded him — he had shouted into the opened tomb: 'Lazarus, come forth!' And this apparition, four days already into stinking decomposition, swathed in white linen, his face also bandaged, had staggered, blind, free momentarily from the clasp of death, clowning back to life. And everyone was happy at this surreal farce, for profane time and oblivion had been restored.

Except for Mary of Bethany, who had at last been awoken — she, not Lazarus — by his shout, by the sacred rage. He now shone for her, just as he would at Emmaus, more than teacher and friend, so she, assuming some of the wisdom of her greater namesake from Magdala, understood his *I am*, although it had been spoken to her sister, understood that it was not somewhere out there but, rather, within her, waiting to be possessed. The next time he visited Bethany — indeed, it was only a week ago — she set about anointing his head with her precious oil. She had spent all she had on it, storing it away for his death. It was here and now, she finally saw, where it was, and that *it* was the breath, the sacred *pneuma*, that had touched her. It enabled her to move, to fill the room with fragrance.[16]

She at least had learnt, and that his *I am* was no more than the wind that bloweth, his medium, the *pneuma* which was all of breath, spirit and wind. He had had such difficulty making them understand that the essence of being has nothing to do with family — when he told them, if they were to follow him, they must reject mother, as he himself did at Cana, spouse, children, friends — indeed, all personal bonds. He taught the same about communal and political ties, even the obligations of honour and virtue, the ethical self merely another evasion. Not the stone tablets of the moral law, but the crucible cup of fire!

What he was doing was stripping away the veils of identity.[17] He knew Salomé had danced for Herod, and stripping away her veils, flirting naked before the political head, had seduced him into forgetting that good man John the Baptist. Conjuring up the demons of *eros*, she had whispered to the trembling tetrarch: 'I am. Don't fear!' Jesus had then decided to follow Salomé's example, and as recorded in the same chapter by Mark, he glided across the water, inviting the twelve to see him as luminous spirit, his own nakedness — they saw only a ghost — instructing them that if they had courage, they would know and their fear would be gone.

The wind that bloweth had shape. His form was in it. Io saw it, during her rapture in the embrace of Zeus — the divine seduction that would curse her life, Zeus appearing to her disguised as a cloud. Io, like Danae, could make out the god's eyes, his sparkling mouth, his fondling hands, in the grey vapour that engulfed her.[18] So it is to be ravished by holy breath. But just as lightning strikes earth, when the *pneuma*, which is life, seizes hold, it impregnates the soil. Out of this ecstatic fusion of body and soul — nothing chaste here — there was fertility: Io would later give birth.[19] His form in the shower of golden fire begat form.

It had been there in the beginning, descending from above, swooping like a dove, when John the Baptist anointed him — only he, Jesus, had seen it — then metamorphosed into a blasting gale, it had driven him into the wilderness, where he gathered himself. Then, once he started, it was all around, needling, that ever-present *pneuma*, this time in the form of broken, tormented spirits,[20] ones inhabiting the sick, the mad and the lost, which it was part of his task to cure. And the cure itself was the dynamism, ready to spring, crouching compressed inside his own breath. There was fire in that breath, fire free from impurity, which gives off, except when enraged, no fumes.

The *I am* was the magnet that drew the charged air — itself *life* — catalysing it. He could never succeed unless the other was exposed, defenceless before him, a Magdalene who loved much. Her own spirit he awakened, the truth slumbering under the mists of oblivion, under the choking fog of her wayward life, his truth, which was as simple as that breath of wind. In flight, it bore the light imprint of the god's fleeting form — just what the disciples had failed to recognise when at night he whirled upon them over the water, his dancing spectre taunting: Courage. *I am*. Don't fear!

His usual method of healing was epitomised in the high drama of the paralysed man. The friends of this prostrate humanity, finding themselves unable to force their way through the crowds, in their desperation hauled his stretcher onto the roof, where they proceeded to remove a section of tiles and then lower him through the hole. Interrupted in his teaching by this pole-rigidified corpse-like contraption descending from above his head in precipitous jerks, a parody of divine *pneuma*, all horizontal immobile body — how could he resist? So he spoke, releasing the paralytic from his failure of spirit, then ordered: 'Arise, take up thy bed, and go home!' At this, the fallen form, slumped in its lethargy, regained its way. It stood up, lifting its stretcher into the vertical as if it were a victory lance or his own cross, and strode off. And that, in a nutshell, was what he had come for — to take those who had lost their place to stand, or never found it, those who were flat out in the horizontal, as if dead, and raise them.[21]

All this he had sought to bring to light, and the two Marys, of Magdala and Bethany, had learnt; and so would John, the young and favoured disciple, slowly over the years, digesting it in preparation to write his account of the story; and Luke and Matthew would get glimpses; and the stranger, Mark, the other lion, he would somehow, stripping the story back to its spare essentials, do it best of all.

The greatest failure was Peter, or was it? — about this he is least sure. He had chosen the slow and methodical, swarthy peasant fisherman named Petros, the rock, for his stolidity, and joked that this was the rock on which his Church was to be built.[22] He would need a ritual community, for people depended on regular guidance, and in dark eras, fortress walls might guard the inheritance, but Peter himself stood for what transforming the sacred rage into an institution would actually mean, his own breath at risk of turning to stone. That episode during the baptism by fire was it, Peter's profane convulsion of activity erecting tabernacles, temples and churches, a reflex in manic fear by one who feels the breath in his vicinity but cannot hear.

'Petrified' should have been the nickname — all that time at Jesus' side, seeing every miracle, hearing every teaching, present at the Last Supper, alerted by the word 'betrayal' but not understanding who or why. Then yesterday, the day of his arrest, it became clear that Peter would flee, and when challenged, would deny knowing him three times before the rooster would announce today's dawn. Jesus told him. Of course, the Rock spluttered with outrage at the lack of trust, pledging he would die with his Master. But the pledge itself, that he needed to make it, was sign that his denial had already begun.

Three times last night, within hours of him having sworn, Peter put his hand on his heart, looked the young woman who was accusing him of belonging to Jesus' circle straight in the eye, and lied: 'I do not know that man! That man has nothing to do with me! No, I am not!'[23] Non-entity that he is, he proclaims his own not-being, as if proud of it. Earlier in the evening, just before the arrest, in the Garden of Gethsemane, he had so little sense of the hard *Necessity* that was about to strike, in spite of having it spelt out for him, that when asked to watch while Jesus prayed, he went to sleep. Woken and reprimanded, on this darkest of all nights, the air leaden with foreboding, he promptly went back to sleep. And a third time, he would give form to his own negation of the *I am*.

Was ever a man so craven or so profoundly dull? What begins as the chosen Rock ends with the Cock, announcing this Friday dawn, the crow of that cheerful, cackling, puffed-up, feathered mockery of manliness. A rogue twinkle can still flicker in the fading lion eye. He is learning what he knows, that it is not miracles and healing nor what he taught nor whom he led that counts, but his own life as he lived it, its tragic climax in failure here and now on the Cross.

In the darkness of this early afternoon, his words come back to confront him: 'Take my yoke upon you, and learn of me.' His own yoke is sore upon him now, and he has strapped himself to it just as surely as did his Greek forefather in this one matter.[24] Like Agamemnon, he has placed the huge ox harness over his own head, as if his own life was that same wagon of unbearable weight, which he had to keep moving, and he did, once he had steeled himself — 'a will now to be stopped at nothing'.

A few days ago, between Bethany and Jerusalem, was one time when he himself lost courage, fearing the altar to which he was being dragged. Hungry, he singled out a fig tree, flourishing in full leaf but fruitless — it was out of season. In his petulance, showing off, he cursed it, so that the next day, the sap parched, it had wasted down to the roots. Being true to itself was its crime, its ordinary natural self, making it incapable of miraculously producing fruit on command. He had withered it to what he would soon become — bleach-boned petrified wood swaying in the temporary vertical. It was as if he had cursed himself, in fury fitting himself to the violence of impending crucifixion, like to like.[25]

He had cursed his disciples, too, for they, looking on, led by Peter, were left in little doubt that they themselves, with or without metamorphosis by fire, were that fig tree. His short-tempered passion had freed him to act with calculated cruelty. He had also left those who would hear this dark story standing astounded with him before that pitiful tree, in shock stuck to a spot without redemptive prospect, bewildered by what he was doing. At least they would now identify with the disciples, instead of lounging at a distance, deriding their foolishness.

He had earlier made it clear that his teaching method was to pitch his stories — story — so that those who heard would not understand:

> *But for those outside, shall all things be done in parables; that seeing they may see, and not perceive; and hearing they may hear, and not understand; lest they should turn again, and be forgiven.*[26]

Don't seek to make much sense of what is beyond you, he was saying, or expect to see what you are inwardly compelled to see. Learn to live in fear; learn to live in perplexity.[27] So he branded the image of this wasted fruit tree into the sensitive skin of the agitated imagination.

His last week had begun with a triumphal entry into Jerusalem. Triumph soon gave way to anger — cleansing the Temple, withering the fig tree. Then anger gave way to despair. I am the faltering hushed voice at night in the agony garden, imploring that the cup of my destiny be taken away, that my hour pass by. There will be no reply. So bring on the darkness; bring on the apocalypse; if I go, I will take the rest of you with me, like Samson crashing the palace roof down on himself and on all of those within. You thought I was a teacher of heavenly order and peace. No, I who was transformed by fire on the mountain and took its power here show what I can do, what I will, and it is destruction.

Look again on this petrified tree. In this, my last week, I am the raging fire, I am the razing whirlwind, I am the earth-shaking thunder. I am the heavy artillery that will devastate Flanders and northern France, barrage by daily barrage, in the time to be, of First World War. Where there were forests, a few stumps; where there were villages, piles of rubble; where there were fields of corn, craters, lice and rats, the flower of Western youth tangled in barbed wire, its corpses sinking in trenches of mud. Human hopes and pleasures and attachments all blasted to nothing — for in this Passion Week, I prepare the wasteland. Then the Cross!

All is still. And time, time itself, falters, then stops. The failure and the loneliness in the eerie mid-afternoon darkness, here upon the Cross, finally sinks him. He sees tears in his own five-year-old eyes as he holds the candle for his father's work; he sees below his young mother's shoulders slump; he sees a broken old man loitering in the distance — Peter, eyes dead with the shame of what he has done. He shuts his own eyes, his body swollen with pain, so raw, so heavy and so weak that he just wishes to fade away, not to be any more.

Pneuma has left him, his hands pinned, detached from it all and yet not, wheezing for a gasp of mere profane breath. A wave of lawless nothing has crashed over him, and he feels himself reeling and spinning, plunging downwards — drowning. The trembling lips break free and wail out anguish: 'Why hast thou forsaken me!' Intimately he speaks it, whispering of his once-secret love, which is no more and that is not to bear. In response — or is it an echo? — not far away he hears the screech of the sacred cloth in the Jerusalem Temple tearing apart. He will cry out again, then *expire*.[28]

How can this be? If even he could not stare into the eyes of his *Necessity* and keep sound, what chance is there? But perhaps that is not it; perhaps we are being told not to be so rational, that the story, which is its own authority, leaves the imprint of a different, more paradoxical truth? 'Don't seek to make sense of what is beyond you.'

How, then, are we supposed to respond to this, the story of Western stories? And especially we, the here-and-now-bound sceptics who inhabit the modern world! His emphasis was simple: *I am*. But the mists lie thick over the river of the truth about the nature of being. Some of the veils he stripped away — family, tribe, property, virtue, communal ritual. The way, he also said, is not through seeing. If you can live towards me, near me, as Magdalene did, the breath will stir and you may hear it, miraculously finding yourself fitted to its form. *I am* my life, my story — that is all there is to know. Courage!

He is the tragic humanness of failure — strip away that veil, too. Through this very fallibility, without God, without magical resurrection, from time to time off-balance, leaving a trail of fear, he was accompanied by some sort of knowing — such as the two at the Emmaus table learnt. He was it, whatever that enigmatic *it* is. All he has, all he leaves, is *I am*, a presence, a charged thereness within the world. Of course, it is now gone, in the fleshly existential sense. It remains, however, as Story, somehow to be tapped for its *pneuma*. The two who find themselves inexplicably driven to flee Jerusalem on a road to nowhere represent all those thereafter who will be swept away by the

Dreaming wave. It will come in the form of a mysterious stranger who walks by their side for a stretch of the way, reveals himself, then is gone.

This Jesus is far from perfect. He is not in the tradition of the Indian guru, in spite of sharing some of the powers and wisdom. The model of the charismatic Hindu teacher includes detachment from normal human relations and emotions, so that for him or her, death becomes unproblematic, merely release from the constraints of material being, release into paradise and bliss. Whilst this may constitute a purer religious way, it is not that of the West. If Jesus were divine — in essence, superior to common humanity — then the Crucifixion would be much ado about nothing. There is no cause for fuss if death is a freeing to return to the heavenly domain. It is, rather, a celebration. However, for he who is human and fallible — just a man — the Passion is tragic. It is a *mythos* in which all suffer unto death.

From the outset, the Church that took his name raised the expectation of a Second Coming — that Christ would return. But he has returned, and many, many times, his story forcing itself since then incessantly upon the West. Even during the twentieth century, its *midrash* resurfacings were to be spotted far and wide. That century opened with its definitive crisis-of-meaning story, shadowed by the death of God — Joseph Conrad's *Heart of Darkness* (1899). It flees the absurd modern city ruled by coffee-time to journey in search of the one who might point the way. The hope is that in his new guise, he has discovered how to live, how to be. But Conrad's stranger turns out to be a soul gone mad, one who has kicked the world to pieces and cannot save even himself, one whose dying words, summing up all he has learnt about human existence, are: 'The horror. The horror!' This is the wasteland of the withered tree without the Cross.

In the century that came close to losing its Dreaming, Conrad's dark tale spawned countless derivatives. There were, just to name some in film, *The Third Man* (1949), *Apocalypse Now* (1979), *Blade Runner* (1982), *Dead Poets' Society* (1989) and *Fight Club* (1999). The most influential play of the century, Beckett's *Waiting for Godot* (1955), hinged on what happens when the stranger fails to arrive. Also, the tradition of the film Western, led by *The Searchers*, conjoins the hero archetype with the one who is so complete in his *I am* as to be free to sacrifice himself to allow others to be reborn, touched by the charged *pneuma*.

But all the modern attempts at *midrash* are as nothing next to the foundation story. My Dreaming, it seems that he said, is indeed like a tidal wave rearing behind you, about to obliterate the ephemeral — except that water is not the element. I am more like a bushfire raging across the land, incinerating everything in its path. Out of the fusion of gale and inferno, in its withering trail, the old is turned into a wasteland of charcoal stumps. Out of the blackened trunks, however, and within days, out of the parched sap of seemingly dead trees, new shoots sprout — figs will fruit once more, and in profusion.

Look for me in that tattered pocket of your life, in the time when your cosy town becomes submerged, and you find yourself a stranger in a foreign land, although it is your own, not speaking the language, the locals staring at you with uncomprehending hostile intent. There, you too can find me, as does the mad boy, awakened from his nightmare by sight of the saving fury sweeping over the sea. At that conjunction of eternity and ordinary being — yours — I shall be you. *I am*. Don't fear!

L et us return to the story, where we left off. Forsakenness is not all. It is surely late, close to three in the afternoon. His breath is weak. Magdalene still to come, she will be the one, there outside the empty tomb early on Sunday morning, waiting for him, mistaking him for the gardener. That encounter will be easy. How he loves her. But after her, there will be Thomas, too — with a groan, he wonders whether he has the strength.

Is Thomas worth it? He is everyone, unsure, out of balance, glimpsing then not seeing, touching then empty-handed, seeking yet afraid to know. He is the human condition. Thomas will not believe his fellow disciples who will tell him in a week's time that they have seen their Master risen from the grave. He has experienced their gullibility before. Moreover, he does not trust his own sight. Thomas is shrewd and sceptical, knowing that there are hallucinations, that there are wishful thinking and nightmare fears, which conjure up spectres before the eyes — as he himself saw walking on the Sea of Galilee — and there are dreams that one believes to have been real. He turns his doubt into a loud proclamation. He will believe only once he has felt the wounds, stuck his own fingers inside the nail holes in the hands and the spear wound in the side. He requires tangible proof. Jesus knows he will have to appear, for Thomas, and he does.

Thomas is suddenly quiet. Jesus beckons to him. He moves forwards, sheepishly. It is not that he believes. But the atmosphere has changed. Thomas does not know what he believes. However, a man who looks like his Master, if it is true that he has a Master, is there, calling him. Out of the corner of his lowered eyes, he stares at the hands, which are open, welcoming him. He is now near enough to touch, but awkward, awkward Thomas, one foot forward and the other away, as if ready for flight. He cannot face him square on. He notices with horror that Jesus' left hand moves slowly to pull his robe aside, half revealing a spear gash in his side, inflicted by a soldier, they say, when he was up on the Cross. His Master's hand is close to the wound; two fingers lightly touch one side of it, inviting Thomas to examine it himself. He reels in dizzy shock, neck feverish with beetroot humiliation, eyes delirious, stuck staring, stammering with fear, wanting to sink into the earth — please, let me be nobody — yet also yearning to be forgiven, like Magdalene, somewhere in the back of his mind wondering why the need to be forgiven is suddenly pressing on him.

His own right hand trembles as it moves towards the wound. Surely, he is not going through with this? He does not know what he is doing. He is an automaton. His hand continues, but not onto the exposed flesh. It stops on the lower edge of the robe; two fingers ease it back — they are quite assured now, their movement delicate. Thomas stares straight at it, straight into the gash. What greater intimacy and trust could there be, he now understands, than to bare one's wounds to another, to let him touch them, and when they are *the* wounds, what more could this man do for him, Thomas? He trusts his eyes, although his sight is misty.

Suddenly, he realises that Jesus' right hand is over him, the palm open, the nail wound exposed, the wound gaping above his, Thomas's head. It is releasing him. Power has returned to the hands, although the fingers are claw-like, contorted stiff. Thomas is loved.

What Jesus sees in his last hour on the Cross, looking forward nine days to this last encounter, eludes Thomas — the aching spasm in the crippled hand, the sorrow in the face, the choked-back lamentation.[29] Thomas is caught up in Thomas — after all, he is everyone. Yes, Jesus has forgiven him. Yes, he has recognised that he is young, and in his youth unsure of what he does. He knows, too, that the need to test the Master is a good sign, that Thomas is close to believing, closer than the others.

There is also, however, the quiet, reflective admonition that if Thomas, who companioned him, doubts, what of all those who never met him, or who never shall meet him? How can they be expected to know? Jesus is reminded of the importance of his calling of Matthew, and now of John there down below, comforting his mother, whom he will take into his house. Much depends on them, more than on Peter, for he has just learnt again it will not be a human institution, a church, that will carry the *pneuma*, catching the print of its fleeting form. It will be the word as Story, and then all those who become possessed by that Story, learning that it is their own, within themselves.

The Cross has accomplished all things. *It* is the sorrow on his face, the sorrow felt by Mary in the nape of her neck — she does not need to see it. The triumph of powerful evil in alliance with the fogginess of the human spirit has intimidated Peter into denying him and his dear young Thomas into doubting him. He has to bear it, the complete human fallibility. Enveloped in the gravity of his sadness, he shall, in nine days' time, have to smile at Thomas, hold him, forgive him. Here, at the very end, is his caring self: 'Come unto me, all ye that labour and are heavy laden, and I will give you rest.'[30]

High and alone above this wasteland of his own making, he is finally free again to love. Welling up out of his crushed form, the abundance, the warmth, is what he now gives. He remembers his father, Joseph the Carpenter, at his frenzied work, born into the vocation to craft the instrument of torture on which his son would die. Once upon a time, five years old, Jesus held the light for him. He sees his mother beneath him. He helps her now. Joseph and especially Mary, they were true to him; they were the best that fathers and mothers can be. Then there was John the Baptist, whose death hurt him so much, and Magdalene — yes, her above all — how he came to love her. They were sound, those two — nothing could crack them. The rest are all Thomases, and so they shall be for generation upon generation, demanding to feel the holes in the hands, the spear wound in the side. It was for the Thomases that he came. The wounds are for them. The Story is for them. The love is for them.

It is calm and still now, high on the Cross. He hears muffled in the distance the veil in the Temple ripping from top to bottom. He looks down on his mother, on the quiet determination with which she holds her sacred infant, knowing what she has to do. All is fine and well. He sees it in its entirety, the close of the cycle, in the shadow of the Crucifixion: afterwards, when he returns, the climax of the second of his two meetings, when he smiles at Thomas, and lifting his right hand, he feels from the open sore in the palm grace irradiating the bowed head. Thomas will not doubt again. He has taken courage. Thomas will be able to live.

Once Upon a Time Now

Of course, we have to recover the Dreaming. Of course, we have to rediscover the Stories, connect our everyday lives in to them, so their *pneuma* may overwhelm our ordinary coffee-time. In the Emmaus inn, two men suddenly find their inconsequential lives lit up with meaning. They could be the modern waitress, or Princess Diana. *Mythos* is pathos. This, by now, goes without saying.

But how are we to do it? How are we to attract the Dreaming wave? The road to Emmaus is one guide, providing encouragement mixed with caution. It says: Courage! It will happen, likely at an off-guard moment. One day, the stranger will be there, walking by your side. Yet, is there anybody who has trudged that stony track and not remained blind to the one who accompanies? Be sure you are alert enough to recognise him, or her, when the heart burns within, not that you have any choice —either you will be alert or you won't. The caution is against trying to force it, force anything. Conscious, deliberate moves are futile — remember Oedipus! That path leads to the churches, and in the modern West, they are empty. Or it leads to the pursuit of knowledge, the civilised expression of loss of nerve, under the illusion that it has something to do with wellbeing.

But how can I live if I cannot find my fate, my hero, my soul mate, my work, which altar to bow down before? I need to know. You cannot know — thus speaks the Western Dreaming. It is not its way to wake you until it happens, and sometimes, not even then. All you can do is wait and follow and try not to worry. Have faith, which is all to do with what He called the *I am*! Cherish the faint grace notes that come from time to time! Above all, remember Matthew, whose fate welled up inside him one afternoon beside some river, leaving him perplexed and uninspired — frozen where it matters, within, unfree to breathe! There and then, it was that an angel visited him.

Not that we can help ourselves. A craving for the Dreaming funds the passion that is our life energy. It drives. We seek it here, we seek it there — when we travel, when we open a book, when we are drawn to a teacher, to a movement, when we become preoccupied by ancestors, with what has come before! Indeed, the commanding past, the one that haunts us, the one we yearn to know, turning us all into archeologists, devoting our lives to the search for fragments of relics, its secret is not what happened to us as babies, as Freud maintained, nor the antics of some great-grandfather, as the historian might suggest. It is the tablets. They are the buried treasure, the great obscured foundations. Moses' call was less to lead than to discover the law, to lead the people to the law, those ancient slabs of stone on which it was written for all time.

One and all, when we enquire, when we are compelled to know, when we are drawn into galleries and museums as if they were hallowed temples, what we are after are the authorities, the rocks that do not move, the sacred site where, in the beginning, it was given. Our fathomless longing is for the citadel, that towering and inviolable presence whose only physical remains are the site, charged with the sacred powers, and a few scattered fragments. Our lifelong quest, which is our life, is to return to the Dreaming.

Emmaus also tells that to be in the vicinity of Truth, any Dreaming Truth, quickens the breath. Suddenly, the heart burns within and you know instinctively that you are where it matters — although you may understand nothing, see no path, recognise no familiar or even friendly faces. An inverse parallel is the person implicated in serious transgression, although innocent, perhaps caught up on its boundary, like the citizens of ancient Thebes, disturbed to distraction by the pestilence within things around them. The young driver who kills a child running out in front of his car is cursed by this violation of sacred order in which he is implicated. Like Oedipus, completely without culpability, he has nevertheless been cast as the unwitting agent for a terrible act, and is overwhelmed by the fog he has been chosen to shoulder.

To walk in the neighbourhood of Dreaming Truth, to come under its thrall, is to be similarly torn out of the oblivion of being. It, too, may come violently, and inflict a weight of pain, such as to be near-unbearable. Or it may happen surreptitiously, gently, the recipient hardly aware. In response, sure moves may be rebuffed, tentative ones welcomed. However impossible its demands in terms of how to live in the earthbound everyday, it can bestow calm.

The sacred is universal. Each Dreaming is particular, providing its own narrative vehicles for gaining access to the general sacred order. No one order is obviously superior to any other, just different, the singular medium of each culture on its own Emmaus road. When Christ proclaims that his is the way, the modern West may take his words as applying only to itself. Its entire Dreaming is hostile to missionary activity, to active moves to convert others. It is altogether hostile to preaching, which at its best is like the advice given by wise Achilles to his bosom friend Patroklos: not to get carried away in the fighting and lose control, advice which Achilles himself knows to be a waste of breath. Jesus, in particular, taught by example rather than words, by means of his own story, the tragic fated path of his *I am*, his inwardness in response to failure.

But how singular when it strikes is the metaphysical cyclone that is Story? Well, it is particular to each individual, but he and she are shaped to what sweeps across them from their own beginning time, their own everywhen, as it surges up from within themselves and their own timelessness. The waitress at her work becomes Matthew. She is Joseph the Carpenter.

In response to the questions: Who or what rules?, By whose authority? and Which altar?, the answer is the Western Dreaming, which is eclectic. In this, we follow the formative Greek vision, gathering together a loose mix of gods, fates and human doings, weaving out of it a grand elusive story of what it means to be human. Indeed, there was an ancient Greek school of philosophers called the *Eklektoi*, so named because they borrowed from different sources. In the case of Western culture, the sources are not haphazard, and the primary elements are fixed — were fixed in the beginning.

Also, the E*klektoi* were the elect or chosen — literally, 'called out' — of the Jesus narratives. In short, the mythic essence of the West is not caught by the designation 'Christian' or 'Judeo-Christian'. It is quite simply the Western Dreaming. It is *eclectic*. Its method is to call out to those whom it touches — hence the centrality of vocation or calling.

The Third Reformation has played a major role in the Dreaming as we inherit it today. A word needs to be added on what shaped it. It did not spring to life out of nothing. It looked back to the eternal stories. Furthermore, it drew elements from both of the Reformations — Humanist and Protestant — from which it diverged, and itself gained dynamism from wrestling with their different ways.

From the Greek tragic view, it took a range of themes. It was fatalistic, sharing the Protestant hostility to any serious notion of free will, that humans may themselves change their own psychic dispositions — the form of the *I am* — or alter their life paths. It also shared the Greco-Protestant focus on faith and grace as the only things that ultimately matter, and that they cannot be willed — that is, gained by means of human deeds, however virtuous. And it drew on Stoicism, and its principle of accepting without complaint what fate decrees, making the best of *Necessity* — 'Let your will be that things happen as they do.'

It was Greek, rather than Catholic or Protestant, in rejecting any sense of divine providence: the higher forces that determine things should not be assumed to be either just or merciful. Overall, its image of divinity tended towards the presence of *pneuma* in the world and away from that of any Lord God above.

The Third Reformation was at one with the this-worldly focus of Protestantism, and took up its Oedipal doctrine of vocation, but earthed it in human stories, ones that it borrowed in the main from the Catholic tradition but also from the Hebrew Bible. The very Catholic figures of Magdalene and the Madonna were vital to it, and in this domain, it was strongly at odds with Protestant asceticism. In general, it took the best from both Catholic and Protestant Christianities, while replacing God the Father with *pneuma*, losing interest in 'eternal life' and, indeed, in all doctrine and dogma. It also reworked strains from ancient Judaism. And it turned its back on churches.

Some Humanist themes were incorporated. Its focus, too, was on the *I am*, here and now, in this life. It acknowledged the Humanist ego, with its celebration of how huge and splendid I am, how free to achieve great things. It tended to share

Aristotle's view that success in the world, the gaining and enjoyment of its goods, including sensual pleasures, is a necessary part of the good life. Its own *I am*, however, was counterbalanced by Jesus' insistent and repeated use of the same two words, his *ego eimi*, alluding to the vital spot, individual spirited being, as it moved in his particular person, becoming radiantly manifest at the Emmaus table. Moreover, the men and women whose stories were told knew full well that the logic of soul, contra that of ego, is fatalistic, thriving on lack of freedom, wherein moves the sacred rage and the possibility of grace.

The Third Reformation begins in Padua in the 1440s with Donatello, and ends in Rome in 1665 with the death of Poussin, the decade in which it continues to resonate in Protestant Holland. It is its works. It picked up fragments of old stories and strands of existing themes, which it rethought and repictured. It did so freely, taking liberties, for instance, with the Jesus narratives, a bit like Jacob wrestling all night with the angel, trying to win a blessing — wild, not too rational, but with an instinct for how to gain the truth that matters. The outcome was a pantheon of masterpieces that eclipse all but the rarest of the ancient tablets. These stories gained their own integrity of form, and a greatness not reducible to the sources from which they sprang.

It is as if the Greek gods had opened their doors for a time and let a few newcomers into their company. What those initiates then told breathed with the lightness, and the gravity, of the Olympian air. Or it was as if the demi-god Prometheus had once again stolen fire from his immortal brethren, descended to earth and given it to a few select humans. This was the fire of sacred rage. They and their truths became like the classical heroes, half human and half divine, like the stranger himself as he appeared on the Emmaus road, journeyed with the two to the inn, showed himself, and was gone.[1]

Third Reformation art belongs to high rather than popular culture. The distinction is partly in the virtuosity of technique and the philosophical depth of the questions being put. Most of the works are inaccessible to the untutored eye — entry into their narratives requires some teaching. This is, indeed, high art, and most of it is difficult.[2]

Not all of the Western Dreaming is erudite. Mark, for instance, wrote his *Life of Jesus* in common Greek, simple and everyday in its style. Homer, while benefiting in English from repeated translation, just to get him right — a characteristic of high culture — is open to everybody who can read. The better the translation, the more likely they are to appreciate and enjoy the text. Bach's *St Matthew Passion*, in spite of its complex virtuosity, may speak to everybody, written for the composer's ordinary church congregation in the small provincial town of Leipzig. Moreover, all the stories are to be found bubbling away in popular culture, told and retold in ever-new guises.

High culture remains in the West the supreme vehicle for the Dreaming. Its stories in their archetypal form, bearing the charisma of everywhen, are like Achilles riding his chariot into battle, 'shining like the flare of blazing fire or the sun in its rising'. To shake the very fibre of being, they must be magnificent. Athena, who presides over this domain, decrees that the work has to be of such quality that the god or the angel floods it with light.

It has been speculated that the Australian Aborigines, because they lack a counterpart to the god Dionysus in their own *Dreaming*, lack 'grog stories', have had no means for handling alcohol and are, as a result, defenceless against it — their lethal *Lethe*.[3]

Failure in Dreaming brings on its own symptoms. The landscape is wasted by such failure, sometimes unleashing evil.[4] The twentieth century was a case in point, our own recent past being, as Hamlet put it, out of joint. Disenchantment shadowed the West, compelling a series of attempts to find belief and purpose in the wrong places. Its most catastrophic ventures were in politics.

The event that set the stage was the First World War. Most histories stress that the 'Great War' was the product of political rivalries. They underestimate the effect of the troubled cultural climate that had set in. It was spawned from the 'God is dead' crisis of meaning that had dominated the 1890s, under the shadow of Nietzsche. The last philosopher, as he has been called,[5] set the challenge with his script for modern *nihilism* — the view that the essential truth about existence is that there is no meaning, nothing, that the human condition is either horrible or absurd. The challenge was: Find your way out of this or you are doomed.

The great sociologist Max Weber, in the opening decades of the century, also saw the impending crisis. His best work struggled with the gravity of Nietzsche's case. Weber provided a historical dimension. He argued that the modern West was a product of the Protestant work ethic — its stress on vocation, backed by a belief that industry and hard work were the way of enacting God's will. However, by the start of the twentieth century, the higher purpose — faith in God — was disappearing as his churches began to empty.

Weber pointed to the rational bureaucracy as the typical modern organisation, full of 'specialists without spirit' and 'sensualists without heart'. He went on to sum up the whole modernisation trend as the *disenchantment* of the world.[6]

Put simply, the case was that the 'rationalisation' principle drives modern society and its workings, making everything more calculable and, therefore, efficient. Whenever we start to think rationally or scientifically about any human activity, as we inevitably now do, the magic goes out of it. Once a person knows, for instance, that the magpie's dawn song is a tactical warning in defence of its territory, the wonder will be lost.[7]

In effect, this was a Dreaming argument. Individuals, under threat by grey water, without anything existing beyond them, are left disenchanted, with nothing to believe and nothing to obey. The modern secular predicament is that they are stranded alone with themselves — with 'me'. If it is not to reduce to puny little *me*, insecure and directionless, it had to find some way of turning itself into a centre of meaning, into *Me*. Or it would be compelled towards the many means of inducing oblivion on which the century gorged itself, ranging from alcohol and drug addiction to obsessional work to manic consumerism. Once again, we would be confronted by the pivotal role of *I am*, accompanied by the age-old advice that immersion in Dreaming is the only way to discover its teaching.

Back at the start, the Great War had been supported enthusiastically, even fanatically, by the cultural elites on both sides, including the sober and practical Max Weber. It was championed as a redemptive means of both finding something to believe in — nation — and clearing away the torpid middle-class decadence which, it was believed, had grown out of decades of comfortable peace. The ambition was to get the blood moving, restore vitality — but blood is not *pneuma*, violence is not therapeutic, and *nation* is not a story that is going to save anyone.

Times that were dead to the Dreaming would find themselves overwhelmed by it, but in negation. One of the archetypes rose from the Unknown like some awakened monster enraged at the disturbance and the neglect, driven to wreak vengeance. This was the story of Christ withering the innocent fig tree. It would set its determining stamp on the entire twentieth-century West. Two millennia on from the beginning, its image became reality between 1914 and 1918, as apocalyptic shelling devastated the fields and forests of northern France and Flanders. They were turned into wastelands of mud and denuded stumps, craters filled with the broken bodies of the flower of European manhood and the fragments of millions of tons of twisted metal. Villages and towns reduced to rubble, it was as if Christ's curse had been set on a whole civilisation, the withered fig tree its signature.

This obliterating wave of wind and fire left a wasteland,[8] but not one that would see the Cross rising from its fallenness. What it led to was not: 'Courage. *I am*. Don't fear!' but Hitler on the one side and Communism on the other. Even more extreme attempts at redemption through politics were born — beyond understanding in the evil they would let loose.[9]

The golden age of the twentieth-century West in terms of prosperity, justice and relative equality — the 1950s and 1960s — resulted when politics returned to its own important and necessary but narrow, practical realm, not trying to save the world. It produced stability and optimism, but also a disaffected upper-middle-class youth wanting more out of life than comfort and the predictable routines that it saw reducing its parents' lives to mediocrity and tedium. It didn't know what it sought, just that what was given was not what it wanted. Restless and discontented with summer plenty, it was cast back into the autumn of Moses' scouts, journeying after the light — after the lost Dreaming. It, too, took the wrong path. A new burst of hot politics followed.

That youth had found itself in a similar situation, half a century later, to that of the great cultural and literary critic Georg Lukács, who had been a regular visitor to the Weber household. In December 1918, aged thirty-two, the War just finished, Lukács returned to his native Budapest. He had taken Nietzsche's argument to heart. In particular, he read the novels of Thomas Mann — and especially *Buddenbrooks* (1902) — as charting the cultural collapse of the entire Western liberal, middle-class order based on home, family, career and civic duty. It had lost its higher justification, leaving it increasingly empty and banal.

Lukács saw Communism as the alternative to nihilism, its cause the only higher one left after the death of God. He knew that the honest man could not live in a nihilistic world, so he took a 'leap of faith' and joined the Party.[10] He would support this, his attempt at Dreaming — even in its Stalinist form — for the rest of his long life.

It was not only in politics that the twentieth century sought an answer — a new faith. There was science, and the hope that it would not only make the human condition more comfortable but would explain the cosmos and the meaning of life, somehow easing terrors of death. But science at this level is no more than a dazzlingly powerful recording and organising of coffee-time facts — 'specialist without spirit'.

There were recurring *modernisms* — movements in art, literature, music and philosophy — celebrating nihilism as a triumph over the repressions and superstitions of religion, absolute morality, social hierarchy and tradition. Out of touch with the Dreaming, they also went the way of the scouts. Steadily running out of energy, their main vitality was *pneumaphobic*, scorning what remained of the crumbling old order. They were led by Marcel Duchamp, who in 1919 drew a moustache on a reproduction of the *Mona Lisa*, implying how ridiculous she looked, and with her, all of Western high culture. Where there was breath, they sought to snuff it out.

There were moves to enchant the *me* directly, by for instance imagining cataclysmic *eros* as enough to provide an entire philosophy of life. There were tactics in withdrawal, cultivating one's own garden, in its many guises. And there was a characteristic psychic defence — resort to therapy and counselling, treating anguish within to ordinary coffee-time, as if disturbance of *pneuma* might be talked away.

A century of negative Dreaming would leave in its wake an indifference to politics — its effects seen to be like the withered fig tree. That false way was finally abandoned, freeing the modern West to accept its failure at Story. It might now open its eyes to re-enchantment.

Everything hinges on the nature of being — of *I am*. But this is not a question for philosophy, which, in its intellectual abstraction, at most plays a minor navigational role on the expedition beyond all charted territory. We travel by Story. Our guides are its brilliant imagery, its characters, its charged intent, and the unknown path each story lays down as it picks its way along, the path set without exit.

The hero establishes that it is possible to be alone, huge and splendid, in the dusk on the plains of Troy. He is what it means to 'stand tall', beyond great deeds and glory, in the poise of reflection as the enemy king, that aged, magnificent sir, kisses the hands of the man who has killed his children. After a life of doing, it means to become the shaft of silver lightning spearing through the drenching greys.

The story of the Western hero does not follow the fairy-tale model of the good victorious over the wicked, the principals living happily ever after. Although many of its surfacings in popular culture — in Westerns, in police and detective television series — do centre on baddies being killed and criminals being caught, the Western Dreaming includes no justice stories. This is surprising but true.

Homer makes it plain that the hero exists to fulfil his own destiny. Duty to family, tribe, community is principally a device for articulating the nature of this vocation and its particular engagement with the *I am*. The community is in itself a lower-order entity — like its own body of limits, the moral law. The great epic story of India, fundamental to Hinduism, the *Mahabharata*, is even more explicit on this point, making it a part of the way of the warrior that its exemplar, Arjuna, must slaughter some of his own family and even be prepared to kill his beloved archery teacher.

The archetypes, led by the hero, all instruct that there are three ascending levels of truth. The coffee-time facts, as studied by science, constitute the base material plane. In the middle belong the moral laws, the 'thou shalt nots', the most important of which are universal. Then there is capital 'T' Dreaming Truth.

The soul mate projects being as a condition of togetherness. I am not all I can be, ought to be, without you. To lose you would be to have part of my self shut down. With you who are, in being, beyond me, I glow within. In loving you, who are over there, complete in your thereness, I move close and possess you. Singular and solitary in my own steadiness of being, I am myself only with you — a 'with' that does not necessarily require dwelling in the same place. You are the stranger who is not strange. All these paradoxes exist and are possible because I somehow know you, the essence of your *I am*. Unlike Poussin, who found himself able to picture his 'beautiful beloved', whoever she was, my actual eye makes out no distinct shape. I just know that you *are*, and that I am not alone.

The mother shows how it is possible to give to the other, and what that means in terms of affliction. At the planting of the seed, she is crucified in her ecstasy — for she knows what is to come, yet still has the courage to say: Yes, I will! It is not hers to enjoy for long before her son's toes begin to flex and he wants to be off, turning back with his parting words: 'Woman, what have I to do with thee!' The sorrow and sadness set in like an endless midwinter night, overlaying the love that is constant and without boundary. And so she drifts away from her earthly self, with its leaden sense of futility and superfluousness, back to join her ancient tribe of shades. Born out of archetype to die back into it. How else could she bear it? Losing herself in that oneness beyond suffering, she joins with all those women dressed in black wailing out of eternity over the bodies of their children.

Magdalene pours into the lifeless hand all the *pneuma* shaped by him, accumulated in the year during which she could not move. It was those months stalled, tortured in confusion, not knowing where to go, what to do. It had been growing within her from that time at the villa of Simon the Pharisee when she wept and kissed and wiped away her old self and was touched back to life by her own capacity for love, which had finally been recognised. The awareness, that is, was growing in the time between then and the week of his death, leading to the climax in the garden, the meeting when he addressed her intimately by name and chided: 'Touch me not!' The command equally meant its opposite. So she did touch him, and with such intensity as to bring his dead hand back to life.

Touch became her mission. Through it, she reveals her *I am* to others. Yet in her case, she was already from birth the someone who loves much. All she is, all she became, was given in the beginning. He just had to look her way to redirect that love — although metamorphosed, she did not really change. Now, when she enters the room, people instinctively move closer, their spirits lifting. It is a force of presence, a being there, something in the air around her that may be touched, does touch. Her warmth consoles the anguish of existence, making life precious.

Matthew is different, in his embryonic being torn out of oblivion, wrenched from nowhere. He resists his call because it demands extreme metamorphosis. After all, he is the uncouth, carefree tax collector, shrivelling up in protest that he is too young, too unfinished, too unsure, too much at odds with himself — just little me. But *he* is the one invited to serious and solitary mission. Just as this person here when confronted by grey cloud showering sparks sees gold coins, that one over there recognises king divinity. So Matthew must undergo a sea change out of ordinariness. It is asking a lot.

He will need a second visitation. Years of resistance, seemingly wasted and in aimless loss, he drifted from this to that, nothing absorbing him for long. Whatever he has taken up he has dropped. Then, half a life on, it moves within, and he sits down in the midst of a ruined temple by some river, feeling driven to write the story. But even now, and with the best will in the world, he cannot. He is clogged up. He needs the angel to blow the breath onto the page.

Joseph the Carpenter does not resist, but he would be finished without his blindness. He can hardly move as it is, and only at night, so weighed down is he by the shadow looming up over him, the horror cast backwards over his entire life from thirty years on. He struggles to turn the gimlet of his vocation, his task to meditate on the fate of his son, the wonderful little boy who lights up his life and his work.

Alternatively, the Story may appear without line or gloss, in the form of *Necessity* imposing a fate that is the sheer edge of the tearing iron. Cassandra is little else than a voice of suffering wailing out her lament, she who would give anything to be blind to the truth. What deeper, more harrowing course for mortals could there be than seeing the yoke around their own neck as they are dragged slowly along an endless way to the sacrificial altar? We know her as pure, spare concentrate of mortal being, stripped of any superfluity of character or story. All we may do is stare in silence at her from lowered eyes.

Oedipus is also governed by *Necessity*, but the inflexion to his story is different. He is the one who is tested. The fates invite Oedipus to try out his own two prodigious powers — will and intelligence. He thinks he is big enough, smart enough, to become a hero. I, Oedipus, am up to becoming such a man! The recognition, however, is forced upon him that he is, rather, the one who murdered his father, then married his own mother and conceived four children with her — the one who did not see. What he learns about his true *I am* makes him freeze in horror. His test is how he bears up to knowledge rising out of the Unknown to embrace him, as he is helplessly drawn towards it. It is knowledge about the nature of identity, his own.

In retrospect, it was a foolish ambition for Oedipus to be king, to gain the esteem of others, to wield power, even if benevolently. It was a foolish ambition to be husband, and father to four children, two of them daughters, whom he loves. That is all ego, all-too-human ego in search of happiness, and not who he is. His normal human pleasures, desires and ambitions, his pride at what he has done, his loves — all are obliterated as he is subjected to remorseless, lingering death by grey water. And at the end of this story, too, a translucence from beyond shimmers through the sheeting rain, a silver shaft spearing over his eyeless visage. Surprisingly, the image that lives on after, the Dreaming image, is not of extinguished being but of a big man with prodigious courage. Oedipus is the one who did not flinch in his insistence on knowing the truth. Athena acknowledges him.

The archetypes of the Western Dreaming may not include any justice stories, of good winning out over evil. They do, nevertheless, concern themselves with order. Oedipus cannot follow his wife/mother in killing herself. That would be too easy an exit, given the horror of his acts, and premature — selfish. He has unfinished business, to redress the cosmic violation for which he has been unwittingly responsible. There is tragic disturbance in the ether, crazed *pneuma* — pollution. Things out of joint have to be put right.

Even god-like Achilles completes his story with two acts of penance for his own excesses: he organises funeral games and he respects the request of the enemy king. Homer sets his story squarely within higher order, and closes with its restoration. However, what disturbs that order is more like sacred impropriety than transgression of moral law. As Jesus teaches, the moral or ethical plane is a lower one, that of water religion, and it does not belong to the Dreaming. His concern is with fire and *pneuma*.

The trajectory of being is required to move in harmony with that encompassing order. So each individual *I am* is known not by its character traits nor by its virtue, but by how it responds when it strays, losing its way. To put on its own yoke, fitting itself to its fate, may be what matters. Matthew, Danae, Captain

Vere, Magdalene, all belong here, in what they learn. This is why the Western Dreaming is preoccupied by the relationship of *I am* to right order, its two favourite categories.

Oedipus, however, with his heroic self-sacrifice in the service of higher order, does little more than prepare the way to the nature of being. All roads converge on one spot. That is the teaching of Jesus by means of his own example. It leads into the central enigma, as elusive as the identity of the stranger on the Emmaus track.

He is clearest about what is not. He is not the hero, who by definition succeeds in worldly achievement and glory. Indeed, Achilles is straightforward by comparison, simple to characterise, the man who must live his vocation, huge and splendid, fulfil it, brute that he is, then gentleman, before a reflective distance comes to him in his twilight hours. This metaphysics of *Live your life!* is not that of Jesus.

Jesus moves, rather, in parallel with the Oedipus story, stripping away all normal attributes of identity — except it is not fate or *Necessity* that directs. He himself does. The parable is that of the withered fig tree, Jesus personifying the obliteration of ephemera. In his story, virtually everything is ephemeral, his legacy the wasteland. First, he targets family, tribe, religious practice and the moral laws. He also tells a rich man that he will have to give away all his money — his problem is not wealth in itself but his attachment to it. Then he turns on his disciples, showing them up, like Simon the Pharisee, as foolish. He deliberately confuses those he has chosen, arousing their most petty superstitions, as when he danced across the Sea of Galilee and they took him for a ghost. The more familiar he becomes to them, the more strange, and the more they fear. So disoriented by the end are Peter and Thomas that both sink into pleading:

'I am not!' His cyclone of annihilating fire reduces everything back to where it began, in oblivion.

Does he ask too much? Is anyone up to what he demands? Indeed, is anyone up to Story — when it comes full on and athwart?[11] In response to the *Who are you?* challenge, Magdalene succeeds because she does not need to assert: 'I am Mary, from Magdala, and have been a prostitute, who now repents and wants to carry out good works.' She remains silent, knowing only that she, too, is not. When she sinks to her knees, weeping over his feet, her own self vacant with shame, of no value to her, he sees that there is one truth. She loves much, and always has. In her case, nothing else matters.

Thomas is initiated through his doubting, his resistance, and then at last seized by Story. He represents everyone, except that his tenacity, his drive to test, is special. Everyone is potentially Thomas, living on the margin of Dreaming, wanting to enter, yet not, fearfully timid. Story is for him, if he is ready and up to it, for them, and the path is left open.

In fact, all Jesus ever adds to 'Courage. *I am*. Don't fear!' is 'I am the Light!' and 'The *pneuma* bloweth where it wills, and thou hearest its sound, but canst not tell whence it cometh, and whither it goeth.'

What Light? He makes it clear to his disciples, in the Lazarus story, that his motive is not compassion for his sick friend. He delays setting out for Bethany, thereby letting Lazarus die. His purpose is 'that ye may believe.' But believe what? It cannot be the flamboyant miracle with which he completes the episode, shouting into the open tomb: 'Lazarus come forth!' The disciples have already witnessed his magical powers many times. No, he is focussing in on the question he asks others about himself: 'Who am I?' Peter attempts to answer — You are this. You do that. Jesus is enraged. It is as if he requires blankness, and silence.

As a teaching story, Lazarus contains two notable encounters. There is Jesus' confrontation with Martha, telling her she parrots the conventional beliefs of the time, all of them barren. Yet it is to she who is absorbed in coffee-time gossip that he speaks his central lesson — '*I am*!' The essence of being, Martha, is within *you*! He might as well be addressing the wind.

The second meeting is with Mary grieving over her dead brother. He responds to her with an angry snort, soon displaced into his extravagant shout to the four-day-old corpse swathed from head to foot in white linen. She is attached to her own passion, little different from Mozart's lovers in love with love. Her self-indulgence must be burnt away.

The Lazarus story is introduced with a cluster of sayings. They include: 'But if a man walk in the night, he stumbleth, because there is no light in him.' John opens his *Life of Jesus* by identifying his Master with the Light: 'In him was life, and the life was the light of men, and the light shineth in the darkness, but the darkness comprehendeth it not.' His anger at Mary of Bethany in her grief was that she had stumbled into the wrong night.

There is a new darkness, and it is born of the Light. Once the infant boy appears from behind green curtains, sacred rage gleaming in his eyes, *pneumaphobia* germinates. It grows, deepening evil, which is no longer primitive and brutal, the simple lust of the raping and pillaging warrior, the murderous jealousy of the jilted wife. It is Judas, who is fully human and for whom being has become everything. Like a moth drawn towards the Light, unable to help itself, he learns that he himself is irrecoverably *not*. He learns the vital human *either-or*. Jesus confronts him at his last meal, as he tightens the strap on his own yoke, challenging the betrayer-to-be: 'I know whom I have chosen. That thou doest, do quickly!' So Judas bows his head, turns away and slowly trudges towards the last door. He is the incinerated tree, for whom one truth remains: 'And it was night.'

In the Western Dreaming, it is from out of that blackest of all darkness that there was Light. The boy draws on it to illuminate his father's work, which is to chisel the Cross on which that son will die, he whose own child hands already bear, for those who can see, the translucent crimson glow of the nail wounds to come. Here, it is not just fate and *Necessity* that drive tragedy, but humans and their evil, and they conspire on a grand scale.

Back at the start, others were drawn to a charismatic light in him, that of *pneuma*. By the middle of his mission, it is exhausted, so with his own energy dim, he climbs the mountain to receive external illumination. It is largely for show. The light within begins to take over only as he approaches death, his desolation stripping away his own human attachments. The scorching of the fig is principally a lesson to himself, a reminder. Then, fed by the light within, he may become the fire feeding the candle flame and the uplifting breath.

The Western view is of a lifelong exchange between attachment and detachment, between fallen worldliness and metamorphosis, between living in the thick of the human and gaining a poise beyond it, between *pneuma* and fire. Even Jesus belongs here, having found himself, in the brief two years of his public work, plunged into the thick of his own story, his engagement with it and the few who came close. At the same time, detachment was lodged deep in his *I am*, and it grew within, bound up with his yoke — the violent hatred he attracts and his own lonely forsakenness.

At Sunday dawn, two days after the Cross, his composure restored, he speaks his ultimate command. It is to detachment, that Magdalene's love is now disembodied, separated from her ego and its desires, even from personal love for him. Let go, he tells her, for you do not need me any more, and in any case, there is no-one left to touch. Equally, he murmurs to her: Love here and now, love me intimately, as I do you, and then let that soul-mate love enable you to give yourself to the world — through your living presence. Her capacity to love, her attachment here and now, frees her *pneuma* for the world and for the beyond. Yet she, too, will find herself like him, in the impending years: scorched back to the essence, her features gaunt, changing, her face becoming that of her beloved in his final hour — spare, withered by suffering, the Light glowing in the dark of deep-set eyes.

The Jesus narratives, taking their cue from the Hebrew Bible, open 'in the beginning'. At the foundation was the word, the story. Mark is specific: In the beginning Jesus Christ, the great announcing of the story I shall tell.

Homer took a different tack. He selects a short episode from the tenth and final year of the Trojan War. He opens with a seemingly minor incident. He stops before the death of his hero — nor does he include the Greek victory and the fall of Troy. In short, he breaks conventional narrative form and excludes both of the obvious climaxes, and with them the famed legend of Odysseus and the Trojan horse. It is as if he is saying that the story of stories has no beginning and no ending, that it could start and finish anywhere. Beginnings are arbitrary. It is, rather, that the described events — while located at a precise historical place and time, the participants all real personages who were born, lived, suffered and died — happened 'once upon a time'.

What, then, is the truth? A clue is contained in the strange fact, which we have stumbled across on a number of occasions, that we may know the stories without ever having been told them. We sometimes recognise the form without having, with our own eyes, seen it traced, and even when it bursts to our own surface like Captain Ahab's cursed white whale, Moby Dick, raging up from the heaving deep to smash his flimsy longboat and reap away his leg.[12]

Furthermore, those stories may start with a couple of fragments, as from an archeological dig. It may then take centuries for the missing parts to accumulate — that is, be imagined — before they are finally pieced together, bit by bit. Perhaps a better metaphor is the modern technique of cloning — starting with a single cell, from which the whole may be grown. The Magdalene, mother and Judas stories are cases in point — needing a millennium and a half to bring to fulfilment. *Midrash* comes in bursts, its awakening punctuating long periods of dormancy. Moreover, all of us become authors, in that we are inwardly driven to complete those timeless stories, unable to help ourselves, in thrall of their blueprint, authors for whom the script is written into our own lives. Indeed, what is not written?

The implication is that the archetype precedes the first actual telling. It is simply given, lodged in some primal Unknown. A parallel was Michelangelo's claim that the complete work of sculpture lay buried in each lump of marble, and he simply had to recognise its shape, then chisel away the concealing superfluous chips. Each individual is born into the primal *lethe* — awaiting the removal of the concealing mists. Thus, Dreaming chronology is that of everywhen. It is something like *once upon a time now*. John's Jesus puts it cryptically: 'Before Abraham was, *I am*.'[13]

Even further, the particular story may not matter. The archetype will find its housing form in its own good time, and it may be any time. The flame that lit up the night work of Joseph the Carpenter might well flare up now, large and compelling, the modern story the one. Indeed, the dying Captain Vere prays for the light that Billy Budd holds. Likewise, stories of failed vocation are strewn around everywhere, as autumn leaves — ours just happens to have been that of Moses as interpreted by Michelangelo.

The nine stories coalesce out of the primal mist, their forms like the profile of Zeus as glimpsed by the swooning Danae, in swirling cloud and gold sparks. How distinct are they? In the eternal flux of shaping, dissolving, reshaping, two of the nine seem to predominate — the hero and Magdalene. The stories of the one who does and the one who loves, on their separate paths but with intersections and a converging end, are not to convert or reduce. They are, furthermore, irrepressible. Vocation and fate may be included under either or both. So may *pneuma*. Soul-mate love and the mother share close affinities with Magdalene. But neither story includes evil, its genesis remaining separate. And Jesus dwells constantly as the enigmatic *I am* pivot to the Western Dreaming.

At every turn, the causal logic underpinning human reason, including the law of non-contradiction, is astounded. We are advised not to think we know, just not knowing, hope to see — unless, that is, Cassandra is our path. Every telling is a retelling, addressed to we who do already somehow, behind our blindness, see. Plato's explanation was that the all-knowing soul when born into a mortal body passes into a condition of forgetting. Like Oedipus, we carry our stories within — or, perhaps, are carried by our stories, into the world and out of it. George Steiner puts it, in reflecting on Kafka's parable 'Before the Law': 'It is not so much we who read Kafka's works, it is they who read us. And find us blank.'[14]

So there was no 'in the beginning' in any literal sense. It is, rather, that a moment arrives of being ready, which means being open enough to receive the great announcing, whether it is to be hero, mother, or metamorphosis out of fallen worldliness, whether to embrace vocation, fate or the soul mate. It is all a question of recognition. It may even be that what is recognised has always been there, in waiting, everthere in the everywhen, which is once upon a time now.

When the gods are present, Story begins. They choose the moment. The innocent object of their attention is ripped out of time, out of logic, out of the comfortable oblivion of all security of placement and definition its lifetime has been spent in building up. Often kicking and screaming, trembling and shaking, the perplexed human would not have it any other way. Fated man! 'The gods get bored with men who have no stories.' To reject the invitation is to have the gods turn away in dismay. How, then, might those humans possibly recover any exuberance, any enchantment, any capacity for living?

The gods, once engaged, appear at times to take some care with their human protégés. Matthew's angel did, as did Poussin's beautiful beloved, if austerely, and so may Athena, she who sang the Dreaming in the beginning. All personages from the stories, including Jesus, wait on her, the Truth goddess.

Under Western skies, where the wind bloweth where it wills, one and all return some day, called to death by grey water, return to meet the silver shaft of lightning under the steady olive gaze. All who are creations of *pneuma* and fire come themselves, when it breathes through them, the sacred rage, to echo: 'Courage. *I am*. Don't fear!' All, like us, are Dreaming.

acknowledgements

The generosity of friends helped in the conception and writing of this book. Stephen Crittenden read draft chapters and took part in suggestive conversations. He alerted me to the significance of the 'Road to Emmaus'. Sally Warhaft has shown special affinity with the entire work, and her judgement and taste were vital at a number of points and with key terms. It was she who questioned whether, in the big stories, there is ever a 'beginning'.

I have been aided in some of my orientation by the La Trobe Reading Group, and especially its spirited 1998 company, which took on Mark's *Life of Jesus*, discussing it a chapter at a time, week by week. I am also indebted to Vidisha Bagchi, and to Gay Bilson, Wendy Bowler, Nigel Cooper, Charles Dempsey, Jennifer Johnstone, Pierre Rosenberg, David Tacey and my daughter, Khadija. Intangible but profound is my obligation to the influence from years ago of my two great teachers George Steiner and Philip Rieff.

HarperCollins Australia has been, as always, a pleasure to work with. This has been especially the case with my publisher in Melbourne, Cathy Jenkins.

the works

God is Dead — *Pneuma*
Poussin, *Winter*, c.1664, Louvre, Paris
Poussin, *Matthew and the Angel*, 1640, Staatliche Gemäldegalerie,
    Berlin
Titian, *Danae and the Shower of Gold*, 1553, Prado, Madrid

Magdalene
Poussin, *Sacrament of Penance*, 1647, National Gallery of
    Scotland, Edinburgh
Raphael, *Deposition*, 1507, Galleria Borghese, Rome
Barocci, *Noli Me Tangere*, 1590, Uffizi, Florence
Donatello, *Magdalene*, 1454, Museo dell' Opera del Duomo,
    Florence

The Hero
Homer, *The Iliad*, c.700BC

Soul-Mate Love
Plato, *The Symposium*, c.384BC
Mozart, *Così Fan Tutte*, 1790
Poussin, *Self-Portrait*, 1650, Louvre, Paris
Shakespeare, *Much Ado About Nothing*, c.1598

The Mother
Poussin, *Annunciation*, 1657, National Gallery, London
Raphael, *Sistine Madonna*, c.1513, Staatliche Gemäldegalerie,
        Dresden
Bellini, *Pietá*, c.1470, Brera, Milan

Vocation
Caravaggio, *The Call of Matthew*, 1600, San Luigi dei Francesi,
        Rome
Michelangelo, *Moses*, c.1515–42, San Pietro in Vincoli, Rome
Herman Melville, *Billy Budd, Sailor*, 1891 (first published 1924)

Fate
Sophocles, *Oedipus the King*, c.426BC
Aeschylus, *Agamemnon*, 458BC
La Tour, *Joseph the Carpenter*, c.1640, Louvre, Paris

The Genesis of Evil
Poussin, *Spring, Summer* and *Autumn*, c.1660–64, Louvre, Paris
Poussin, *Confirmation*, c.1638, Belvoir Castle, Leicestershire
Titian, *The Flaying of Marsyas*, 1575–76, National Museum,
        Kromeriz

'Courage. *I am*. Don't Fear!'
Donatello, *High Altar*, c.1444–50, Basilica del Santo, Padua
Mark, *Life of Jesus*, c.70
Verrocchio, *Christ and Thomas*, 1483, Orsanmichele, Florence

notes

For Want of Story

1   The theme of the god manifesting on earth in the form of the stranger
    is already to be found in Greek mythology — Zeus, for instance,
    appearing on a number of occasions disguised as an unknown guest
    (Roberto Calasso, *The Marriage of Cadmus and Harmony*, trans. Tim
    Parks, Vintage, London, 1994, p. 53).

2   Frank Kermode reflects at length on the ending to Mark's *Life of Jesus*,
    in *The Genesis of Secrecy* (Harvard University Press, Cambridge, Mass.,
    1979, especially Chapter 3).

    The term 'Gospel' will not be used in this book. The original
    Greek titles, as in *KATA MARKON*, which are second century AD in
    any case, simply mean 'According to Mark'. In reality, the four
    canonical works are *Lives of Jesus*, and whereas 'gospel', etymologically
    'good news', does pick up one theme, it is far from the major one.
    Raymond E. Brown in his study of the core of the Jesus story, the
    Passion — *The Death of the Messiah* (Doubleday, New York, 1994, Vol.
    1, p. 11) — stresses that what he is dealing with is *narrative*.

3   *Phaedrus*, 250a.

4   For example, Martin Heidegger: '*Platons Lehre von der Wahrheit*',
    Wegmarken, Klostermann, Frankfurt, 1967, pp. 109–44. Drawing on
    the same Greek, he also refers to *beauty* as that which 'tears us out of the
    oblivion of being (*der Vergessenheit des Seins*) and grants us a view of that
    being' (*Nietzsche*, Vol. 1, Neske, Pfullingen, 1961, p. 228).

5   'Energy' was an important category for Aristotle, who for instance
    taught that 'we exist by energy' and that 'happiness is a form of energy'
    (*Nicomachean Ethics*, trans. H. Rackham, Heinemann, London, 1934,
    Book 9, Chapters 7–9).

6   Plato's term, used in his *Symposium* (215e), at least as rendered in a very
    free translation of *ta paschontas* by Michael Joyce (*The Collected Dialogues*

of Plato, ed. Edith Hamilton & Huntington Cairns, Princeton University Press, Princeton, 1963, p. 567). Henry James introduces the term explicitly in his masterpiece *The Ambassadors* — see John Carroll, *Humanism*, Fontana, London, 1993, Chapter 11.

7   The famous *'Noli me tangere'* phrase in the original Greek is *Me mou haptou*, with the range of scholarly translations ranging from 'Cease from clinging to me' through 'Do not hold me' to Tyndale's 'Touch me not', continued in the King James Bible. As we shall consider at length later on, if the whole Magdalene story is taken into account, Tyndale's three-word invocation is the most apposite — its economy and pungency also telling.

In general, Tyndale's translation of the *Lives of Jesus* will be used throughout this book. Occasionally, the King James or Authorised Version did make improvements, and when its rendition of the original Greek appears flawed, I will draw on the Revised Standard Version or, with an eye on modern biblical scholarship, provide my own translation.

8   As the Peggy Lee hit song from 1969 put it. *Is That All There Is?* draws upon a story titled *Disillusionment*, by the twenty-year-old Thomas Mann.

9   This is close to one aspect of Jung's theory of archetypes. Jung argues, for example, that the authority and numinosity of a particular mother draws much of its force from the 'mother archetype' projected by the child on to her — 'Psychological Aspects of the Mother Archetype', *Collected Works*, Vol. IX, Part 1, trans. R. F. C. Hull, Princeton University Press, Princeton, 1959, pp. 80–84.

One of a number of principal ways in which this book is at odds with the Jungian schema is in its working hypothesis that each culture has its own sacred sites and its own sacred stories, rather than there being a common source of all human archetypes — a 'collective unconscious'.

My use of 'archetype' is in some senses closer to that of Northrop Frye, who defines it as a 'typical or recurring image ... which connects one poem with another and thereby helps to unify and integrate our literary experience.' (*Anatomy of Criticism*, Princeton University Press, Princeton, 1957, p. 99). However, my basic unit is *story* not *symbol*, and Frye's definition does not include any primordial 'sacred site' force.

10   Calasso, pp. 243 & 387.

11   The genre of 'reality television' does the opposite — shows in which ordinary people, not actors, are pitted against each other in contrived situations — for example, on an island competing to survive or find buried treasure, or in an exotic villa to find their perfect match. Without the guiding hand of Story, the participants tend to stumble around, their everyday selves humiliated, their normal pursuits shown up as even more absurdly profane than they feared.

12   The first appearance of this term with which I am familiar was in 1872. The German philosopher Friedrich Nietzsche, in Section 23 of his book *The Birth of Tragedy*, argues that culture is founded on myth, and myth depends on 'a fixed and sacred primordial site' (*ein fester und heiliger Ursitz*).

13   Among the multitude of possible meanings for *logos* is 'tale', a usage found in Herodotus and Heraclitus, 'fable' as in those of Aesop, 'grand narrative', as in Luke's *Life of Jesus* considered as a totality — and 'story' (H. G. Liddell and R. Scott, *Greek–English Lexicon*, 9th edition with Supplement, Oxford University Press, London, 1996). For a thorough scholarly overview of Johannine *logos*, see Raymond E. Brown, *The Gospel According to John*, Doubleday, New York, 1966, Vol. 1, Appendix II.

14   Deborah Bird Rose, 'Ned Kelly Died For Our Sins', in Max Charlesworth (ed.), *Religious Business*, Cambridge University Press, Cambridge, 1998, p. 111.

15   R. B. Onians notes the presence of *Necessity* in modern English usage (*The Origins of European Thought*, Cambridge University Press, Cambridge, 1951, p. 333).

16   For example, two of the greatest of eighteenth-century English landscape gardens — Castle Howard and Blenheim — accompany houses capped by statues of Athena.

17   Robert Fitzgerald's translation of Homer, *The Odyssey*, Heinemann, London, 1962, line 1. The first translation is Richmond Lattimore (University of Chicago Press, Chicago, 1967, lines 9–10). 'Muse' does appear in the first line of the Greek original, as does 'goddess, daughter of Zeus' in the tenth. That daughter may be merely the muse who sings through the poet, but this seems too literal, the goddess in the tenth line speaking directly, not through some human intermediary. Athena, protector of Odysseus, is writ everywhere in the story that follows.

18   Kermode, pp. 81–96.

19   *The Republic*, Book 10, is the principal reference.

20   Michael Grant employs this same principle in his overview, *Myths of the Greeks and Romans* (Phoenix, London, 1994).

21   The Emmaus story failed to inspire any great paintings, in spite of a number of attempts by Caravaggio, Velazquez and Rembrandt, amongst others. However, the theme of the two lost wayfarers unaware of what they carry was picked up obliquely in Raphael's *Deposition* and Poussin's *Autumn*, both singular masterpieces.

22   The anthropologist W. E. H. Stanner titled a book of his essays *White Man Got No Dreaming* (Australian National University Press, Canberra, 1979). The second essay in that collection remains the classic outline of 'the Dreaming' (pp. 23–40) — there, Stanner coins the word 'everywhen'. Judith Wright includes the line 'We too have lost our dreaming' in her 1973 poem 'Two Dreamtimes'.

I. God is Dead — *Pneuma*

The principal sources for the story are Poussin's *Winter*, Poussin's *Matthew and the Angel* and Titian's *Danae and the Shower of Gold*.

1 Homer, *The Iliad*, trans. Richmond Lattimore, University of Chicago Press, Chicago, 1951, Book 17, lines 446–47.

2 Aeschylus, *Agamemnon*, trans. Richmond Lattimore, University of Chicago Press, Chicago, 1953, lines 182–83.

3 *Winter* has been Poussin's most celebrated painting for many observers, and for much of the time since its first hanging, in 1664. While it has a surface Romantic beauty, reworked variously in the nineteenth century by Turner and Gericault, amongst others, it also contains within it the lynchpin to modern metaphysics. It is, obviously, a *midrash* of Noah's flood.

4 *Concluding Unscientific Postscript*, trans. D. F. Swenson, Princeton University Press, Princeton, 1968, p. 483.

5 *The Gay Science*, s. 125, trans. Walter Kaufmann, *The Portable Nietzsche*, Viking, New York, 1954, pp. 95–96. A. N. Wilson has charted the nineteenth-century story of the waning of belief among influential English intellectuals — *God's Funeral*, Norton, New York, 1999.

6 This follows Freud's model of two clusters of instincts: one that draws people towards each other, centred on *eros*; the other that drives them apart, centred on violence (e.g. *Civilization and its Discontents*, trans. Joan Riviere, Hogarth, London, 1963).

7 John 3:8. The Christian tradition in capitalising Holy Ghost and Holy Spirit has tended to make obscure and abstract what is a much more down-to-earth evocation in the original Greek of the *Lives of Jesus*. I am avoiding the word 'spirit' as much as possible, with its associations of 'spirituality', on the grounds that it seems to me to be at odds with what the *Lives of Jesus* are sowing in Christ's *I am*.

8 Argued at length, as a major theme, in my *Ego and Soul* (HarperCollins, Sydney, 1998).

9 The best modern critics have acknowledged the superiority of Mark. Frank Kermode devotes his *Genesis of Secrecy* entirely to this *Life of Jesus*. Harold Bloom puts it:

> *A substantial number of Americans who believe they worship God actually worship three major literary characters: the Yahweh of the J Writer, the Jesus of the Gospel of Mark, and Allah of the Koran.* (*Shakespeare*, Riverhead, New York, 1998, pp. xviii–xix)

Bloom would have been more accurate to have written 'should worship', for the Christian Churches, whether Catholic or Protestant and especially those with fundamentalist tendencies, have avoided Mark, preferring the more 'meek and mild', 'sweetness and light' Jesus of Luke.

10 This is one of the many instances in which Tyndale's translation is finer than what has replaced it.

11 Mark's Jesus makes a number of references to God in relation to Old Testament passages — especially in Chapters 7 and 12 — and in disputes with Jewish leaders, using their own language. There are a dozen references to the 'kingdom of god', which could just as readily be translated as 'the divine realm'. The voice of God does also speak during the Transfiguration.

12 Exodus 3:14.

13 Not to be confused with the Humanist 'I am', which was identified with each individual and his or her character, served by reason and free will (see Carroll, *Humanism*, especially Chapter 1).

14 Instances include his 'letter of the law' refusal to minister to a Greek woman because she is not Jewish — he accepts her reproach — and his loss of temper with Peter (Mark 7:26–30 and 8:29–33).

15 The generative archetype here was set by Homer, 'cup' substituting for 'urn'. Achilles consoles Priam after they have paused in their weeping together:

> *There are two urns that stand on the door-sill of Zeus. They are unlike for the gifts they bestow: an urn of evils, an urn of blessings. If Zeus who delights in thunder mingles these and bestows them on man, he shifts, and moves now in evil, again in good fortune. But when Zeus bestows from the urn of sorrows, he makes a failure of man, and the evil hunger drives him over the shining earth, and he wanders respected neither of gods nor mortals.*

> (*The Iliad*, Book 24, lines 527–33)

Raymond E. Brown explores the range of possible meanings of 'cup' in Mark's text (*Death of the Messiah*, Vol. 1, pp. 168–70).

16 Raymond E. Brown, *Death of the Messiah*, Vol. 1, p. 482.

One of the rare redemptive fragments included by Mark is to position a centurion as witness to the death, who exclaims: 'Truly this man was the son of God.' The centurion, who has seen the truth, does not make a normal exclamation, such as: 'Praise the Lord!' Christ, not God, is the object of his new-found faith, although there does remain a rhetorical reference to divine paternity.

17 They do see a young man, clothed in white, inside the tomb, who tells them that Jesus will reappear in Galilee as he had promised. However, he makes little impression on them, if anything adding to their fear. They do not carry out his instruction to report his message to the disciples. To them, the principal witnesses, he is not 'good news'.

18 E.g. Mark 9:42–50, a thematically and stylistically disjointed section, with verses 44 and 46 being corrupt later additions.

19 Luke underlines the point by having the political head, Herod, fearing reports of Christ's power, misread his own vulnerability as ethical — John has accused him of immorality in relation to his brother's wife. He thinks that imprisoning John will protect him from failure in relation to the new power — *pneuma*.

20 Dostoevsky uses the phrase in his first major novel, *Crime and Punishment* (1866). The argument is continued through both of the later works *The Possessed* and *The Brothers Karamazov*.

21 Once upon a time, the Churches sang hymns with vigour — tapping *pneuma*. But they have rarely mobilised the Dionysian force of fire, an exception, perhaps, the pentecostalist tradition, and its ecstatic equivalents, which continue to flourish in pockets of the modern West.

22 Aristotle, *Poetics*, with trans. by S. H. Butcher, Dover, New York, 1951, XIII, 1453a16.

23 Luke 5:32.

24 Luke 3:16. This passage is rare in Luke in that it does not attempt to sugar Mark. Luke characteristically repeats Mark word for word while removing the dark edges. He even restores God to the text: Luke's Peter responds to Christ's 'Who am I?' with 'The Christ of God.' Mark's Peter had simply replied: 'Thou art the Christ.' (Luke 9:20; Mark 8:29)

25 Perhaps this was what Nietzsche was obscurely grappling with when he made 'Death of God' and 'Beyond Good and Evil' two of his main themes — a case of the surfacing of Dreaming in a most unlikely place.

26 Don Cupitt also places the death of God in the late Middle Ages, and contemporary with art getting 'better' — his exemplar being Jan van Eyck (*After God*, Weidenfeld & Nicolson, London, 1997, p. 69).

27 Freud's potent concept, describing the process whereby something that is repressed is tolerated in its opposite form. The patient tells the analyst that the person in the dream 'was *not* my mother'. (Freud, 'Negation', *Collected Papers Vol. V*, ed. James Strachey, Hogarth, London, 1950, pp. 181–85.)

28 For an extended analysis of Holbein's *The Ambassadors* and *Hamlet* in these terms, see Carroll, *Humanism*, Chapter 3.

29 *The Iliad*, Chapter 15, lines 262–68.

30 Contra Kierkegaard, who tied it inextricably, in the modern world, with dread.

31 The author was himself struck by a sort of *metanoia* when first coming across Poussin's painting of *Matthew and the Angel*, in Berlin. It would prove the start of pilgrimages to many places, and many times, visiting the work of Poussin. The first part of Matthew's life will be told in the Sixth Story.

32 Oskar Bätschmann observed the link in Poussin's *Matthew and the Angel* between the white cloth and Matthew's later beheading (*Nicolas Poussin — the Dialectics of Painting*, trans. Marko Daniel, Reaktion, London, 1990, p. 124).

33 Plato's terminology — *Symposium*, s. 202–204.

34 Ovid, *Metamorphoses*, trans. Allen Mandelbaum, Harvest, New York, 1993, Book IV, lines 600–11.

35 Genesis 32:22–32.

36 Seventeenth-century Holland added a footnote to the Third
Reformation, in the works of Vermeer and, to a lesser extent, de Hooch.
Jewels in the corner of its garment, Vermeer's studies of *Lacemaker*,
Geographer, *Astronomer*, *Woman with a Water Jug*, *Artist* and *Kitchen-Maid*
all blend the stories of grace and vocation. They do so under the
classical authority more powerfully tapped by *Winter*. La Tour's *Joseph
the Carpenter*, while also focussing on grace and vocation, is different, in
that it included Jesus. Vermeer's major works are without explicit
Christian trace, perhaps the reason for their coldness.

37 One scholar has argued that the presence of the olive, through its oil,
symbolises the Sacrament of the Last Rites, making this a Christian
death painting in which the Church plays a central role, as *ecclesia
triumphans* (Willibald Sauerländer, 'Die Jahreszeiten', *Münchener Jahrbuch
der bildenden Kunst*, 3, VII, 1956, pp. 181–84). *Winter* is so lacking any
Christian feel, never mind allusions to Christ, the Cross or even the
Church — and everyone is damned, good and bad alike — that this is a
ludicrous reading. Moreover, the olive is a classical reference, far
removed from the Roman Church.

38 Poussin had in an earlier work, *Blind Orion*, painted Diana leaning
nonchalantly up in the clouds, looking scornfully down on the humans
below. Here, he disguises the goddess.

39 Aeschylus, *Agamemnon*, line 160; and Euripides puts it:
> since Aphrodite is nothing but the human lust,
> named rightly, since the word of lust begins the god's name.
(*The Trojan Women*, trans. Richmond Lattimore, University of Chicago
Press, Chicago, 1956, lines 989–90)
Actually, I cannot recall an instance in which it is Athena herself
whose existence is questioned — maybe the Greeks did not dare.

40 Homer, *The Iliad*, Book 5, lines 1–8.

41 Those Greeks were more certain about *Necessity*, and her three
daughters, the Fates, who weave the thread of each individual destiny,
the thread that can be neither cut nor loosened. Life had taught them
that lesson, the story of Oedipus emblazoned over their entire culture,
branded into their central nervous system. We, too, know just as surely
that Oedipus is our own secret self, a theme to be explored in the
Seventh Story.

2. Magdalene

The principal sources for the story are Poussin's *Penance* (the second
one, of 1647, painted for Chantelou), Raphael's *Deposition*, Barocci's
Noli Me Tangere, and Donatello's *Mary Magdalene*. Luke's narrative of
Magdalene's forgiveness at the house of Simon the Pharisee (7:36–50)

and John's of the meeting in the garden (20:11–18) are both seminal. For all the scholarly ink spent in arguing whether the woman in Luke is Mary Magdalene, Third Reformation art, following Gregory the Great in the sixth century, then medieval mainstream interpretation, consistently portrays her as such. It takes a petty scholar even to contemplate wrecking one of our greatest stories with such pedantry.

What is more, a feature of archetypal story, as Frank Kermode has pointed out in the case of the Judas narrative, is that it compels those who come under its thrall to bring it to its logical completion (Kermode, pp. 81–96). It demands to be filled out. That the *Lives of Jesus* provide no more than fragments of the Magdalene story forces those who retell it to fill in the gaps, including how she spent the rest of her life.

This archetype has sometimes been referred to as the 'Holy Sinner' — for instance, by Dostoevsky, who employs it repeatedly in his major novels (e.g. Sonia in *Crime and Punishment*). But the orthodox Christian notion of the 'sinner' perverts the story.

1   For an extended interpretation of the 'Diana cult', see Carroll, *Ego and Soul*, Chapter 14.

2   For a fuller reading of 'Marilyn Monroe', see *ibid.*, pp. 71–76.

3   Hegel, *Die Phänomenologie des Geistes* (1807). For one account of the significance of *aufheben*, see Walter Kaufmann, *Hegel*, Weidenfeld & Nicolson, London, 1966. To reduce modern philosophy to a footnote to Magdalene requires two clarifications. That *modernism* has some of its origins in Hegel excludes Hegel's great predecessor, Kant, from the judgement — Kant kept one foot in the old order, defending the absolute moral law. Secondly, Nietzsche is a partial exception in spite of him being the patriarch of *modernism*, and having his own redemptive notion, 'the transvaluation of all values', merely another absurd and abstract reworking of *aufheben*. He saw the problem — nihilism — with chilling clarity, became its master diagnostician, predicted the dead-end of his own route, yet managed to stake out in passing the nature of vital culture, with his constant reference point the ancient Greeks. Finally, he became increasingly deranged by the return of his own repressed — Christian truth.

The 1998 Papal Encyclical, *Fides et Ratio*, argued lucidly for inextricable links between philosophy and theology — the case here is that both are under the presiding authority of *mythos*.

4   Indeed, it was the Left intelligentsia in the twentieth century, seeking redemption through politics, that was explicitly drawn to *aufheben* — as if Magdalene were some system of socioeconomic institutions. For example, Max Horkheimer and Theodor Adorno gave their most influential work an Hegelian title — *The Dialectics of the Enlightenment* (1944) — and Herbert Marcuse devoted his first Book to Hegel — *Reason and Revolution, Hegel and the Rise of Modern Social Theory* (1941).

5 It is worth noting in surveying some of the notable twentieth-century manifestations of Magdalene that the year 1899 saw the publication not only of Joseph Conrad's nihilistic masterpiece *Heart of Darkness* but also of Tolstoy's third and last novel, *Resurrection*. *Resurrection* is pure Magdalene *midrash*, the central woman driven in shame and despair into prostitution, the central man, her seducer, driven to spend the rest of his life seeking forgiveness.

6 Alban Goodier, *The Public Life of our Lord Jesus Christ*, Burns, Oates & Washbourne, London, 1930, Vol. 1, pp. 263–73.

7 Some scholars have explained the reversal away as Luke's clumsy drawing together of different elements from Mark and Matthew, with the riddle or parable imported into the story (Michael D. Gouldner, *Luke, A New Paradigm*, Sheffield Academic Press, Sheffield, 1989, p. 404; C. F. Evans, *Saint Luke*, SCM, London, 1990, p. 364).

8 Gouldner, p. 399.

9 As in Poussin's *Penance*. Elizabeth Cropper and Charles Dempsey have provided a translation of the Hebrew on the headscarves (*Nicolas Poussin*, Princeton University Press, Princeton, 1996, p. 117).

10 A trope used by John Ford in his 1953 film *Mogambo* to indicate the principal character's security of being.

11 The basic metaphor is from *The Odyssey* (trans. Robert Fitzgerald, Heinemann, London, 1962, Book 23, p. 406).

12 For the authoritative survey of modern scholarship on John 20:1–18, the 'Touch me not' story, see Brown, *Gospel According to John*, Vol. 2, s. 68. John's recording of his own belief, without having seen the risen Jesus, is an obvious contrasting prelude to the story of doubting Thomas, which he is about to tell.

13 John's *Life of Jesus* makes explicit that after Jesus' death, his spirit will return in a different guise, that of the *Paraclete* — on the nature of the *Paraclete*, see Brown, *op. cit.*, Vol. 2, Appendix V. Moreover, Magdalene is the one who is intimate with Christ in all three of his forms — alive man, dead body, risen spirit.

14 In the account told from close to Christ's own consciousness, that of Mark, his failure to find any affinity of companionship with his own disciples plays a big role in rattling his composure. At times, Mark evokes a poignant sense of Christ's loneliness. The *midrash* of a human Christ in love with Magdalene, and even consummating the union, appears in medieval folklore and is repeatedly hinted at in Third Reformation art. Stephen Crittenden has speculated that D. H. Lawrence's *Lady Chatterley's Lover* is a modern retelling of the story, the central character, who has an older, impotent husband, falling in redemptive love with the gamekeeper/gardener.

15 Western art has sometimes included a fourth story, that of Magdalene weeping under the Cross (see Ingrid Maisch, *Mary Magdalene*, trans. Linda M. Maloney, Liturgical Press, Collegeville, Minn., 1996, p. 70). This is not the case for the great works of the Third Reformation.

16 The *Lives of Jesus* provide an alternative motif of transgression and forgiveness. Peter is awakened from cowardly denial by an outraged young woman confronting him with the fact he is barefacedly violating a major law. Thou shalt not lie, certainly about a matter of ultimate importance — in this case, knowing the man who has changed your life! This is Peter's Fall, exposure crushing, Magdalene-like, his own weak, pitiful and blind self.

   Like her, he is so ashamed, he will never again break the law. Death in the blast furnace of humiliation has made him, forged at long last his own courage. But there is no explicit forgiveness in this story, and little grace. Peter spends the rest of his life doggedly building the Church. His reform, by means of a life of practical penance, is perhaps better depicted as Fall followed by stumbling survival, striving for higher recognition. Ultimately, there is little affinity between him and the ethos of Magdalene.

17 The *Magdalene* is a late work, from 1454. John Pope-Hennessey argues that a post-1966 restoration has 'domesticated' the harsh effect of the original (*Donatello Sculptor*, Abbeville, New York, 1993, p. 277.)

18 Indeed, she may be also read as the Western prototype of initiation, with obvious parallels with Australian Aboriginal ritual. It subjected boys at puberty to symbolic death, through months of physical torture, before bringing them back to new life, metamorphosed into adulthood, through teaching them the sacred truths.

19 This is Titian's projection, in his late *Pietá* (1570–76).

20 I have excluded the formative Christian story of 'goodness', that of the Good Samaritan, from the archetypes on the grounds that in relation to the modern West, it is subsumed under Magdalene. The turn from Mother Teresa to Princess Diana indicated a rejection of the Catholic tradition of ascetic, self-sacrificing charity, deriving from the Good Samaritan, as culturally obsolete. The modern West is attracted to a more complex — indeed, blemished, even compromised — ideal of pure goodness.

   Moreover, the great art of the Third Reformation did not take up the Good Samaritan story — the exception being Rembrandt, but in his case, not with telling effect.

21 All four *Lives of Jesus* themselves work indirectly, by displacement, in turning away from describing any of the gruesome details of crucifixion. The tradition thus, once again, invites artists and others to follow their own intuition and select from between the lines.

22 Notably in Baroque art (Maisch, p. 69), and most incisively Georges de la Tour's *Repentant Magdalene* (c.1630), held in the Louvre.

23 The full implications of this metaphysical either/or are spelt out at length in my book *Humanism*, Humanism's dependency on the laws of Nature and its own different 'I am' having failed to save it.

24 John records Christ during the Last Supper using the expression 'the spirit of truth' — *to pneuma tes aletheias* — to refer to the Paraclete (16:13).

25 The large number of preparatory drawings for the *Deposition* that have survived indicates just how seriously Raphael took this work, labouring again and again to find the right position for his figures. There was much more to the genius of the 'divine Raphael' than a single flash of inspiration followed by breathtaking virtuosity with the brush.

26 I have included some elements from Poussin's version of the story, his own great expressionist *Lamentation over the Dead Christ* (1657) painted in the shadow of Raphael's *Deposition*. Poussin, in addition, revises the method of Magdalene's triumph. He depicts her leading a group of four others around the body lying on the ground at the entrance to the tomb. There is the mother collapsing in grief, the third Mary looking on in despair, John cradling the head, and a completely bewildered Joseph of Arimathea beckoning him into the dark and hopelessly black, empty tomb. Magdalene is on her knees, bent low over the corpse — just as she was bent low a year earlier in Simon's villa — tenderly raising its left hand, which she is kissing. Everything is focussed on this hand, the hub of the entire world, and on whether she can halt its downward motion, matter plummeting under the force of gravity. The power here is not that of Magdalene alone, but of the sacred community she has built, now bound together by their common task, working with her to will the hand to rise.

Poussin's *Lamentation* is theologically powerful on a number of fronts, not the least of which is the founding of a sacred community quite different in its logic from that of the Church.

3. The Hero

The single source for the story is Homer's *The Iliad*.

1 As part of the Australian bicentennial, in 1988, a thorough survey of community groups was organised to discover which people, it was believed, had contributed most to building the nation. A war hero, Weary Dunlop, received more nominations than anyone in the country's history.

2 The interview is from Studs Terkel's classic study of Americans at work — *Working*, Peregrine, London, 1977, p. 479.

3 Wayne received double the vote of the contemporary star of his type, Mel Gibson, who came third, after Clint Eastwood (Gary Wills, *John Wayne*, Simon & Schuster, New York, 1997, pp. 11–12).

4 *Ibid.*, p. 27.

5 The epitome of this is the John Wayne character in Ford's masterpiece *The Searchers* (1956), the one twentieth-century work to reflect with some conviction the Homeric original. Significantly, *The Searchers* reverberates through many later films — as acknowledged by the director, Martin Scorsese, in relation to his *Taxi Driver* (1976).

6 W. H. Auden, *A Lullaby* (1972).

7   This is almost exactly the case for my own football sacred site, the Melbourne Cricket Ground. If there were ramparts on the outer top wall, one could imagine what it was for the terrified citizens of Troy looking down as Achilles chased their hero, Hektor, three times around the outside of their citadel before killing him.

There are, of course, variations between the different football codes. Most notably, there is little physical contact in soccer, although the primitive chant of its crowds is one of their leading traits. Some commentators at Australian Rules football games, led by Jack 'Captain Blood' Dyer, have developed a style that has affinities with wild Homeric incantation.

8   *The Iliad*, Book 16, lines 345–50. The magisterial American translation by Richmond Lattimore will be used throughout.

9   One of the most distinctive hybrids was the Christian knight — as in the legend of King Arthur. A knight of Arthur's round table, Sir Galahad, moves the hero type close to that of the saint. Don Quixote extends this tradition, part *midrash*, part parody.

10   Notable Third Reformation representations of the hero include Donatello's *St George* (c.1418) and *Gattamelata* (c.1447), Titian's *Young Englishman* (1545) and *Charles V at Mühlberg* (1548). Poussin's *Landscape with the Ashes of Phocion* (c.1648) reflects the hero indirectly, through Phocion's widow attending to his remains. She herself is a heroine in the tradition of Antigone.

Shakespeare projected telling First Reformation, or Humanist, characterisations of the hero — notably, Henry V and Brutus.

11   George Steiner, 'Homer in English', *No Passion Spent*, pp. 88–107. Steiner's essay is of immense cultural significance, its question 'Why?' vital to the Western Dreaming. There are a range of allied questions — for instance, why the legacy of the West's other towering literary figure, Shakespeare, should have needed counterbalance in his own language culture. Or is it that the English world, when it matters, prefers Homer to Shakespeare, ranking him higher in the pantheon?

12   Germany had staked its own competing claims, whether through the poet Hölderlin, the archeologist Schliemann, or the philosopher Heidegger — who asserted a unique affinity between German language and culture and that of ancient Greece.

13   The vitality in English continues just as much outside England. The best modern translations of Homer have been American. In John Ford's tribute to American war hero Spig Wead, *The Wings of Eagles* (1957), the director positions a copy of *The Odyssey* behind the crippled hero. Also signalled is that Ford's immediately preceding film, *The Searchers*, had been his *midrash* of *The Iliad* — no accident that it stands as his masterpiece.

The one episode in Australian history to have gained mythic weight in the national imagination is celebrated as Anzac Day. On 25 April 1915, troops landed in the Dardanelles. In rational terms, the ensuing Gallipoli campaign was a miserable failure. From the outset, the army fell far short of its objective, then spent months tied down by the Turks, making no progress, before finally withdrawing in defeat. And the location has no geographical significance for a continent set on the other side of the world. But if the Australian troops had reached their first main objective, the hilltop of Mal Tepe, they would have been able to look due south across the Hellespont to see, on a clear day, with the help of binoculars, the ruins of the ancient city of Troy. In *The Iliad*, the King of Troy is referred to as Dardanian Priam. The Anzacs found their war close to the West's first sacred site. Moreover, C. E. W. Bean's two-volume account of their campaign stands as the Australian *Iliad*, unique and masterful in its style of history — faithful to the facts, which Bean knew first-hand, yet told with mythic intensity (*The Story of Anzac*, *The Official History of Australia in the War of 1914–1918*, Vols 1 & 2, Angus & Robertson, Sydney, 1933–34).

14 Calasso, pp. 324 & 335.

15 *The Iliad*, Book 5, lines 87–94.

16 Akira Kurosawa, *Sanjuro* (1962).

17 Jasper Griffin, *Homer on Life and Death*, Oxford University Press, Oxford, 1980, p. 105.

18 *The Iliad*, Book 21, lines 106–12.

19 *The Iliad*, Book 24, lines 539–42.

20 It was Aristotle who made 'greatness of soul' his central moral attribute (*Nicomachian Ethics*, Book IV, Chapter 3). He was merely following his great artistic predecessors in fifth-century Athens.

21 A major dimension of the Hebrew Bible is thus non-Western — its focus on tribe, on the collective salvation of the 'chosen people'.

22 Christopher Hibbert, *Wellington*, HarperCollins, London, 1997, p. 231. The theme of the son crushed by having to live in the shadow of a father who has done everything is explored in Racine's *Phèdre* (1677), a *midrash* of Euripides' tragedy *Hippolytus*. Racine's Hippolytus puts it: '*Et moi, fils inconnu d'un si glorieux père . . .*' (Act III, Scene V).

23 *The Iliad* has not commonly been regarded as a tragedy — one exception was Plato, who recognised Homer as the father of tragedy, but argued that his work should be banned as barbaric (*Republic*, Book 10).

24 Every serious modern sportsman and woman knows this experience — a partial exception is teams that celebrate after victory. More generally, the experience is an aspect of vocation.

4. Soul-Mate Love

The principal sources for the story are Plato's *Symposium*, Mozart's *Così Fan Tutte*, Poussin's *Self-Portrait* (the second one, from 1650) and Shakespeare's *Much Ado about Nothing*.

1   *It Must Be Him* (1967) sung by Vikki Carr; *I Fall to Pieces* (1961) sung by Patsy Cline.

2   Edgar Morin, *The Stars*, trans. Richard Howard, Grove Press, New York, 1960, pp. 144, 157 & 172. It is unnecessary to document the prominence of the archetype in Hollywood films. Suffice it to note that *Casablanca* was true to the type, with the addition of the hero theme cutting through it. Moreover, arguably the most successful novel/film of the twentieth century, *Gone with the Wind*, while it followed the turbulent life of the selfish but vivacious heroine, was also driven by the stock love motif. Scarlett O'Hara realises only at the end, when it is too late, that she had misdirected her irrepressible scheming to get the man she thought was the one. Mr Right was, in fact, her by now estranged husband.

3   Homer, *The Odyssey*, Book 23, lines 158–66.

4   Plato, *The Symposium*, with trans. by W. R. M. Lamb, Heinemann, London, 1925, s. 203c–e. Plato told the fable of the splitting of humans in half through Aristophanes. This may have been intended as a distancing device, in that the real-life Aristophanes was the master dramatic satirist of the age.

5   Denis de Rougement, *Passion and Society*, trans. Montgomery Belgion, Faber, London, 1956; Robert A. Johnson, *The Psychology of Romantic Love*, Routledge & Kegan Paul, London, 1983.

6   Kierkegaard, *Either-Or*, trans. D. F. & L. M. Swenson, Anchor, New York, 1959.

7   Kierkegaard, *Fear and Trembling*, trans. Walter Lowrie, Princeton University Press, Princeton, 1954, pp. 103–105.

8   Poussin would honour marital fidelity once, indirectly. The story was from Plutarch, that of Phocion, an Athenian statesman and general (402–318BC), who had been called upon by his city many times in his long life to advise and lead it. In 318, he was tried on trumped-up charges of treason and condemned to death. Furthermore, it was decreed that the body be disposed of outside the city and no Athenian provide wood for the funeral pyre. Poussin, in two paintings, and especially the second, his *Landscape with the Ashes of Phocion* (c.1648), casts Phocion as the selfless Stoic hero treated with crushing injustice. He questions what sense there can be in human life and society if this can happen.

Phocion's widow is shown, Antigone-like, defying Athenian law by kneeling just outside the city walls over her husband's ashes, gathering and cradling them. In the story, she is reported as having replied to an Ionian woman who was showing off her jewellery: 'My ornament is Phocion.' Here, the artist transplants the *Deposition* theme — Magdalene holding the dead hand of Christ — into a secular setting. It is the loyal wife, as hero, who strives to find more than death in death, as if trying to kindle a spark out of the ashes, one that will soar with *pneuma* up to the vivid-blue heavens over her head. For a fuller reading of this painting, see John Carroll, 'What Poussin Knew', *Quadrant*, Vol. 41, No. 7, July 1997.

9 Duc de la Rochefoucauld, *Maxims*, trans. Constantine FitzGibbon, Millington, London, 1978, No. 75.

10 Freud, *Group Psychology and the Analysis of the Ego* (1921), trans. James Strachey, Hogarth, London, 1959, Chapter 8; *Civilization and Its Discontents*, pp. 3 & 19.

11 Vermeer is atypical in painting himself into the canvas in his *Artist and His Model* (c.1662–68).

12 Titian established himself as the master of the nude, his vast output including many high points — the enigmatically seductive *Venus of Urbino* (1538), for instance, or the young *Magdalene* (1535), voluptuous and uninhibitedly lusty, but convincing. He also produced dignified portraits, from the reverent homage of *La Bella* (1536) to the posthumous idealisation of *Isabella of Portugal* (1548).

The painting masterpiece in the domain of the artist celebrating his model is the *Rokeby Venus* (c.1645–48). Velazquez employs his own virtuosity to create a peerless tribute to Aphrodite/Venus — a beautiful young woman reclining naked, back to the viewer, on a bed covered by austere leaden-grey drapery, which highlights the fine pallor of her skin. But for the mortal woman, love is inextricably tied to suffering. We glimpse before us, in the depths of a mirror into which she gazes, a soul flickering in its hurt.

13 The actual prod was from two of his main patrons pestering him for a portrait of himself. He decided the available painters in Rome were all hacks, so he reluctantly painted two *Self-Portraits*.

14 Cropper and Dempsey note that Poussin would have used a mirror to paint his *Self-Portrait*, and that he builds this reflection into his work (Elizabeth Cropper & Charles Dempsey, *Nicolas Poussin — Friendship and the Love of Painting*, Princeton University Press, Princeton, 1996, p. 189).

15 The oldest and most enduring hypothesis — first put by a friend of Poussin's, Bellori — is that she represents Painting. Poussin is allegorising his own vocation.

16 Charles de Tolnay, observing the Greek attributes, suggested that the woman represents Hera in the embrace of Zeus on their wedding day, an allusion to Poussin's own marriage ('*Le Portrait de Poussin par lui-même au Musée du Louvre*', *Gazette des Beaux-Arts*, 1952). Hera — or her Roman equivalent, Juno — is often shown wearing a crown or diadem, as queen of the gods. Rubens used her in a title page of a book published in 1613, François Anguilon's *Opticorum Libri Sex*, to represent *Optica*, and had her holding a sceptre with a brilliant single eye set at its crown, her other hand touching a pyramid — the stone in Poussin's ring is in the shape of a pyramid (Matthias Winner, '*Poussins Selbstbildnis im Louvre als Kunsttheoretische Allegorie*', *Römisches Jahrbuch für Kunstgeschichte*, Vol. 20, 1983, pp. 45–46). Jacques Thuillier, in his biography of Poussin, has questioned the identification of the woman with the painter's wife, on the grounds that none of the contemporary biographers who knew the painter remarked on a resemblance

(Thuillier, *Nicolas Poussin*, Fayard, Paris, 1988, p. 134). However, the link with Hera/Juno has been consolidated by Elizabeth Cropper and Charles Dempsey, with the eye in the crown shown to represent Perspective, thus suggesting that Poussin was weaving a complex theory of seeing and understanding for his friend and patron, Chantelou (Cropper and Dempsey, pp. 189–92).

17 The phrase is Nietzsche's (*The Genealogy of Morals*, First Essay, s. 11, *Basic Writings of Nietzsche*, trans. Walter Kaufmann, Modern Library, New York, 1968).

18 Quoted by Alain Mérot (*Poussin*, Thames & Hudson, London, 1990, p. 187).

19 Elizabeth Cropper, 'Painting and Possession: Poussin's Portrait for Chantelou and the *Essais* of Montaigne', *Der Künstler über sich in seinem Werk*, *Actes du Colloque de la Bibliotèque Herziana*, Rome, 1989.

20 Poussin, *Correspondance*, ed. Ch. Jouanny, F. de Nobele, Paris, 1968, pp. 383–85 — letter of 22 June 1648.

21 Henry James, *Selected Letters*, ed. Leon Edel, Hart-Davis, London, 1956, pp. 216–17 — 1894 letter.

22 The literary exploration of this theme is exemplary in Patrick White's novel *Riders in the Chariot* (Eyre & Spottiswoode, London, 1961).

23 The expression to 'grow them up' is borrowed from the Australian Aborigines — they use it in the context of the rite of initiation of boys at puberty.

24 Harold Bloom questions this, reading Benedick's final reference to marriage as being linked with cuckoldry as a portent for the future (pp. 200–201): 'Prince, thou art sad; get thee a wife! There is no staff more reverend than one tipped with horn.'

   This is to misunderstand the trial of trust that finally brings the principal couple together. It is more likely that Benedick is throwing in a rueful reflection on his own past character. His last, pointed words to the frivolous Romeo figure, Claudio, were: 'Love my cousin.'

25 This dimension of soul-mate love is read here from the male perspective. I am unsure to what degree the female point of view differs in its essentials.

5. The Mother

The principal sources for the story are Poussin's *Annunciation* in the National Gallery in London, Raphael's *Sistine Madonna*, and Bellini's *Pietá* in the Brera in Milan. The *Sistine Madonna* was preceded by other great Raphael Madonnas, notably the *Grand Duke* (1504) and *La Belle Jardinière* (1507).

1 Bruno Bettelheim, *Symbolic Wounds*, Free Press, Glencoe, Ill., 1954. The theory's main weakness is the orthodox Freudian one of rashly assuming that girls are less overwhelmed by their mothers.

2 Jung makes this point — e.g. 'Psychological Aspects of the Mother Archetype'.

3 Here was the great flaw in ancient Greek culture. Even in *The Iliad*, in which Achilles' mother, Thetis, is devoted to her son, Thetis is little more than a helper, portrayed with little of the warmth Homer lavishes on Hektor's devoted father, Priam. On the dread of women among classical Greek men, see Philip Slater, *The Glory of Hera*, Beacon, Boston, 1968.

4 Luke especially, and Matthew. Mark not only excludes any birth or childhood stories, but in his only major reference to Mary, implies that she is a nuisance, Jesus dismissing her: 'Who is my mother.' One is tempted to extend pathological resistance to the mother from the Greeks into the heartland of the *Lives of Jesus* — the narratives of both Mark and John.

5 A partial qualification to this judgement is the Hebrew Bible, which while heavily patriarchal in ethos does provide a number of antecedents to Mary. The main point is that Mary is less a creation of the *Lives of Jesus* than of medieval and Renaissance European culture.

6 That modernity is less sceptical about the existence of 'angels' than of the other supernatural entities, including God, that appear in the Bible is born out in Rainer Maria Rilke's major work — *The Duino Elegies*. That *Ein jeder Engel ist schrecklich* ('every angel is frightful') is one of Rilke's opening images.

7 Poussin's portrait of an *Annunciation* Mary in whom sensual and spiritual are equally powerful brings to completion a Third Reformation tradition that begins with Raphael's Madonnas and marks one of the major shifts away from the Catholic orthodoxy. The pure and virginal, other-worldly Madonna of Catholic imagery right through to the twentieth century was systematically overturned by the Third Reformation.

   Poussin's down-to-earth fleshy angel, while drawing on sixteenth-century precedents (e.g. Titian), is unique in its radicalism — although his contemporary, Rembrandt, is moving in the same direction. An irreverent modern use of the angel is provided by Frank Capra in his film masterpiece *It's a Wonderful Life* (1946).

8 Titian's image, in his huge *Presentation of the Virgin* (1534–38). The age of five is not arbitrary, linking in one direction with the boy Christ, and in the other with the extraordinary princess that Velazquez celebrated in his own masterpiece *Las Meninas* (1656).

9 It was Kierkegaard who wrote of how dreadful it would have been to be Mary (*Fear and Trembling*, trans. Walter Lowrie, Princeton University Press, Princeton, 1954, pp. 75–76).

10 Calvin put it that even the purest of good works are blemished (John Calvin, *The Bondage and Liberation of the Will*, trans. G. I. Davies, Baker, Grand Rapids, 1996, pp. 26–27).

11　As portrayed in Aeschylus' *Agamemnon*, to be considered in the Seventh Story.

12　Thus the story locates the fearful power of the mother in her spiritual vocation, in direct contrast with the materialist, scientific theory, derived from Freud, which prevailed in the twentieth century.

13　The allusion is to the Aesop fable in which a vixen boasts to a lioness of how many children she has, before asking: 'And how many do you have?' The lioness replies that she has only one, but it is a lion.

14　Poussin directly equates an ineffectual Joseph with the donkey in his *Egyptian Madonna* of 1657.

15　In Raphael's version, this is not true, the two famous cherub/angels doubling up as Christ and John the Baptist as young boys, both with a pensive sadness to their look — they, too, know the future. In spite of what they know, they are off to play. The popularity of the two Raphael angels in the late twentieth century — reproduced endlessly on gift cards and calendars — was another sign of modernity's peculiar acceptance of these supernatural entities.

16　Some Third Reformation art underlines the point by using ordinary men and women, sometimes with the physiognomic attributes of peasants, as models for Joseph and Mary — e.g. Caravaggio and Rembrandt. This is less true of the Italian mainstream, and especially of Raphael Madonnas, although Joseph is almost universally portrayed as a simpleton, and usually much older than his wife — e.g. Poussin.

　　Mary is also sublimated into the secular mother — especially in seventeenth-century Holland. For instance, De Hooch's *Woman Delousing a Child's Hair* (c.1658–60) projects the interior of the home as itself a hallowed order when under the authority of a mother's right presence.

17　The tradition of the collapsed Mary, lost in her own grief, goes back at least as far as Giotto. Poussin employs the device of the two selves in his *Landscape with the Body of Phocion* (c.1648), splitting Phocion's widow into two characters, one bent in grief, the other alert and active.

18　Some of these themes are depicted by Tiepolo in his *Venus and Time* (c.1753–58) — especially the equation of soaring in flight with giving birth, the whole experience a liberation from mundanity.

19　The archetypal story of the sacrilege of felling the sacred oak is that of Erisychthon, told by Ovid (*Metamorphoses*, Book 8).

6. Vocation

The principal sources for the story are Caravaggio's *Call of Matthew*, Michelangelo's *Moses*, and Herman Melville's *Billy Budd, Sailor*.

1　The example is from Studs Terkel's *Working* (pp. 249–53). I have used it as a leitmotif in my *Ego and Soul*, in relation to the nature of modern work (especially Chapter 2).

2 Nietzsche, *The Birth of Tragedy*, s. 4.

3 Many art historians have mistaken this figure for Matthew — a beautiful irony, true to Caravaggio's purpose. Vocation is mysterious, and at many levels. For the real Matthew, see Angela Hass, 'Caravaggio's *Calling of St Matthew* Reconsidered', *Journal of the Warburg and Courtauld Institutes*, Vol. 51, 1988.

4 Caravaggio is unique amongst the painters in being able to represent a convincing adult Christ, one with presence and authority, and he does so again in his huge *Raising of Lazarus* (1609). The Ninth Story will draw on two sculpture Christs, by Donatello and Verrocchio — and Raphael and Poussin were both successful in depicting powerful boy Christs, notably in the *Sistine Madonna* and *The Plague of Ashdod* (1630).

5 Ernest Jones, *Sigmund Freud, Life and Work*, Hogarth, London, 1954–57, Vol. 2, p. 407. The current author should at this point confess his own fascination with the riddle of the power of Michelangelo's *Moses*.

6 Charles de Tolnay refers to 'a cataclysm made man', and continues lyrically:

> *This man is a volcano and the elements of fire and water are unleashed in him: the beard has become a torrential river, the hair takes on the aspect of flames, the leg is like a rock born from the flowing lava of the cloak which surrounds it.*

> (*Michelangelo, Volume IV: The Tomb of Julius II*,
> Princeton University Press, Princeton, 1970, pp. 39–40)

7 This is consistent with Michelangelo's five marble Madonnas. Robert S. Liebert remarks that critics have repeatedly noted that in all of them, the Virgin is cold and detached (*Michelangelo, A Psychoanalytical Study of his Life and Images*, Yale University Press, New Haven, 1983, p. 407). A thorough Freudian analysis of Moses/Michelangelo would start with the cold, neglecting mother.

8 It has been widely argued that the horns, grotesque to the modern eye, are merely a continuation of a common medieval practice of portraying a 'horned Moses', in which they represent rays of divine light, a symbol of the Old Testament hero's sacred mission. It was St Jerome's ambiguous translation of a phrase from the Hebrew into the Latin Vulgate Bible that triggered off this tradition (Ruth Mellinkoff, *The Horned Moses in Medieval Art and Thought*, University of California Press, Berkeley, 1970).

The 'horned Moses' explanation will not wash. Michelangelo's work is acclaimed by art historians for its innovation, its sheer originality of both conception and execution. Michelangelo had no need to include horns to indicate that this was Moses — the tablets make that plain. Raphael, in the same period, does not bother to put horns on Moses in his *Transfiguration*. Moreover, Michelangelo was not so clumsy as to suggest the fineness of the sublime with these fat, diminutive outgrowths.

9   The horns may also carry a fourth projection, that of the cuckold. If the story were of Moses and the Golden Calf, then the horns could be read politically, of him being betrayed by his fickle people. Then again, the cuckold is a figure of mockery, hardly fitting for the powerful leader. My interpretation of the statue as autobiography does allow for some unknown personal reference, to Michelangelo himself having been jilted. Liebert speculates that the self-punishment in the late painting of the *Last Judgment* in the Sistine Chapel is in part homosexual guilt over relations with the much younger Tommaso (pp. 355–59).

10 This is not the place to deal properly with Freud's complex identification with Moses/Michelangelo. Other elements that would need to be considered include the father of psychoanalysis' own ambivalent relation to — and identification with — the father/prophet/great leader of his Jewish people, and to religious authority in general; repressed homosexuality; parricidal paranoia; and repression of the mother.

11 The interpretation here is quite different from that offered by the many who have written about the statue. They divide into roughly two camps as to Michelangelo's intention. One tradition, which includes Freud, interprets this Moses as responding in anger to having just seen his fickle people dancing around the Golden Calf. There is a range of opinion on the significance of gesture and expression, but agreement that Michelangelo has chosen the moment of wrath after Moses has come down from Mount Sinai carrying the two tablets of the law.

    The other tradition, led by Erwin Panofsky, argues that this Moses is, rather, in communion with his God ('The Neoplatonic Movement and Michelangelo', *Studies in Iconology*, Harper & Row, New York, 1962). Moses is here idealised as leader and inspired prophet, an exemplary synthesis of action and vision. Panofsky describes this particular Moses as in a state of 'supernatural excitement', having seen 'the splendour of the divine light'.

12 This is a stock Christian and Third Reformation theme, deriving from John's *Life of Jesus* and Paul's Epistle to the Romans, that the Old Testament path, that of law, was superseded by that of Christ, the path of faith. Michelangelo, in choosing Moses to represent failed vocation, joins this tradition, which will receive later reworkings — notably by Poussin, in his *Crossing of the Red Sea* (c.1635), and in his *Autumn*, which plays a central role in the Eighth Story, *The Genesis of Evil*. Poussin would have known Michelangelo's statue well. So would Caravaggio. In both cases, it is reasonable to assume profound influence — in relation to the theme of vocation.

    Yet Michelangelo remains different from a Christianity that separates itself in hostility from Judaism, in that he himself identifies with Moses. Moreover, there is textual support in the biblical story for an unheroic Moses. There are three different character stages. The key change comes when God first appears to Moses and speaks to him from the burning bush (Exodus 3:1–4:17). The Moses sketched before this encounter with divinity had been a courageous and independent man, shaping up in the hero mould. During it, he loses his nerve, repeatedly protesting that he is not up to what is being asked of him — a prototype for Matthew. In the end, God becomes angry at his lack of spirit and, soon after, even seeks to kill him (Exodus 4:24). The bumbling, ineffectual Moses, low in faith, uncharismatic and with a speech defect, then undergoes a long initiation into leadership — all symbolised in the extraordinarily rich image he uses of himself, 'I who am of uncircumcised lips' (Exodus 6:12).

13 Shelley's line from *Ozymandias*, a poem that might have been written with Michelangelo's *Moses* in mind, describing 'that colossal wreck':
> *Half sunk, a shattered visage lies, whose frown,*
> *And wrinkled lip, and sneer of cold command,*
> *Tell that its sculptor well those passions read*
> *Which yet survive, stamped on these lifeless things . . .*

14 This Moses may be observed from an angle standing ten degrees left of square on to the statue. In general, to see the different movements of the sculpture depends on finding the right position, in terms of distance and angle.

15 Vermeer paints this explicitly in his *Lacemaker* (c.1668).

16 Paul Barolsky, *Michelangelo's Nose*, Pennsylvania State University, University Park, 1990, p. 39.

17 If the viewer inverts the head, taking the horns to be the chin or, even more freely, breasts, then the image is of a woman upside down. There are other works in which Michelangelo deliberately built in a second face. John T. Paoletti finds a mask that when turned upside down reveals a caricatured self-portrait ('Michelangelo's Masks', *The Art Bulletin*, September 1992).

18 Herman Melville finished writing his story *Billy Budd, Sailor* just before his death in 1891. It was not published until 1924.

19 Max Weber spells out in similar terms this 'ethic of responsibility' as central to any political vocation — 'Politics as a Vocation' (1918), included in *From Max Weber*, eds. H. H. Gerth & C. Wright Mills, Routledge & Kegan Paul, London, 1948.

20 Terkel, pp. 421–24.

21 Roger Scruton, 'Some Principles of Vernacular Architecture', *Quadrant*, Vol. 36, No. 1, January 1992.

22 That culture always works to establish the vertical over the horizontal is a theme developed by Philip Rieff — e.g. 'By What Authority? Post-Freudian Reflections on the Repression of the Repressive in Modern Culture', *The Feeling Intellect*, ed. Jonathan B. Imber, Chicago University Press, Chicago, 1990, pp. 330–51.

23 Martin Heidegger reflects on the relations between building, dwelling and thinking in an essay, '*Bauen, Wohnen, Denken*', *Vorträge und Aufsätze*, Neske, Pfullingen, 1954, Part II, pp. 19–36.

7. Fate

The principal sources for the story are the Oedipus legend as told by
Sophocles, Aeschylus' *Agamemnon* and La Tour's *Joseph the Carpenter*.

1   One painting does partial justice to the richness of *Oedipus the King*,
    Ingres' *Oedipus and the Sphinx* (1808), painted obediently under the
    neoclassical authority of Poussin. In turn, it is subject to minor *midrash*
    in Gustave Moreau's *Oedipus and the Sphinx* (1864).

2   Sophocles, *Oedipus the King*, trans. David Grene, University of Chicago
    Press, Chicago, 1942, lines 981–82.

3   Aristotle, *Poetics*, especially VI–XIV.

4   Nietzsche, *The Birth of Tragedy*, especially ss. 7 & 22–23.

5   A number of literary critics have made this observation — e.g. Frye, pp.
    209–11. Here is the main reason that Shakespeare's 'tragedies', with the
    partial exception of *Macbeth*, are not tragic in the deep sense.

    George Steiner coins the term 'absolute tragedy' for those rare
    works of unmitigated 'negative ontology', ones that imply it is better
    not to be born or to die young. He includes *Oedipus the King* in this
    category, 'founded rigorously on the postulate that human life is a
    fatality.' ('Absolute Tragedy', *No Passion Spent*, pp. 129–30.)

6   Sophocles, *Oedipus Tyrannus*, ed. Hugh Lloyd-Jones, Harvard University
    Press, Cambridge, Mass., 1994, lines 471–72.

7   In the Sophoclean tradition, the Sphinx of Thebes is a monster sent by
    Apollo.

8   There are parallels in the story of Job from the Hebrew Bible. God
    scornfully asks Job, when he complains about the injustice of his
    afflictions: 'Where were you when I laid the foundation of the earth?'
    The main difference with the Oedipus story is that the Hebrew God is
    doing what he does for a reason. He remains essentially a just divinity.

9   Modern Western legal thinking hinges on the doctrine of *mens rea*, or
    the guilty mind — persons who are not conscious of what they are
    doing cannot be held to be criminally culpable. For an extended
    discussion, see John Carroll, 'Against Free-Will', *The Salisbury Review*,
    June 1995.

10 Calvinism hinged on the paradox that everything is predestined,
    determined in advance, by an all-powerful God, but individuals are
    nevertheless completely responsible for what they do — every
    transgression increasing their Fallenness (see Carroll, *Humanism*,
    Chapter 4).

11 Kierkegaard, *Either/Or*, trans. D. F. & I. M. Swenson, Anchor, New
    York, 1959, Vol. 1, pp. 135–62.

12 Calvinist *predestination* was a central axiom of the Second Reformation.
    In fact, it was merely an Oedipus *midrash*. It is in the logic of this
    archetype that, with the magisterial exception of the Sophoclean
    original, it prefers to articulate itself as philosophy, and theology.

13 Primo Levi, *If This Is a Man*, trans. Stuart Woolf, Penguin, London, 1987, pp. 146 & 161.

14 Bernard Williams, *Shame and Necessity,* University of California Press, Berkeley, 1993, Chapter 1.

15 Aeschylus, *Agamemnon*, lines 57–59. The Lattimore translation will be used throughout, except for line 218, referring to Agamemnon putting on the yoke of *Necessity*.

16 Lines 773–75.

17 Lines 926–27.

18 Lines 463–66.

19 Euripides is more explicit than Aeschylus, in his play *Iphigenia in Aulis* making it clear to Agamemnon that if he tries to spare his daughter, the army will mutiny and probably kill all of his family.

20 J. D. Deniston & D. L. Page, *Aeschylus, Agamemnon*, Oxford University Press, Oxford, 1957, p. 88.

21 Williams, pp. 130–36.

22 *Agamemnon*, line 1149.

23 Kierkegaard, in his *Fear and Trembling* reflections on Abraham and Isaac, attempted to vindicate the obeying of faith in what one does, even if it leads to the worst ethical and personal consequences.

24 For example, a marble copy (first-century AD) held in the Louvre, taken from an original fifth-century BC bronze statue by Kresilas — the *Pallas of Velletri*. In this copy, which is of course all we today can know, the face is crude while the gestures of the arms and hands are perfect. As often, we can but imagine what clarity about these vital things must have shone in fifth-century Athens — and especially in relation to the nature of the presiding divinity.

25 'Faith alone' and 'no free will' were propounded by Luther, 'individual conscience' and 'vocation' by Calvin and later, English neo-Calvinists. The main argument of my *Ego and Soul* is the continuing dominance of the Protestant cultural blueprint over the modern West, long after belief in the God of Luther and Calvin has lapsed.

26 The great painter of secular vocations as a religious mission was Vermeer, working in Calvinist Holland a couple of decades later than La Tour — he provides the 'Protestant ethic' with its icons. His *Geographer*, *Astronomer*, *Lacemaker*, *Kitchen Maid* and *Artist* all show anonymous individuals in deep meditative concentration at their chosen life tasks. The link with the Cross is no more than a hint in Vermeer — above the geographer's shoulders, for instance, on top of a cupboard, is a globe mounted in a wooden frame shaped like a cross.

27 An Oedipal link, the Sphinx posing as its riddle: What is it that walks on four legs in the morning, two at noon and three in the afternoon.

8. The Genesis of Evil

The principal sources for the story are Poussin's *Spring*, *Summer* and *Autumn* — the first three of his *Four Seasons*. This trilogy was the crowning philosophical statement of his life work, completed a year or so before his death in 1665. There is more in these paintings than the theme of genesis of evil. Poussin's first *Confirmation* is also loosely drawn upon, as is Titian's *The Flaying of Marsyas*.

1   Ovid tells the story of Proserpine, abducted and raped by Pluto (*Metamorphoses*, Book 5). The pomegranate was taken as a symbol of rebirth and in the Christian context, resurrection — as in paintings of the infant Christ holding one of the fruit. For the many symbolic associations of the pomegranate, see Mirella Levi d'Ancona, *The Garden of the Renaissance*, Florence, 1977, pp. 312–18.

2   A counterbalance to Camille Paglia's thesis, 'If civilization had been left in female hands we would still be living in grass huts' (*Sexual Personae*, Penguin, London, 1991, p. 38). Paglia's implication is that it was much more likely that Adam was the restless and curious one. Perhaps so — the rational facts, biological and historical, would support her. But the Dreaming is insistent that Eve led, just as the Jesus cycle would single out a couple of women as the ones transformed by Christ's presence, however much the Catholic Church, in its insistence on a celibate male priesthood, would try to deny the fact.

   The 'Garden of Eden' is a fantasy of those who labour, who are slaves to the material necessity of eking out a living — in an endless cycle of labouring, consuming, sleeping, labouring and so on until death. Eden is a paradise of consumption without labour (Hannah Arendt, *The Human Condition*, University of Chicago Press, Chicago, 1958, Chapter 3).

3   Numbers 13:1–30. Dreaming is our master, and its *mythos* disregards rational time.

4   An engraving by Hieronymus Wierix, titled *Typus utrisque S. Legis*, from 1607, portrays the two scouts carrying a pole bearing a bunch of greatly enlarged grapes. Resting on top of the pole, directly above the grapes, is the foot of the erect Cross. The Cross bears the crucified Christ, and is looped by vines carrying further bunches of grapes, this time of normal size (Sauerländer, pp. 177 & 178). This image, of Christ as a bunch of grapes linked with Moses' scouts or spies, is found in medieval art — e.g. a thirteenth-century bas-relief on a church door in Sion in Switzerland. Poussin must have come across this tradition.

5   Poussin would have picked up cues for the argument from Raphael's *Deposition*. In the Raphael, there are also two bearers, but what they carry is the actual dead body of Christ, not symbolically displaced into grapes on a pole. Raphael's rear bearer has malice written all over his face. For him and his companion, the body is a terrible and profane weight, contrasting with the lightness of the hand that Magdalene

holds — and, indeed, the whole body seen from her perspective. Here is another major example of Poussin carrying out a *midrash* on Raphael.

6 Nothing like the caricature Jew later Christian times would make of him. The caricaturing is there in the Old Masters of the Third Reformation, although less extreme than in vernacular cartoons. Christ the Jew is never given similar physiognomic attributes — nor are any of the other principals in the Jesus narratives, who were all, apart from Pilate, Jews.

7 A modern film revival of the Judas archetype was *Amadeus* (1984), which portrayed Salieri, a composer gifted enough to recognise the genius of Mozart but not good enough to match its least creation. In this *midrash*, Salieri's entire existence is consumed by envy of the 'divine Mozart'.

8 One reason that Shakespeare's *Othello* is not really tragic.

9 Milton, in *Paradise Lost* (1674), projects the same role onto Satan, who would rather be lord of hell than second to God in heaven — a *midrash* of the Judas story. The line: 'Better to reign in Hell, than serve in Heav'n' (Book 1, line 263) could serve as a motto for Judas.

10 Melville speculates in his *Billy Budd, Sailor* about the evil in the master-at-arms, concluding that it is inborn, a sort of 'natural depravity'. The story is a straight *midrash* of Judas as interpreted here, finding the trigger for envy in *being*, in the pure *pneuma* and goodness of Billy.

11 Kermode speculates that the Judas story is a later addition to the gospel cycle, but once included, it behaved true to archetype, demanding to be filled out until it was complete (pp. 84–96). On the likely historicity of Judas Iscariot, see Raymond E. Brown, *Death of the Messiah*, Vol. 2, Appendix IV.

12 Matthew 27:3–10.

13 The amount is specified in a fragment in John (12:1–8), displaced into the Mary of Bethany sequence.

14 John 13:29.

15 George Steiner makes the point, noting the later caricatures, from Shakespeare's Shylock to T. S. Eliot's Jew who squats on the windowsill, in *Gerontion* ('Two Suppers', *No Passion Spent*, pp. 416–17).

16 In the Christian Bible, the most powerful story of sibling rivalry is that of the Prodigal Son (Luke 15:11–32) — and as with Cain, it is the father who is the key parent. The dutiful elder brother spits rancour when his wastrel sibling is embraced by their father, welcomed home and celebrated. This parable has been, with the Good Samaritan, Christianity's best-known and most influential story outside the direct Jesus narrative. It has much more to it than envy, and may be read from the standpoint of any of the three principal characters (Rembrandt, in his great late work *The Return of the Prodigal Son* (c.1667) concentrates on the father). Its motif of reconciliation–rejection–envy is, I am suggesting, subsumed under that incarnate in the Judas story.

17 There is a case to be made that sibling rivalry is more basic than competition for the parent's attention. For instance, George Steiner notes that *Antigone* was of greater interest to the nineteenth century than *Oedipus*, indicating a focus on horizontal sibling relations rather than vertical parent-child ones (*Antigones*, Oxford University Press, Oxford, 1984, pp. 1–19).

18 A leading twentieth-century *midrash* of Cain was John Steinbeck's novel *East of Eden* (1952).

19 Steiner evokes the darkness of Judas' fate, and the deeply anti-Semitic cast of this Johannine passage, Judas' own name insinuating him into the Christian imagination as Judaism incarnate.

Poussin's second *Eucharist* (1647) places Judas at the door, head bowed, dressed in a red cloak, back turned to the others, exiting, the entire scene cast in ominous shadows. However, the painting fails to deepen the Johannine text.

20 Twentieth-century philosophy, led by Heidegger and Sartre, spent a lot of energy writing about 'nothingness', at a level of dizzy and misty abstraction absent from the concrete drama of the Judas story.

21 Steiner is surely right to link John's Judas narrative with the greatest Western evil of the twentieth century, the Holocaust: 'his exit is the door to the Shoah' ('Two Suppers', p. 417). The links are multiple, deep and obscure — starting with the rationalisation for Christian anti-Semitism. There is something in the pressing darkness of the imagery, the shadows literal and psychological that pervade the scene, Christ's hammering away about betrayal, and Judas' almost helpless obedience to his role, that throws a cloak of such tragic blackness over the Judaic traitor as to find some obscure affinity with the all-too-real modern history of Auschwitz. A different dimension of Story confronts us here. The archetype itself seems to play a role in the later evil.

22 *The Iliad*, Book 20, lines 490–503.

23 It was Darwinism that postulated the basic principle of both Nature and life as 'struggle for survival'. As its materialist star rose to metaphysical ascendancy in the West, it shifted the ground from one extreme, of the happy Edenic garden, to the other, of survival of the fittest and most successfully violent.

24 Goya, *Cudgel Fight* (1820–21).

25 Freud raised the 'death instinct' in many places, most fully in *Civilization and Its Discontents*. His followers have never been short of interpretative words in relation to almost everything else he ever wrote.

26 Quoted by Bloom, pp. 442–43.

27 The great philosopher of rancour and its psychological origins was Nietzsche — above all, *Beyond Good and Evil* (1886) and *The Genealogy of Morals* (1887). He missed the Dreaming origins. Moreover, it was Nietzsche who introduced the term 'will to power'.

28 A common theme in modern Western fiction. For example, Dostoevsky
    portrays the utterly cold political operator Peter Verkhovensky, in *The
    Possessed* (1873), as having two pleasures in life — destruction and
    eating. In Peter Bogdanovich's film *The Last Picture Show* (1971), the
    principal female character, Jacy, is so humiliated by having to strip
    naked at a swimming-pool party that she turns into a viciously cold
    manipulator, repressing all warmer feelings, determined never to lose
    control again. In the boredom that then swallows her up, a life without
    love, sadistic power remains her one pleasure.

    Herbert Hendin examined the widespread strategy amongst
    American college students in the late 1960s and early 1970s of
    repressing feeling in order not to lose control — *The Age of Sensation*,
    Norton, New York, 1975.

29 Alban Goodier's reconstruction — *The Public Life of our Lord Jesus
    Christ*, Vol. 3, pp. 147–48. Raymond E. Brown is more circumspect,
    locating Gethsemane as, most likely, a plot of land or a garden with
    olive trees on the Mount of Olives (*Death of the Messiah*, Vol. 1, p. 149).

9. 'Courage. *I am.* Don't fear!'

The principal sources for the story are Donatello's *High Altar* in Padua,
Mark's *Life of Jesus* — with supplements from Luke and John — and
Verrocchio's *Christ and Thomas*.

1   The authority for this adaptation of the story is Third Reformation
    images, but also the narrative accounts, especially that of Mark. Mark
    invites us, his readers, to feel ourselves inside Christ's skin and
    experience the story as he lives it. We are surreptitiously asked to
    identify with Christ the man. Mark is not much interested in the
    impact his Master had on others, nor even in what he taught — there
    are no sermons, few parables, negligible moral advice. He does not
    bother with normal biography, omitting any reference to birth or
    childhood. The narrator is recording Christ's own consciousness,
    implying that in essence, he is no different from we who look on.

    John's narrative — and to a lesser degree, Luke's — present a
    rather different Jesus — triumphant, never doubting, and in control of
    his destiny.

    The Dreaming Jesus is a composite figure. Mark tells his basic story.
    Luke adds some episodes — notably, Magdalene at the villa of Simon the
    Pharisee, and the road to Emmaus. John completes the written story, by
    recording the raising of Lazarus, the confrontation with Judas at the Last
    Supper, the encounter between the gardener and Magdalene, and the
    doubting of Thomas. He also places the greatest stress on *pneuma*.
    Moreover, Jesus' direct presence, unlike that of Magdalene, is more
    powerful in the original texts than in Third Reformation *midrash*.

2 The configuration is that of the Padua High Altar. Donatello sculpted the *Madonna and Child* c.1450 after the *Crucifixion*, which appears to have been mainly done in 1444–45 but was not finished until 1449. The placement of the *Madonna and Child* directly under the *Crucifixion* dates from 1895, and has been hotly disputed by some scholars — see Pope-Hennessy, *Donatello*, Chapter IX. As I suggest here, the current placement has to be right, perfect for Donatello's deeper meaning — he, almost alone of artists, could have imagined this wonderful conjunction.

3 John 2:4.

4 Mark 4:13. See Kermode, pp. 28–33.

5 Mark 6:45–55.

6 Mark sets up this reading by including the seductive dance of Salomé earlier in the same chapter, a pair of Dionysian moments that strike fear into those who witness them. The norm in Third Reformation art is to portray Salomé as a fully developed, attractive, sometimes lascivious young woman. In this, it is in conflict with the implication in Mark and Matthew, who both refer to her as *to korasion* — a young girl.

7 Mark 6:50. The five Greek words read: *Tharseite, ego eimi me phobeisthe.*

8 Mark's phrase (e.g. 8:12) — John has Jesus weeping in frustration. On the disappointment with the disciples, see e.g. Mark 4:40.

9 The orthodox translation of the Greek word *metemorphothe* is 'transfiguration', which lacks any resonance in modern English usage.

10 The La Trobe Reading Group in its 1998 study of Mark collectively picked up a rich series of initiation themes, including the 12-year-old girl linked with the woman who had been bleeding for twelve years and is cured by touching Christ's robe (Mark 5).

Moses' God first appears to him as fire — in the burning bush. The contrast here is that it is Jesus himself, not God, who incarnates fire. In *mythos* terms, the one who prepares the way for Jesus is Moses, not John the Baptist. There is explicit antecedence in that the second time Moses comes down from Mount Sinai with the stone tablets of the Law, the skin of his face was shining, so he had to wear a veil before his people (Exodus 34:35).

11 It is Raphael, in his *Transfiguration* (1518–20), who conjoins the stories of the metamorphosis and the curing of the mad boy.

12 Mark 9:22.

13 John 11:1–12:8.

14 Francis Moloney, following Bultmann, makes it clear that when Jesus 'weeps' in this scene, it is not out of sympathy for Mary and her grief, but out of frustration at her lack of understanding — that the Jews take his weeping to be compassionate is a supporting cue to read it otherwise, for in this sequence, they get everything wrong (*Signs and Shadows, Reading John 5–12*, Fortress, Minneapolis, 1996, pp. 165–69).

15 T. S. Eliot used the image of the tiger, in *Gerontion* (1920):
>   *In the juvescence of the year*
>   *Came Christ the tiger.*

The most 'Christ the lion' *Life of Jesus*, that of Mark, was written by the evangelist who had the lion as his own symbol. It is quite at odds, as is much of John, with the orthodox picture of Christ as 'innocent' (e.g. Bruce Wilson, *Reasons of the Heart*, Allen & Unwin, Sydney, 1998, pp. 211–12).

16 There is a long tradition of conflating Mary Magdalene and Mary of Bethany. Alban Goodier makes a heroic modern attempt to do this, suggesting that this Mary spent her young womanhood in the town of Magdala, renowned for its lax morals and common prostitution, then, having been forgiven by Christ, returned home, to reappear later as the Mary of the Lazarus story (*The Public Life of our Lord Jesus Christ*, Vol. 2, pp. 266–68 & 357–65). The problem with this reading is that Mary Magdalene would not have been as obtuse as the Mary in Bethany, who is much lower in the hierarchy of the chosen. The episode with Mary of Bethany is more plausibly understood as a parallel subplot, in the Shakespearean mode, to the master narrative of Magdalene.

For a different argument for separating the two stories, see Raymond E. Brown, *The Gospel According to John*, Vol. 1, pp. 450–51.

17 Mark 3:31–35 & 6:1–6; Luke 14:26.

18 The scene is evocatively painted by Correggio, *Jupiter and Io* (1530).

19 The story of Io is retold in Book 1 of Ovid's *Metamorphoses*.

20 Mark's terminology is unclean or impure spirits — literally, uncatharted *pneumata*.

21 The Christian concept of 'resurrection', with all its portentous — and, in modern times, meaningless — abstraction, derives from the simple Greek of 'standing up', as in the concrete and timeless story of the paralysed man.

22 This audacious reading of Christ's famous remark about this being the rock on which I shall build my Church (Matthew 16:18) is not fanciful. It is in keeping with the entire manner in which Christ treats Peter, at its most scornful and belittling in Mark. Mark's Christ simply does not take Peter, who is such a dolt, seriously. Moreover, he is almost systematically hostile to anything that might symbolise a church.

23 *Ouk eimi* — John 18:17.

The story is brilliantly captured by Caravaggio in his *Peter's Denial*. This painting is usually not attributed to Caravaggio himself, but the spiritual weighting and psychological truth are so precise that it is hard to credit it to a lesser artist.

24 Whenever the word 'yoke' (*zugos*) appears in a classical Greek text, the immediate association is with *Necessity*. There is some deliberate linking here of the Cross with the yoke of *Necessity*.

25 One reason for the curse is that Moses' scouts had carried figs. Poussin in his depiction of the scouts includes only grapes and pomegranates — both fruit initiated by evil and thereby transformed. Figs are excluded, because they are to receive their metamorphosis at the hands of Christ himself.

26 Mark 4:11–12. Those 'outside' are contrasted with the disciples, but it is soon made clear that the 'insiders' do not understand any better.

Mark is unique in that he writes his narrative in such a way as to induce the very perplexity that he has Christ proclaim as his method. His story has an uncanny disquieting brilliance. In part, the reader is placed in Christ's own shoes; then, as the story progresses, the identification shifts towards the disciples, and even Peter. By the end, the reader has joined the three women at the empty tomb, too afraid to speak of what they know.

The Mark passage about teaching in order to perplex is reworked by Matthew so as to soften it. Calvin in his *Institutes* was to recapture some of Mark's endemic unrest with his repeated insistence that to feel assured of salvation may itself be a symptom of the opposite.

27 A wisdom similar to that expressed by the Greek choruses of Aeschylus and Sophocles.

28 Mark uses *exepneusen*, which translates literally as 'expire', or 'breathe out' (15:37). Matthew's words are *apheken to pneuma* (27:50) — literally, let go his last breath, or yield up, dismiss the spirit.

29 On which day Christ appears to Thomas, see Raymond E. Brown, *The Gospel According to John*, Vol. 2, p. 1025.

30 It is this episode in the *Life of Jesus* in which he himself embodies the parable of the Good Samaritan. His curing of the sick, his miracles and his raising of Lazarus are all principally instrumental — teaching devices rather than motivated by compassion. This is not true of the care he shows to everyman Thomas when he blesses him.

Once Upon a Time Now

1 The history of why the Third Reformation did not play a more overtly prominent role in the ensuing centuries is not one for this book. Suffice it to say that Humanism and the Protestant Reformation dominated the West right through until the end of the twentieth century. Moreover, Catholic Christianity turned its back on the renewal, retreating back into its medieval doctrine — the key dates in the seventeenth century under the Papacy of Urban VIII (1623–44). Urban had two great artists residing in Rome to choose between, and he gave his patronage exclusively to Bernini, not Poussin — who from that time found most of his patrons in Paris, to where the Western centre of cultural gravity was shifting.

Bernini's Baroque style, in its fountains, sculpture and church architecture, exemplified the rejection of serious metaphysics — Luther's 'vital spot' — for theatrics and decoration. It became its own caricature in the interior of St Peter's, a celebration of imperial monumentalism in the tradition of secular, egomaniacal Caesars. Bernini's *Baldacchino* formed the centrepiece, as it still does. Huge, heavy and ornate, it is an extravaganza of coloured marbles, looking like some monster creation of a Roman gelateria, grotesque in its vulgarity.

Having said that, the peerless urban beauty of Rome as any visitor may experience it today owes more to Gian Lorenzo Bernini than to any other man — with the partial exception of his great patron, Pope Urban VIII.

2 In fact, the Old Masters are not difficult to teach. It is a question of the viewer getting the hang of how to work a way into the narrative. The stories are, as we have seen, basic to everyday life — its joys, its trials and its tragedy. Some painters in whom this is obviously the case — for instance, Rembrandt and Vermeer — have retained and strengthened their appeal. The nihilistic credo of modern art has failed to win many outside the cultural elites — indeed, there is widespread popular resentment against the technical crudity and metaphysical barrenness of *modernism*. Likewise, a rapport with the ethos of the Old Masters has survived, a sense that their intention was serious and right. This is in the context of a culture returning to a preference for the visual image over the written word. Finally, once interest is aroused, it is not an onerous task to learn of the classical and biblical stories upon which particular works draw — indeed, James Hall's 350-page *Dictionary of Subjects & Symbols in Art* (Murray, London, 1979) will usually suffice.

3 Craig San Roque (with Barry & Elva Cook), *Story about Intjartnama*, National Drug Strategy, Commonwealth Government of Australia, Alice Springs, April 1994.

4 'Soul-Mate Love' considered individual cases of failure in Dreaming, such as *femme fatale* and Don Juan figures.

5 Heidegger, *Nietzsche*, Vol. 1, e.g. p. 469.

6 Max Weber, *The Protestant Ethic and the Spirit of Capitalism*, trans. Talcott Parsons, Unwin, London, 1930, especially pp. 181–83; and 'Science as a Vocation', *From Max Weber*, trans. H. H. Gerth & C. Wright Mills, Routledge & Kegan Paul, London, 1948, pp. 129–56.

7 Charles Darwin confessed in his *Autobiography* that as a young man, he had stood in the midst of the grandeur of the Brazilian forest filled with wonder, but after years of scientific scrutiny, such feelings had completely left him (Carroll, *Humanism*, pp. 144–52).

8 T. S. Eliot's *The Waste Land* (1922) became perhaps the most influential poem of the century, drawing implicitly on the imagery of the First World War as a metaphor for the general condition of the West. It opens with an epigraph asking the Cumaean Sibyl what she wants. Her reply, in Greek, is: 'I want to die.' Eliot's own personal response,

prefigured in the last section of *The Waste Land*, where he puts the Emmaus question: 'Who is the third who walks always beside you?', was to turn to an orthodox Anglo-Catholic Christianity — articulated in his *Four Quartets* (1944).

9   This is not the place to explore the perversity of Hitler's own negation, whereby the awakened Dreaming concentrates modern evil against the people of Judas — and of Jesus.

10 Personal account from Agnes Heller and Ferenc Fehér, who were students of Lukács. Agnes Heller, in her autobiography, puts it that Lukács became a Communist not out of sympathy for the poor but out of need for an ideology of salvation (*Der Affe auf dem Fahrrad*, Philo, Berlin, 1999, pp. 118–19).

11 I owe this phrase to the poet Les Murray, from a personal dedication.

12 Herman Melville, *Moby Dick* (1851), in itself a great Dreaming presence.

13 John 8:58.

14 George Steiner, 'A note on Kafka's 'Trial', *No Passion Spent*, p. 251. Steiner is, in effect, making a case for including Kafka among the seminal contributors to the Western Dreaming.

bibliography

Aeschylus, *Agamemnon*, trans. Richmond Lattimore, University
of Chicago Press, Chicago, 1953

Hannah Arendt, *The Human Condition*, University of Chicago
Press, Chicago, 1958

Aristotle, *Nichomachean Ethics*, with trans. by H. Rackham,
Heinemann, London, 1934

Aristotle, *Poetics*, with trans. by S. H. Butcher, Dover, New York,
1951

Aristotle, *Rhetoric*, trans. H. C. Lawson-Tancred, Penguin,
London, 1991

Paul Barolsky, *Michelangelo's Nose*, Pennsylvania State University,
University Park, 1990

Oskar Bätschmann, *Nicolas Poussin — the Dialectics of Painting*,
trans. Marko Daniel, Reaktion, London, 1990

C. E. W. Bean, *The Story of Anzac, The Official History of Australia
in the War of 1914–1918*, Vols 1 & 2, Angus & Robertson,
Sydney, 1933–44

Harold Bloom, *Shakespeare*, Riverhead, New York, 1998

Raymond E. Brown, *The Death of the Messiah*, Doubleday, New
York, 1994

Raymond E. Brown, *The Gospel According to John*, Doubleday,
New York, 1966

Roberto Calasso, *The Marriage of Cadmus and Harmony*, trans.
T. Parks, Knopf, New York, 1993

John Calvin, *The Bondage and Liberation of the Will*, trans.
G. I. Davies, Baker, Grand Rapids, 1996

John Calvin, *Institutes of the Christian Religion*, trans. Ford Lewis
Battles, Westminster Press, Philadelphia, 1960

John Carroll, 'Against Free-Will', *The Salisbury Review*, June
1995

John Carroll, *Ego and Soul*, HarperCollins, Sydney, 1998

John Carroll, *Humanism — the Wreck of Western Culture*, Fontana,
London, 1993

John Carroll, 'What Poussin Knew — *Landscape with the Ashes of
Phocion*', *Quadrant*, Vol. 41, No. 7, July 1997

Max Charlesworth (ed.), *Religious Business*, Cambridge University
Press, Cambridge, 1998

Joseph Conrad, *Heart of Darkness*, Heritage, New York, 1969

Elizabeth Cropper, 'Painting and Possession: Poussin's Portrait
for Chantelou and the *Essais* of Montaigne', *Der Künstler
über sich in seinem Werk, Actes du Colloque de la Bibliotèque
Herziana*, Rome, 1989

Elizabeth Cropper & Charles Dempsey, *Nicolas Poussin —
Friendship and the Love of Painting*, Princeton University
Press, Princeton, 1996

J. D. Deniston & D. L. Page, *Aeschylus Agamemnon*, Oxford
University Press, Oxford, 1957

Euripides, *Iphigenia in Aulis*, trans. Charles R. Walker,
University of Chicago Press, Chicago, 1958

Euripides, *The Trojan Women*, trans. Richmond Lattimore,
University of Chicago Press, Chicago, 1956

Fides et Ratio, Papal Encyclical Letter, Vatican, Rome, 1998

Sigmund Freud, *Civilization and Its Discontents*, trans. Joan
Riviere, Hogarth, London, 1963

Sigmund Freud, *Group Psychology and the Analysis of the Ego*,
trans. James Strachey, Hogarth, London, 1959

Sigmund Freud, 'Negation', *Collected Papers*, *Vol. V*, ed. James
    Strachey, Hogarth, London, 1950
Northrop Frye, *Anatomy of Criticism*, Princeton University Press,
    Princeton, 1957
Alban Goodier, *The Public Life of our Lord Jesus Christ*, Burns,
    Oates & Washbourne, London, 1930
Jasper Griffin, *Homer on Life and Death*, Oxford University Press,
    Oxford, 1980
James Hall, *Dictionary of Subjects & Symbols in Art*, Murray,
    London, 1979
Angela Hass, 'Caravaggio's *Calling of St Matthew* Reconsidered',
    Journal of the Warburg and Courtauld Institutes, Vol. 51, 1988
Martin Heidegger, *Nietzsche*, Neske, Pfullingen, 1961
Martin Heidegger, *Vorträge und Aufsätze*, Neske, Pfullingen,
    1954
Martin Heidegger, *Wegmarken*, Klostermann, Frankfurt, 1967
Herbert Hendin, *The Age of Sensation*, Norton, New York, 1975
Christopher Hibbert, *Wellington*, HarperCollins, London, 1997
Homer, *The Iliad*, trans. Richmond Lattimore, University of
    Chicago Press, Chicago, 1951
Homer, *The Odyssey*, trans. Robert Fitzgerald, Heinemann,
    London, 1962
Henry James, *Selected Letters*, ed. Leon Edel, Hart-Davis, London,
    1956
Robert A. Johnson, *The Psychology of Romantic Love*, Routledge &
    Kegan Paul, London, 1983
Carl Jung, 'Psychological Aspects of the Mother Archetype',
    Collected Works, Vol. IX, part 1, trans. R. F. C. Hull,
    Princeton University Press, Princeton, 1959
Franz Kafka, *Die Erzählungen*, Fischer, Frankfurt, 1996
Frank Kermode, *The Genesis of Secrecy*, Harvard University Press,
    Cambridge, Mass., 1979
Soren Kierkegaard, *Concluding Unscientific Postscript*, trans. D. F.
    Swenson, Princeton University Press, Princeton, 1968

Soren Kierkegaard, *Either-Or*, trans. D. F. & I. M. Swenson, Anchor, New York, 1959

Soren Kierkegaard, *Fear and Trembling*, trans. Walter Lowrie, Princeton University Press, Princeton, 1954

Primo Levi, *If this is a Man*, trans. Stuart Woolf, Penguin, London, 1987

Robert S. Liebert, *Michelangelo, A Psychoanalytical Study of his Life and Images*, Yale University Press, New Haven, 1983

Georg Lukács, *Soul and Form*, trans. A. Bostock, Merlin, London, 1974

Martin Luther, *The Bondage of the Will*, trans. J. I. Packer & O. R. Johnston, James Clarke, Cambridge, 1957

Martin Luther, *Commentary on St Paul's Epistle to the Galatians*, ed. John Dillenberger, Anchor, New York, 1961

Ingrid Maisch, *Mary Magdalene*, trans. Linda M. Maloney, Liturgical Press, Collegeville, Minn., 1996

Francis Moloney, *Signs and Shadows, Reading John 5–12*, Fortress, Minneapolis, 1996

Ruth Mellinkoff, *The Horned Moses in Medieval Art and Thought*, University of California Press, Berkeley, 1970

Herman Melville, *Billy Budd, Sailor*, Chatham River Press, New York, 1987

Alain Mérot, *Nicolas Poussin*, Thames & Hudson, London, 1990

Edgar Morin, *The Stars*, trans. Richard Howard, Grove Press, New York, 1960

Friedrich Nietzsche, *Beyond Good and Evil*, trans. W. Kaufmann, Modern Library, New York, 1968

Friedrich Nietzsche, *The Birth of Tragedy*, trans. W. Kaufmann, Modern Library, New York, 1968

Friedrich Nietzsche, *The Genealogy of Morals*, trans. W. Kaufmann, Modern Library, New York, 1968

R. B. Onians, *The Origins of European Thought*, Cambridge University Press, Cambridge, 1951

Ovid, *Metamorphoses*, trans. Allen Mandelbaum, Harvest, New
York, 1993

Camille Paglia, *Sexual Personae*, Penguin, London, 1991

Erwin Panofsky, *Studies in Iconology*, Harper & Row, New York,
1962

John T. Paoletti, 'Michelangelo's Masks', *The Art Bulletin*,
September 1992

Plato, *Phaedrus*, trans. R. Hackforth, *The Collected Dialogues of
Plato*, Princeton University Press, Princeton, 1963

Plato, *The Republic*, trans. Paul Shorey, *The Collected Dialogues of
Plato*, Princeton University Press, Princeton, 1963

Plato, *The Symposium*, with trans. by W. R. M. Lamb,
Heinemann, London, 1925

Plutarch, *The Lives of the Noble Grecians and the Romans*, Dryden
translation, Encyclopaedia Brittanica, Chicago, 1952

John Pope-Hennessey, *Donatello Sculptor*, Abbeville, New York,
1993

Nicolas Poussin, *Correspendance*, ed. Ch. de Jouanny,
F. de Nobele, Paris, 1968

Racine, *Phèdre*, Garnier-Flammarion, Paris, 1965

Philip Rieff, *The Feeling Intellect*, ed. Jonathan B. Imber,
University of Chicago Press, Chicago, 1990

Rainer Maria Rilke, *Duino Elegies*, trans. J. B. Leishman and S.
Spender, Hogarth, London, 1968

Duc de la Rochefoucauld, *Maximes et Réflexions*, Gallimard, Paris,
1965

Pierre Rosenberg, *Nicolas Poussin*, Réunion des Musées
Nationaux, Paris, 1994

Denis de Rougement, *Passion and Society*, trans. Montgomery
Belgion, Faber, London, 1956

Craig San Roque, *Story about Intjartnama*, National Drug
Strategy, Commonwealth of Australia, Alice Springs,
April 1994

Willibald Sauerländer, *'Die Jahreszeiten'*, *Münchener Jahrbuch der bildenden Kunst*, 3, VII, 1956

Roger Scruton, 'Some Principles of Vernacular Architecture', *Quadrant*, Vol. 36, No. 1, January 1992

Philip Slater, *The Glory of Hera*, Beacon, Boston, 1968

Sophocles, *Antigone*, trans. David Grene, University of Chicago Press, Chicago, 1954

Sophocles, *Oedipus the King*, trans. David Grene, University of Chicago Press, Chicago, 1942

Sophocles, *Oedipus Tyrannus*, ed. Hugh Lloyd-Jones, Harvard University Press, Cambridge, Mass., 1994

W. E. H. Stanner, *White Man Got No Dreaming*, Australian National University Press, Canberra, 1979

George Steiner, *Antigones*, Oxford University Press, Oxford, 1984

George Steiner, *No Passion Spent*, Faber and Faber, London, 1996

Studs Terkel, *Working*, Peregrine, London, 1977

Jacques Thuillier, *Nicolas Poussin*, Fayard, Paris, 1988

Charles de Tolnay, *'Le Portrait de Poussin par lui-même au Musée du Louvre'*, *Gazette des Beaux-Arts*, 1952

Charles de Tolnay, *Michelangelo, Volume IV: The Tomb of Julius II*, Princeton University Press, Princeton, 1970

Max Weber, *From Max Weber*, trans. H. H. Gerth and C. W. Mills, Routledge & Kegan Paul, London, 1948

Max Weber, *The Protestant Ethic and the Spirit of Capitalism*, trans. Talcott Parsons, Unwin , London, 1930

Patrick White, *Riders in the Chariot*, Eyre & Spottiswoode, London, 1961

Bernard Williams, *Shame and Necessity*, University of California Press, Berkeley, 1993

Matthias Winner, *'Poussins Selbstbildnis im Louvre als Kunsthistorische Allegorie'*, *Römisches Jahrbuch für Kunstgeschichte*, Vol. 20, 1983

index